Jihadism Constrained

Jihadism Constrained

The Limits of Transnational Jihadism and What It Means for Counterterrorism

Barak Mendelsohn

ROWMAN & LITTLEFIELD
Lanham • Boulder • New York • London

Published by Rowman & Littlefield
An imprint of The Rowman & Littlefield Publishing Group, Inc.
4501 Forbes Boulevard, Suite 200, Lanham, Maryland 20706
www.rowman.com

Unit A, Whitacre Mews, 26–34 Stannary Street, London SE11 4AB

Copyright © 2019 by Barak Mendelsohn

All rights reserved. No part of this book may be reproduced in any form or by any electronic or mechanical means, including information storage and retrieval systems, without written permission from the publisher, except by a reviewer who may quote passages in a review.

British Library Cataloguing in Publication Information Available

Library of Congress Cataloging-in-Publication Data

Names: Mendelsohn, Barak, 1971- author.
Title: Jihadism constrained : the limits of transnational jihadism and what it means for counterterrorism / Barak Mendelsohn.
Description: Lanham, MD : Rowman & Littlefield Publishers, [2019] | Includes bibliographical references and index.
Identifiers: LCCN 2018031639 (print) | LCCN 2018035084 (ebook) | ISBN 9781538118498 (electronic) | ISBN 9781538118474 (cloth : alk. paper) | ISBN 9781538118481 (pbk. : alk. paper)
Subjects: LCSH: Jihad. | Terrorism—Prevention—International cooperation. | Terrorism—Religious aspects—Islam. | International relations.
Classification: LCC HV6431 (ebook) | LCC HV6431 .M4446 2018 (print) | DDC 363.325—dc23
LC record available at https://lccn.loc.gov/2018031639

To My Haverford Students Past and Present

Contents

Abbreviations ix
Acknowledgments xi
Introduction 1

1 The Emergence of Transnational Jihadism 9
2 The Power of National and Tribal Identities 19
3 Grand Plans Collapse on the Walls of Reality 47
4 Intra-Jihadi Conflicts 77
5 The Way Forward 107

Notes 125
Bibliography 145
Index 157
About the Author 163

Abbreviations

AQAP	al-Qaeda in the Arabian Peninsula
AQC	al-Qaeda Central
AQIM	al-Qaeda in the Islamic Maghreb. Formerly the GSPC
ASL	Ansar al-Sharia Libya
AST	Ansar al-Sharia Tunisia
EIJ	Egyptian Islamic Jihad
GIA	Armed Islamic Group (Algeria)
GSPC	Salafist Group for Preaching and Combat (Algeria)
HTS	Hayút Tahrir al-Sham. Succssor to Jabhat Fatah al-Sham (Syria)
ISI	Islamic State of Iraq. Evolved from al-Qaeda in Iraq, predecessor to ISIS and the Islamic State
ISIS	The Islamic State of Iraq and al-Sham, also known as the Islamic State
JFS	Jabhat Fatah al-Sham, also known as Jabhat al-Nusra (Syria)
JN	Jabhat al-Nusra, also known as Jabhat Fatah al-Sham (Syria)
LIFG	Libyan Islamic fighting Group
TWJ	al-Tawhid wal-Jihad. Predecessor to al-Qaeda in Iraq

Acknowledgments

At the time of the September 11 attacks, I was a second year graduate student at Cornell University and an enthusiastic observer of Middle East politics. Since that day, I have tried to understand the phenomenon of terrorism and the jihadi groups using terrorism, particularly the jihadi banner-carriers al-Qaeda and the Islamic State (ISIS). My ideas and thoughts have evolved over the years. As my knowledge deepened, so did my understanding that the jihadi movement is intricately complex and my commitment to demonstrating this complexity. In a way, the book in front of you is the culmination of this exploration process. Equipped with tools from international relations theory and many primary and secondary sources, I set out to propose a strategic analysis of the jihadi threat to the United States and to the international order.

In a sense, this project is an attempt to set the record straight; rather than a caricature of a united front of evil-doers, I sought to bring to light the diversity of the jihadi movement and the numerous disagreements between its components. While jihadi violence is a threat, I am hoping that this study will help put it in perspective. Al-Qaeda and ISIS are a danger, but not of the magnitude U.S. counterterrorism policies in the past 17 years would suggest. Far from a robust and unified movement, the components of the jihadi movement are struggling as they fight against states and a world order that are much stronger and more resilient. Not only does the international community benefit from critical material and ideational advantages over their jihadi opponents, the latter's inability to unify behind one objective and one strategy—or to at least avoid infighting that exhausts jihadi resources—further compounds their difficulties.

I would like to thank the Foreign Policy Research Institute (FPRI) for its support of the *After the Caliphate* project conducted by its Program on the Middle

East. Alongside *Jihadism Constrained*, the project includes a series of articles in the journal *Orbis: FPRI's Journal of World Affairs* and several podcasts.

Many thanks go to the people of FPRI. I am indebted to my dear friend Mike Noonan who brought me to FPRI over a decade ago. Since I arrived in the Philadelphia area to assume a position at Haverford College, FPRI has become a second home to me. With the chutzpah of a small think tank, but talents of a large one, FPRI always has punched higher than one would anticipate from a relatively low-resource organization. Under the leadership of Alan Luxenberg, to whom I am grateful, FPRI is dedicated to the pursuit of knowledge, pluralism of thought, the education of the general public about questions of national security, and the advancement of the policy conversations in the security realm.

Special thanks go to Tally Helfont and Sam Helfont who together led the *After the Caliphate* project. Tally presents a deadly combination of brains and competence. Her support and guidance were invaluable in assuring that I finished the book on schedule without losing rigor. Sam read drafts of all chapters and his critical comments contributed greatly to the quality of the work. I am also grateful to the other participants of this project, Nada Bakos, Mia Bloom, Chelsea Daymon, Brandon Friedman, Frank Gunter, and Dominic Tierney, for their feedback. I thank Tom Shattuck and Sarah Tarrow for making my prose more readable, Natalia Kopytnik for the cover design, and the amazing Jessica Blitz, Aine Carolan, and Cecilia White for terrific research assistance.

My gratitude also goes to the many research assistants who have worked with me since I arrived at Haverford College: Rob Williams, Cecilia White, Nicolas Sher, Ryan Rubio, Rachel Miller, Nicholas Lotito, Gabrielle Logaglio, Harry Levin, Nathaniel Kennedy, Rose Kautz, Ty Joplin, Hannah Jaenicke, Michael Iacono, Jack Hasler, Rupinder Garcha, Katie Drooyan, Caroline Clowney, Matthew Cebul, Aine Carolan, and Jessica Blitz. In addition to helping me out in my research projects, these students also built and maintained the *Global Terrorism Research Project* (gtrp.haverford.edu), which became an important source for students of al-Qaeda and the jihadi movement throughout the world.

My thanks and love go to my wife Allison for her endless support and understanding in general, but throughout the writing process in particular. My mom Varda, my brother Amit, and my sister Inbal provided support from afar. Finally, I am grateful for the four-legged members of the family, Nina, Marmaduke, and Zoe.

This book is dedicated to my students at Haverford College, past and present.

Barak Mendelsohn, May 2018
Haverford, PA

Introduction

The al-Qaeda terrorist attacks on September 11, 2001, were a watershed event. Their perpetrator, al-Qaeda—largely unknown to most people in the West—suddenly gained worldwide notoriety. Shocked and angry, the American public sought revenge. Their leaders vowed to punish the culprits and cripple al-Qaeda so that it would never again pose such a risk to the U.S. and the American way of life. The magnitude of the attack and the fear that it was only the opening salvo in a planned terror campaign for which—as the surprise of 9/11 revealed—the U.S. was ill-prepared contributed to an outsized assessment of al-Qaeda's strength. Adding to this exaggerated threat assessment was the Bush administration's view that all jihadi groups were enemies of the United States and, consequently, must become targets of its War on Terrorism. This view was based on the recognition of al-Qaeda's vast connections with other jihadi groups,[1] but it suffered from a lack of nuance, particularly a failure to understand the internal dynamics within the broad jihadi movement, which often featured more conflict than unity.

Seventeen years later, the jihadi threat still looms large over the West. The fight has already lasted far longer than both the Second World War and the Vietnam War. During these years, the jihadi threat has evolved, and al-Qaeda's fortune has ebbed and flowed. Its failure to produce another spectacular attack at the level of 9/11, and the loss of many of its leaders—most importantly the death of its preeminent leader and founder Osama bin Laden in 2011—led the Obama administration to declare its impending end prematurely.[2] But the group has continued to operate and even expand, presenting branches throughout the Middle East, North Africa, and Central Asia. The 2014 meteoric rise of the Islamic State (also known as ISIS), al-Qaeda's affiliate-turned-competitor, also shows that transnational jihadism still retains its vitality. Even after the self-styled caliphate has lost most of its previously controlled territory, experts who witnessed the group's recuperation following its crippling by the American surge in Iraq are careful not to write off its potential for recovery.[3]

Have U.S. efforts against al-Qaeda and its associates failed? Did the United States waste the blood and money that were the cost of confronting the jihadi threat? One would be justified in worrying that the answer to these questions is affirmative. After all, relevant datasets indicate that post-9/11 cases of terrorism have ticked up significantly.[4] Just in the last few years, jihadis have been responsible for mass casualty attacks in San Bernardino (2015, 14 fatalities) and Orlando (2016, 49 fatalities), while a wave of jihadi attacks hit European cities such as Paris, London, Brussels, Berlin, Barcelona, Nice, and Manchester. Moreover, since the 9/11 attacks, security services have uncovered numerous other plots against the U.S. and its allies by al-Qaeda, the Islamic State, and jihadi sympathizers. Jihadis now operate in nearly every corner of the globe. Many also have demonstrated willingness to sever their ties to their home countries and travel long distances to support a jihadi cause abroad. Indeed, Muslims from at least 120 countries answered the Islamic State's call to immigrate to its so-called caliphate, despite the long distance and often considerable obstacles.[5]

Prior to 9/11, only six jihadi outfits were designated by the U.S. State Department as foreign terrorist organizations; 35 additional groups had been designated by the end of 2017.[6] Of the 80 groups and entities associated with al-Qaeda and the Taliban currently on the sanctions list formed pursuant to United Nations Security Council Resolution 1267 (1999), 29 were designated during the first couple of years after the attack, 21 other outfits were added between the fall of 2003 and the beginning of the Arab revolutions in December 2010, and 30 others were designated since the beginning of the uprisings.[7]

In this book, I argue that although the existence of a jihadi threat is undeniable, its magnitude must not be overstated. One cannot simply infer the extent of the threat to international peace and stability by bracketing together all jihadi actors and aggregating their numbers. Such an assessment fails to appreciate factors that make a simple conversion of jihadi cumulative capabilities to threat level unwarranted. I identify three interrelated factors that constrain the jihadi movement: First, the "localization trap," the power of state and sub-state identities, which stands as a surprisingly robust bulwark against the transnational agendas of al-Qaeda and the Islamic State. Second, the absence of a viable strategic plan for a global revolution leaves transnational jihadi actors unable to turn violent action into strategic effects. Transnational jihadi groups envision a different organization of world politics, shifting from the nation-state paradigm to a Muslim-dominated religious order; but they cannot hold a state for long, let alone create a sustainable transnational polity that would gradually replace existing states. Finally, intra-jihadi disagreements over objectives and strategy, and struggle for power within the jihadi movement, constrain its development.

THE TWO FACES OF THE JIHADI THREAT

The jihadi threat to the United States has essentially two main elements. The first concerns the threat to American lives and property as a result of terrorist attacks, primarily at home. The second aspect is the jihadi threat to American interests, specifically to the survival of U.S. allied regimes, American business interests, and more broadly to international peace and stability. Whereas the terrorist threat to lives gets most of the attention, the threat to American interests often goes undiscussed. Insufficient attention also is given to the question of jihadis' ability to promote a transnational agenda and achieve their political objectives. Such an omission is problematic. As the prominent terrorism scholar Bruce Hoffmann reminds us, a distinct feature of terrorism is that the acts of violence are carried out in order to accomplish political objectives.[8] Even when jihadi actors turn to other means, such as guerrilla fighting, their violence serves a political agenda. Thus, to assess the jihadi threat properly, looking at its lethality is not enough; we must focus instead on the ability of jihadi actors, whether al-Qaeda, ISIS, or other groups, to produce political effects.

The 9/11 terror attack was the most successful of its kind if measured by the damage caused to its targets. It also succeeded in producing political and strategic effects by dragging the U.S. into quagmires in Afghanistan and Iraq. But as a linchpin of al-Qaeda's strategy to mobilize the Muslim world behind it and cripple the U.S. to enable al-Qaeda to remove ruling regimes in Muslim states and establish a caliphate in their stead, the attack largely failed. The 2004 Madrid bombings is another example of what would seem to be a terrorist success. Not only did it result in nearly 200 fatalities and many more injuries, but it also affected the outcome of the Spanish elections and led to the withdrawal of Spanish forces from Iraq. But in contrast to the perpetrators' hopes, the attack did not create a snowball effect that would leave the U.S. with no allied forces in Iraq, nor did it lead European nations to accept Osama bin Laden's ceasefire offer.[9]

For some, the need to explore the political effects of jihadi violence might appear misplaced. Notwithstanding the carnage terrorism brings, terrorists usually fail to accomplish their political objectives.[10] And jihadi actors who seek to overturn world order set an impossibly high bar for success.[11] Yet, some terrorist campaigns successfully have sent foreign occupiers packing.[12] Moreover, the jihadi threat cannot be seen as limited to the use of terrorism; combining a mix of terrorism, guerrilla, and conventional fighting, armed non-state actors such as the Islamic State did manage to gain control and even govern large swaths of land in Syria and Iraq.

Even if we accept that jihadi groups are unlikely to attain their political objectives, we must recognize the obstacles jihadis face so that states will be able to calibrate their policies accordingly. An accurate—that is, tamped down—assessment of the jihadi threat should inform policymakers' response to the threat, as well as media coverage of terrorist attacks. Since terrorists' success depends on shaping the target's perceptions regarding the costs of terrorist attacks, exaggerated threat assessment, especially when it leads to overreaction, has a self-fulfilling quality and ends up only bolstering the threat. Disproportional response could backfire by increasing the credibility of the perpetrators and expanding the circle of Muslims with grievances against the U.S., ultimately resulting in new recruits to the jihadis' cause, while failing to match officials' unrealistic promises to eradicate terrorism. Additionally, it could lead to misallocation of sparse resources as funds are channeled disproportionally to the fight against terrorism at the expense of other important needs.

In a series of books and articles, John Mueller and Mark Stewart have made a compelling case that the United States has exaggerated the threat posed by terrorism when compared to other threats to American lives. For example, the odds that an American would die from a fall in the bathtub or be shot by a weapon-carrying toddler are far greater.[13] The danger from a public policy subject such as mass shooting is almost unconceivably greater than any terrorist threat to American lives—though it generates much less policy response from the U.S. government. Mueller and Stewart also have demonstrated the inefficiency of U.S. counterterrorism policies, showing an enormous mismatch between the funds dedicated for the many counter-terrorism agencies established or strengthened after 9/11 and their success in thwarting terrorist attacks.[14]

This book's emphasis is different. Far from the dismissive spirit of the work of Mueller and Stewart, I recognize the potency of the threat of terrorism. Just because transnational jihadis are failing to realize their ambitious agenda does not mean that they cannot hurt; just because their attacks often are thwarted does not mean jihadis will not be able to inflict great pain on their targets occasionally. Even though the fear of terrorism has subsided since its peak soon after the shock of 9/11,[15] Americans still appear gripped by it,[16] and jihadis still are determined to strike the United States.[17] Americans may have become accustomed to the much more lethal threat of car accidents to the point of normalizing it, but the threat of terrorism, relying as it is on the production of fear to bring a target to submit to the perpetrators' demands, resonates more strongly as a policy problem. Thus, rather than underscoring the irrelevance of terrorism, I seek to present a nuanced picture of the threat.

In fact, it is exactly because I recognize the centrality of the perceived threat of terrorism that I am convinced it is essential to look critically at its true nature and magnitude and identify the shortcomings of the actors using terrorism. To do so, I focus on structural characteristics that limit jihadis and that are particularly detrimental to transnational jihadi actors such as the Islamic State and al-Qaeda. These constraining characteristics are anchored in the structure of the international system and the power of localism. They are joined by the fragmented nature of the jihadi movement—in part the result of the decentralization of authority in Islam, clashing egos, and disagreements over strategy and priorities—which divides the movement and makes the unification of all jihadi actors' efforts unfeasible. These characteristics operate separately from particular American counterterrorism efforts. But American policies could—and as I argue, should—utilize them as part of the U.S. counterterrorism tool kit. My hope is that the perspective I lay out in the following chapters will contribute to policy debates regarding the best way to amend the American strategy for dealing with terrorism.

This book also differs from existing literature on jihadism. Since 9/11, many excellent books explored different facets of the threat. They often focused on strengthening readers' understanding of particular jihadi groups and individuals, jihad arenas, and jihadi ideology.[18] Some also detailed the story of the War on Terrorism.[19] In contrast, this book joins a short list of studies that focused on the limits of jihadism, particularly the terrific contributions in Assaf Moghadam and Brian Fishman's edited volume *Fault Lines of Global Jihadi*,[20] Vahid Brown's *Cracks in the Foundation*,[21] and Nelly Lahoud's penetrating exposition of jihadism' self-destructive ideology.[22] But it goes beyond intra-jihadi dynamics to also explore systemic features that undercut the jihadi enterprise, linking, in this way, the study of the jihadi movement to international relations theory. It is unique in the conscious use of ideational and material factors, stemming from the nature of the international system as one based on nation-states, to demonstrate the movement's limitations. As such, this work also allows for future comparison between groups such as al-Qaeda and the Islamic State and other armed and peaceful transnational movements.[23]

OVERVIEW OF THE BOOK

The rest of the book is divided into five chapters. In chapter 1, in an effort to orient the reader and introduce the actors standing at the heart of this book, I offer a brief and partial history of the emergence and evolution of transnational jihadism since the 1980s war in Afghanistan. In chapter 2, I examine the power of national and tribal identities. I argue that transnational jihadism's focus on religious affiliation, rather than on national or tribal identities, has had very limited purchase among Muslims. Jihadi leaders reject national and ethnic identities, proudly proclaiming Islam's ability to transcend all non-religious social bonds. Yet, for all their efforts, jihadi groups repeatedly have found that the majority of Muslims still cling to local identities.

In chapter 3, I discuss armed non-state actors' inherent difficulty in producing a viable strategy to promote their ultimate political objectives. Not only have jihadi efforts to overtake existing countries and turn them into Islamic states been unsuccessful or failed to produce enduring regimes, but also their ability to create a transnational polity that would expand and eventually overturn the state-based order has not matched the power of its opponents to thwart it. In making this argument, I examine the shortcomings of al-Qaeda and the Islamic State's strategies for producing world revolution.

The chapter also highlights the international community's ability to repress and socialize challengers to the state-based order. In the aftermath of the 9/11 attacks, the international community came together to fight transnational jihadism and its challenge to the foundations of the international order. Whereas domestic terrorism has been the responsibility of the respective states affected, confronting transnational jihadism (understood as al-Qaeda and associated groups broadly conceived) became a collective duty. Strengthening states' commitment and ability to prevent cross-border terrorist activities implied choking the transnational dimension of jihadi terrorism.

Localization became one way in which transnational jihadi groups responded to these external pressures, but it led them into the localization trap. Local jihadi groups have sought to distance themselves from transnational groups, emphasizing instead their national attachment, and consequently, their limited objectives. Meanwhile, branches of transnational groups tended to focus on local struggles, contributing very little to the jihadi desire to break the international order. In al-Qaeda's case, the ferocity of the American and international response to the 9/11 attacks caught the group unprepared. Severely constrained and in need of demonstrated success, it turned to establishing branches and delegating authority to them. However, in the process, al-Qaeda created competing and locally oriented power centers over which it had very limited control.

In chapter 4, I discuss the limits of intra-jihadi cooperation. I maintain that the inability of the different groups comprising the jihadi movement—and even those belonging to al-Qaeda—to overcome their differences undermines their ability to translate the expanded geographical reach of the movement into the construction of a unified movement under one leadership. These intra-jihadi cleavages are manifested in differences over strategy, interpersonal conflicts involving leaders of the movement, and in the troubled relations between foreign jihadis and the local Muslims they claim to seek to support and to assist.

I pay particular attention to disagreements surrounding religious questions such as the conditions under which excommunication (*takfir*) is required as well as the terms of allegiance (*bay'a*) between jihadis and the conditions under which a pledge of fealty becomes invalid. I argue that the couching of intra-jihadi debates in religious terms exacerbates conflict within the jihadi movement and makes reconciliation and unity much harder to achieve. I demonstrate these points through a discussion of the rivalry between al-Qaeda, the Islamic State, and both groups' former Syrian branch *Jabhat al-Nusra* (JN). The rivalry between these groups undermined inter-jihadi cooperation and hindered the unification of the jihadi movement.

Indeed, despite many ideological similarities between al-Qaeda and ISIS and the latter's initial subordination to al-Qaeda, in 2013, the two groups found themselves deadlocked in a ferocious fight. ISIS branded al-Qaeda operatives apostates for refusing to accept the authority of its leader, the self-styled caliph Abu Bakr al-Baghdadi. At the same time, al-Qaeda admonished its former branch for breaking its oath of allegiance to al-Qaeda's leader and equated it with the notorious *Khawarij*—the group held responsible for the first civil war (*fitna*) within Islam, and the murder of 'Ali, the fourth caliph. In a strange twist, in 2016, al-Qaeda found itself defending its claims for authority over JN, the same group whose conflict with the Islamic State triggered the open spat between al-Qaeda and the Islamic State.

I conclude the book with some policy implications in chapter 5. In a nutshell, I argue for a containment strategy to deal with the threat posed by transnational jihadi groups. The threat of terrorist attacks will continue to occupy the U.S., but the global infrastructure created in the aftermath of the 9/11 attacks has been successful in containing the threat to the international order. I thus call on the U.S. to limit its involvement in overseas conflicts to situations in which a jihadi group threatens to upend the regional and international order.

1

The Emergence of Transnational Jihadism

The central thesis of this book is that notwithstanding the expansion of jihadism, al-Qaeda and the Islamic State—the transnational jihadi groups that have been the focus of the U.S. counterterrorism effort—face considerable structural obstacles that significantly constrain their ability to attain their political objectives. In this chapter I offer a brief, and in no way exhaustive, account of the evolution of the jihadi movement from its emergence on the battlefield in Afghanistan, before moving to a discussion of the limitations of transnational jihadism in the following chapters.

EMERGENCE

The roots of the modern jihadi movement can be traced back to the Soviet invasion of Afghanistan (December 1979) and the resistance it produced. While jihadi groups operated in various Muslim states throughout the 20th century, the Afghanistan war was a turning point, creating a global jihadi movement. Although no more than 20,000 Muslim volunteers left their homes to support the jihad against the Soviets, and their contribution to the war effort was marginal compared with the local Afghan fighters, Afghanistan became a symbol of Muslim unity and resistance.[1] The war also demonstrated the ability of devout Muslims to defeat much stronger powers and to change history. Of particular significance, the war brought together jihadis from different countries, thus producing a transnational movement of battle-hardened, like-minded radicals. It also led to the emergence of a new jihadi elite—most importantly, Osama bin Laden.

With the end of the war, a large group of Arab mujahideen wanted to keep the flame of jihad alive and to use the knowledge and the experience that they had acquired in Afghanistan elsewhere. But they were conflicted about what they should do next. Some, especially those who had previous experience in fighting Arab governments, were inclined to bring jihad back to their home countries. Others argued that the mujahideen should travel to other places where Muslims were oppressed by non-Muslims.[2] These two strands—one focusing on change in Arab states and the other seeking to defend Muslims under occupation—characterized the jihadi movement of the 1990s. Their ultimate failure paved the way for the rise of al-Qaeda's brand of transnational jihad. Veterans of the Afghan war tried and failed to win separate struggles against their home governments in Egypt, Algeria, and Libya. Jihadi arenas in the periphery—Chechnya, Bosnia, and Kashmir—also produced unsatisfying results.

Al-Qaeda, established in 1988 as the Soviet presence in Afghanistan was coming to its end and as the war began to subside, represented a third way. The founders of al-Qaeda knew they wanted to tap the jihadi zeal to accomplish new objectives. The idea was to create a mobile force that would support Islamic and Muslim causes.[3] Bin Laden's proposal that Afghanistan veterans could protect the Saudi border from the Iraqi threat—made after Iraq invaded Kuwait (August 1990)—reflected this line of thinking. To bin Laden's chagrin, the Saudis rejected the proposal and instead asked the U.S. to send American forces.[4] This episode further enhanced bin Laden's hostility toward the U.S. and the Arab regimes, leading him to hone in on al-Qaeda's international orientation and further distinguishing al-Qaeda from most other jihadi groups.

By the end of the 1990s, the failure of localized jihads tilted the balance toward a more globalized view of jihad, focusing on the United States as the main enemy. Bin Laden maintained that local jihads had failed due to U.S. support of the secular regimes. The remedy to this situation was to confront the United States and to bring about its collapse. Once it fell, the Arab regimes would lose their shield, and the believers could take control. The fate of the Soviets served to draw parallels for the coming confrontation with the United States and to embolden the jihadis; it suggested that the collapse of the U.S. was inevitable and that it would weaken the regimes that Washington supported beyond repair.[5]

After a few years in Sudan, bin Laden returned to Afghanistan in 1996. Al-Qaeda was not alone there. Multiple other jihadi groups found safe haven in Afghanistan, building a series of training camps to support the Taliban's war effort and to prepare for their own future terrorist campaigns.[6] Despite al-Qaeda's distinct agenda, bin Laden was careful not to be seen as competing with—or threatening—other non-state armed groups. Instead, al-Qaeda functioned mainly as a facilitator, assisting various other groups. For example, it provided training for volunteers from across the Muslim world regardless of organizational affiliation. Al-Qaeda also provided financial and technical support for their terrorist operations.

Bin Laden knew that the small core of al-Qaeda operatives would be insufficient to achieve the network's goals. In his view, al-Qaeda should function as the vanguard. For genuine change to take place, the various actors comprising the wider jihadi movement needed to collaborate, and the "Muslim street" needed to wake up. After dedicating years to building an independent infrastructure, by 1998, al-Qaeda's leadership was ready to advance to its next phase and announced the establishment of the World Islamic Front for Jihad Against Jews and Crusaders.[7] Still leery of provoking resistance from other jihadi groups, the new front was an umbrella group that brought together Egyptian, Pakistani, Bangladeshi, and Afghan groups. Formally, al-Qaeda's status on this front was equal to its partners—though, in reality, it enjoyed a prominent position.

A few months after announcing the establishment of the Front, al-Qaeda bombed the American embassies in Nairobi and Dar al-Salam as its "coming-out" operation, killing more than 200 people in the process. Retaliatory U.S. strikes on training camps in Afghanistan and a pharmaceutical factory in Sudan were resounding failures, killing neither large numbers of al-Qaeda operatives nor any of its key leadership. Rather, these counterstrikes provided al-Qaeda with tremendous fodder for propaganda. Al-Qaeda's popularity soared, attracting many new volunteers to its training camps and expanding its donor base. Additionally, the American retaliation cemented al-Qaeda's alliance with the Taliban and at least for a while quieted other groups' criticism of al-Qaeda.[8] The October 2000 bombing of the USS Cole in the port of Aden, Yemen, was the group's second significant attack on an American target. This time, the United States elected not to retaliate, avoiding another potential fiasco, but that decision further boosted al-Qaeda's self-confidence and its conviction that U.S. power was a myth.

9/11 AND ITS CONSEQUENCES

Emboldened by its growing stature and popularity, al-Qaeda was ready to launch a cataclysmic event that would expose the "Western war on Islam" and U.S. "occupation" of the Middle East by carrying out an attack that the world could not ignore. The attacks on New York and Washington on September 11, 2001, were designed to change the nature of the battle by provoking greater U.S. involvement in an unwinnable war that would eventually lead the United States to retreat from the region while eroding its base of power. Ultimately, this weakening would result in its demise and open the field to a new power structure in which the Muslim *umma* (the entirety of the Muslim community) would dominate.

But the attack also produced some unintended consequences. Whereas al-Qaeda succeeded in provoking the United States to increase its military involvement in the region, the group underestimated American power as well as American resolve. Al-Qaeda's leaders were surprised and disappointed to find the Taliban unwilling, and the foreign jihadi contingent in Afghanistan unable, to resist the invading forces in any meaningful way.[9] When the United States invaded Afghanistan, it demonstrated its overwhelming military advantage by toppling the Taliban regime and sending al-Qaeda on the run. Even worse, the 9/11 attacks and the subsequent American reprisal failed to produce the expected awakening and mobilization of the "Muslim street." In al-Qaeda estimates, over 2,000 volunteers of diverging commitment levels (equivalent to five times al-Qaeda's strength at the time) arrived in Afghanistan in the aftermath of 9/11, but this number was far from bin Laden's vision of Muslim mobilization.[10]

Despite these failures, the 9/11 attacks did serve al-Qaeda's goals to some extent. The war in Afghanistan increased Muslim resentment towards the United States. In addition, 9/11 helped al-Qaeda in uniting many of the militant groups behind it. The international community's response put all Islamic groups under tremendous pressure. The transnational nature of al-Qaeda's membership and the network's worldwide reach rendered the struggle against it global. Its complex web of connections with groups from around the Muslim world became a defining characteristic of the jihadi movement, pitting governments and militants against one another in a direct confrontation. President George W. Bush's statement that in this battle one must to take sides, not sit on the sidelines, further raised the stakes.[11]

While al-Qaeda was preoccupied with its survival in Pakistan's tribal areas, the organization encouraged its allies and its external operations' cells to carry out attacks against Muslim regimes and Western targets. However, there was no way to hide al-Qaeda's precarious position. Al-Qaeda's fortunes improved after the United States invaded Iraq in 2003. The invasion redirected important U.S. operational and intelligence assets from Afghanistan to Iraq,[12] providing breathing room to al-Qaeda and the Taliban. While the 9/11 attack was generally unpopular among Muslims, the invasion of Iraq appeared to confirm al-Qaeda's claim that the United States was an expansionist aggressor, waging a war against Islam and seeking to take over the Middle East.

Importantly, the American presence in Iraq provided the jihadis with operational opportunities that were particularly critical at a time when their ability to strike the American homeland had declined considerably. Young Muslims, largely from Arab countries, traveled to Iraq to join the fight, taking advantage of Syria's porous border with Iraq and the Syrian regime's blind-eye policy toward it. The U.S. failure to stabilize the country further empowered the radicals, and their increasing confidence strengthened the movement's ability to recruit. The appeal of this recruitment drive became evident in Europe, where well-established networks that surrounded radical imams and jihad alumni capitalized on the anger against the United States. Furthermore, European countries' failure to integrate their disenfranchised Muslim population rendered these youths a receptive audience for al-Qaeda's call. Indeed, some, even if a notably small segment of the Muslim population, made their way from Europe to Iraq. Others focused their terrorist ambitions on European soil, as demonstrated by the attacks on the transportation systems in Madrid (on March 11, 2004) and in London (on July 7 and 21, 2005).

Notwithstanding the opportunities that the American invasion of Iraq presented the jihadi movement, al-Qaeda's predicament following the collapse of the Taliban and the international siege on al-Qaeda's global network did not allow it to participate meaningfully in the military resistance against the forces that invaded Iraq. Although it had some operatives in Iraq such as Abu Hamza al-Muhajir who would later lead its Iraqi branch, al-Qaeda lacked the necessary infrastructure and personnel to operate. Instead, it watched enviously as the Jordanian Abu Musab al-Zarqawi established an organization of foreign jihadis (later joined by many indigenous Iraqis) to fight the American occupation and, by virtue of destabilizing post-invasion Iraq, achieved hero status among jihadi sympathizers.

Indeed, the success of al-Zarqawi's group, *al-Tawhid wal-Jihad* (TWJ), represented a breakthrough for the global jihadi movement: for the first time, a jihadi organization with a transnational agenda had created a base in the heart of the Middle East, one that would become the nucleus of the Caliphate. Moreover, it demonstrated the increased appeal of transnational jihadism. At the same time, al-Zarqawi's success carried with it the seeds of fragmentation even among adherents of the transnational agenda. This fragmentation would manifest a decade later in a bitter fight between al-Qaeda and the Islamic State.

Al-Qaeda responded to its post-9/11 difficulties by pursuing expansion through franchising. In this way, it was able to forge an image of success in which organizational expansion compensated for its inability to strike the American homeland again. At the same time, it offered groups that wished to benefit from al-Qaeda's reputation, operational and logistical networks, and donor base a way to join the group without losing much of their own autonomy. The franchising drive began in 2003 with the establishment of a Saudi branch, *al-Qaeda in the Arabian Peninsula* (AQAP), followed in 2004 by a merger with al-Zarqawi's TWJ. Over the next 11 years, it added franchises in Algeria (2006), Yemen (2009), Somalia (2010), Syria (2011), and the Indian subcontinent (2014).[13]

Al-Qaeda's expansions into Saudi Arabia and Iraq were risky and, as it turned out, self-defeating choices. The premature launching of the campaign in Saudi Arabia and the Saudi people's general aversion to challenging a Muslim regime—especially when a jihad against a foreign invading force was available just across the border in Iraq—resulted in a resounding failure and led to the destruction of al-Qaeda's infrastructure in the Kingdom.[14]

Iraq presented a different set of challenges. It was a cause Muslims could unite behind and thus provided al-Qaeda with an opportunity to recover. However, Iraq also increased the pressure on al-Qaeda to prove its vitality at a time when its operational capabilities were scant and competition was high. The merger with TWJ facilitated al-Qaeda's entry into the Iraqi arena, but al-Zarqawi and his successors were unreliable partners who ended up severely damaging the al-Qaeda brand. Contrary to al-Qaeda's wishes, al-Zarqawi prioritized a counterproductive sectarian approach that undermined al-Qaeda's U.S.-first strategy[15] and pushed the country into a civil war between Shiites and Sunnis, which the Sunnis could not win. The relationship between al-Qaeda and the TWJ haunted al-Qaeda for years to come as the rogue franchise first tarnished al-Qaeda's reputation among Sunni Muslims, and later, as ISIS, it took advantage of the conditions in Iraq and Syria to challenge al-Qaeda's central leadership and upstage it.

Al-Qaeda's Iraqi branch brought chaos to the country, turning the American intervention into a quagmire by sabotaging the state's recovery and reconstruction while bleeding the American forces. But the carnage it produced, particularly the killing of innocent Muslim civilians, gradually undermined the branch's image among Sunnis in Iraq and beyond. The relationship between al-Qaeda in Iraq and local Sunni groups had started straining even before al-Zarqawi's death (June 2006). But his successors, Abu Hamza al-Muhajir and Abu Omar al-Baghdadi raised the ante; instead of seeking reconciliation and accommodations, they attempted to impose their authority on all of Iraq's Sunnis. In October 2006, an umbrella group that served as a front for al-Qaeda announced the founding of an Islamic emirate, named the *Islamic State of Iraq* (ISI) and led by al-Baghdadi who at that point was known to neither al-Qaeda Central (al-Qaeda's central leadership, AQC) nor most of Iraq's Sunnis.[16] Claiming to be the legitimate and sole representative of Iraq's Sunnis, ISI sought to coerce its Sunni opponents into submission.

ISI overreached. It started a sectarian civil war, but could not protect the

Sunnis it dragged into this fight from their Shia foes who were more numerous and dominated Iraq's institutions.[17] Moreover, ISI did not reserve its unrestrained brutality to the Shia and often directed its weapons against fellow Sunnis who refused to accept its impositions. Determined to fight back, some important groups among Iraq's Sunni tribes stood up to the jihadis, even allying with the American forces, which they had viewed as enemies only a short time before. Following the collective effort to rid Iraq of ISI, the jihadi project in Iraq that appeared until 2006 to be a tremendous success story, had faltered.[18] By 2010, almost all the leaders of ISI were dead, including al-Muhajir and al-Baghdadi. Thus, the TWJ affiliation ended up damaging al-Qaeda.

But al-Qaeda learned from its initial mistakes, and in its subsequent expansion, the leadership exercised greater caution in making decisions. In 2006, the Algeria-based *Salafist Group for Preaching and Combat* (GSPC) became al-Qaeda's third franchise. Renamed *al-Qaeda in the Islamic Maghreb* (AQIM), the group failed to carry out a sustained violent campaign in Algeria. However, the franchise proved highly successful in facilitating al-Qaeda's ensuing expansion into the Sahel region, and as such, became an invaluable resource for filling al-Qaeda's coffers, often through kidnapping-for-ransom operations.

In January 2009, al-Qaeda launched a branch in Yemen. An in-house expansion comprised of Yemeni al-Qaeda members and reinforced by Saudis who had escaped government crackdowns, the branch adopted the name al-Qaeda in the Arabian Peninsula to signal continuity with the defunct Saudi branch. Over time, AQAP became al-Qaeda's most important branch as well as its most dependable affiliate. When AQC could not successfully execute foreign operations in the West, AQAP assumed this role: its plan to down a Northwest flight over Detroit (on Christmas Day 2009) did not succeed only because the bomber failed to ignite the explosive properly,[19] and a plan to explode two cargo planes ten months later was thwarted at the last moment.[20] Both operations came closer to success than any planned by al-Qaeda's senior leadership during that period, and their high profile allowed al-Qaeda to claim them as victories, particularly in circumventing Western security measures and drying up Western resources.[21] As a sign of AQAP's importance, in 2013, Ayman al-Zawahiri, who succeeded bin Laden two years earlier as the leader of al-Qaeda, nominated AQAP leader Nasir al-Wuhayshi to the post of al-Qaeda's general manager. It was the first time this position was filled by a branch leader and not an al-Qaeda Central figure.[22]

The Somali *al-Shabab* joined al-Qaeda in 2010.[23] Bin Laden initially resisted al-Shabab's appeals for a merger. When he did accept its pledge of allegiance, bin Laden refused to acknowledge the relationship publically. Al-

Qaeda's position changed only after bin Laden's death when his successor, Ayman al-Zawahiri, faced pressure to demonstrate the organization's relevance at a time when a wave of uprisings challenged governments throughout the Middle East and North Africa.[24]

JIHADISM AND THE RISE OF ISIS

The Arab uprisings facilitated further expansion of the jihadi movement. The turmoil opened space for groups such as *Ansar al-Sharia Tunisia* (AST) and *Ansar al-Sharia Libya* (ASL) to operate. Meanwhile, in Mali, jihadi outfits with strong links to AQIM captured its northern region before being pushed out by a French military intervention (2013). In Yemen, AQAP embedded itself within a broader social movement, taking advantage of the troublesome political transition and later a civil war to capture, and for a time, govern territory in the country's south.

But it was in Iraq and Syria where the most important fronts for jihad emerged. In Iraq, the devastated al-Qaeda franchise, called the *Islamic State of Iraq* (ISI) since October 2006, recovered under the leadership of Abu Bakr al-Baghdadi. It capitalized on the growing Sunni resistance to the sectarian policies of Iraq's Shi'a-led government and started expanding its presence in Sunni areas—even capturing large swaths of territory and important Sunni cities. Meanwhile, in response to Syria's civil war, a small group of operatives, who had fought in Iraq under the command of ISI, started building a new al-Qaeda branch named *Jabhat al-Nusra* (JN). Though JN announced its presence in Syria in January 2012,[25] it continued to deny any formal links to either ISI or al-Qaeda until ISI exposed its subordination the following year.

Over time, JN became increasingly self-sufficient and quite successful in embedding itself within the rebel camp. JN's increased independence not only threatened ISI, but also increased the latter's desire for supremacy over the whole of the jihadi movement. As a result, ISI leader al-Baghdadi announced his group's expansion into Syria in April 2013 under the name the *Islamic State of Iraq and the Levant* (ISIS).[26] Maintaining that JN was subordinate to ISI, al-Baghdadi declared that ISIS would absorb JN. But JN's leader Abu Muhammad al-Joulani rejected al-Baghdadi's words, announcing instead that the group was and would remain loyal to al-Qaeda's chief Ayman al-Zawahiri.[27]

Al-Qaeda tried to arbitrate between JN and ISIS and to keep both under its umbrella, but ISIS did not see itself as subordinate to al-Qaeda. Moreover, it viewed al-Joulani as having rebelled against al-Baghdadi's authority. Finally, in February 2014, al-Qaeda formally distanced itself from ISIS.[28] The split within the transnational jihadi community further escalated after ISIS took over Mosul in June 2014 and subsequently expanded in Syria. On June 28, 2014, ISIS announced the establishment of a Caliphate with al-Baghdadi as the Caliph and changed its name once again—this time to the *Islamic State* (IS).[29]

This move not only reaffirmed its independence from al-Qaeda, but also claimed authority over all Muslims and all jihadi groups, wherever they may be found. The Islamic State's remarkable successes in Iraq and Syria and its proclamation of the Caliphate catapulted it to a position of predominance in the jihadi scene. Revenues from taxing, oil fields, kidnapping-for-ransom, and looting made ISIS the richest terrorist organization in the world. It also became the preferred choice for most of the 40,000 foreign fighters from at least 120 countries who came to join the jihad in Syria and Iraq.[30]

The group collected pledges of allegiance to al-Baghdadi, including from important jihadi groups such as *Boko Haram* and the Sinai-based *Ansar Beit al-Maqdis*.[31] And though ISIS failed to get any of al-Qaeda's franchises to defect, it did chip away at al-Qaeda's membership, especially among the rank-and-file in Algeria, Yemen, and Somalia. As part of its expansion strategy, the Islamic State established 35 *wilayas* (provinces), 16 of which were outside its main zones of operation in Iraq and Syria. Despite this large number of provinces, in reality, the group controlled very little territory outside of its core holdings, and very few of its wilayas possessed elements of governance. For a while, the Libyan coastal city of Sirte served as the Islamic State's main territorial possession outside of the Middle East, but by the summer of 2016, the group was driven away from the town.[32]

The Islamic State's blitzkrieg in Iraq and Syria caught its local enemies by surprise. But the group soon overreached. The combination of the threat it posed to Kurdish autonomy in Iraq, its war crimes against the Yazidis, and the beheading of American journalists and aid workers pushed the United States to intervene. U.S. President Barack Obama vowed to "degrade and ultimately destroy" the group.[33] By the fall of 2017, a combination of U.S. airpower and local forces supported by American special forces on the ground liberated most of ISIS's territory, including the prized cities of Mosul and Raqqa.

Yet, ISIS is far from dead. After a period of relative quiet, it recently increased the tempo of its attacks in Iraq.[34] Hundreds of ISIS fighters have departed Iraq and Syria and relocated to other arenas, bolstering its Khorasan and Sinai provinces.[35] The group's operatives have been carrying out devastating terrorist attacks in the Middle East, North Africa, and Central Asia, as well as in major European cities. Sympathizers have heeded its calls and carried out lone wolf attacks in Canada, Australia, the United States, and

France. The frequency of ISIS terrorist attacks has, in fact, risen at the same time that the Caliphate has been shrinking. Finally, ISIS has built an extensive cyberspace apparatus, resilient enough to survive even considerable setbacks and recover from considerable drop in its media products.[36]

Notwithstanding the Islamic State's defeat in Iraq and Syria, jihadi actors across the world have been expanding their reach and the tempo of their operations. Indeed, between the Islamic State, al-Qaeda and its franchises (the last of which was announced in the Indian subcontinent in September 2014[37]), and other jihadi outfits, the threat posed by jihadism—domestic and transnational—remains a central security challenge to both Western and non-Western countries.

2

The Power of National and Tribal Identities

Transnational jihadi groups struggle to attain their objectives in the face of resilient national and tribal identities. These entrenched identities and the institutional arrangements embodying them—the nation-state and the tribe—conflict with the jihadis' effort to establish religious order and a religious polity—the caliphate—in their stead.

State actors and transnational jihadi groups see the world differently: where most observers see a world populated by sovereign nation-states—with each possessing legitimate exclusive authority within its territory—jihadi actors view a world that was created by God and is divided between forces of good and of evil locked into a cosmic struggle that ultimately will end with the victory of the pious believers.[1] In contrast to the state-centric perspective in which nation-states are the primary actors and the source of collective identification and identity, for transnational jihadis, nationalism and the state are actually tools used by God's enemies to hide the conflict's "true nature" and to marginalize humans' fundamental—that is, religious—selves in order to drive people away from the divine path. Rejecting the nation-state, transnational jihadis see God as the sole source of authority and sovereignty, and states' claims of sovereign authority as usurpers of divine authority.[2]

The prioritization of religion as a source of identity leads jihadis to take aim not only at national identities, but also at all alternative markers of collective identity around which people organize their lives, including subnational and cross-national tribal and ethnic identities. Such identity groups have preceded the nation-state and often have much deeper roots in Muslim communities. Consequently, unlike the claim jihadis level at the state, they do not present ethnic and tribal identities as a manifestation of an intentional anti-

Islam ploy. Transnational jihadis are mindful that the Islamic revelation came in response to a corrupt tribal social and political structure in the Arabian Peninsula. Therefore, they underscore the role of Islamic identity in unifying Muslims of different ethnicities and tribes. Yet, even the most radical among the jihadis largely seek to avoid pitting Islamic identity against tribal affiliation. In fact, al-Qaeda and its affiliates usually seek the assistance of tribal allies in promoting the jihadi agenda. More focused on establishing Islamic governance—and therefore more likely to clash with other actors over questions of authority in its territories—ISIS, and its predecessor ISI, have demonstrated greater readiness to confront violently the tribes that refused submission. However, even ISIS has not designated the tribes as inevitable enemies who must be fought in order to realize the group's religious imperialist agenda.

The attitudes of transnational jihadi groups toward the nation-state and tribalism are central for understanding the ideational component of the jihadi enterprise. Despite the considerable impact of these identity cleavages on the ability of transnational jihadis to promote their agendas, the subject rarely gets sufficient attention.[3] This is unfortunate as transnational jihadis are not only pursuing the physical expansion of an Islamic political entity at the expense of nation-states, but they also seek to reorient people's identities away from nationalism, race, ethnicity, and tribalism. In what amounts to a radical plan of social and political engineering, transnational jihadi groups want to overthrow the state-based order while making Islam people's predominant identity marker.

On the face of it, this jihadi project is overly ambitious. Its end-state requires the Islamic identity to trump all alternatives, at least for all people of Muslim faith. Moreover, transnational jihadism envisions turning all Muslims into subjects of a caliphate that represents an all-encompassing political entity that rejects the legitimacy of national identity or the organization of human beings in nation-states. Given the magnitude of the task, many jihadi groups, from the *Libyan Islamic Fighting Group* (LIFG) to the Syrian *Ahrar al-Sham*—which in principle subscribe to revolutionary Islamic goals—have adopted narrower political objectives. Specifically, many such groups limit their objectives to turning their nations into Islamic states. Such an agenda implies accommodating nationalism, rather than its full rejection.

However, transnational jihadi groups reject such partial solutions. Guided by expansive visions, they engage in a wholesale assault on nationalism. Those engaged in governance may also attempt to transform tribalism. This chapter explores the complicated relations between jihadi groups and national and tribal identities, arguing that the power of these identity markers (primarily nationalism) serves as a bulwark against the expansion of transnational jihadism. It begins with a discussion of the relationship between Islam and nationalism, arguing that notwithstanding their religiosity, Muslims' sense of national identity has been on the rise, support for sharia law conditional, and backing for transnational jihadis' political vision and their version of Islamic law weak. The foreign fighter phenomenon, central to the solidification of Islamic identity at the expense of national identity, is discussed in the following section. In the third section, I present transnational jihadis' negative view of nationalism, followed in the fourth by a discussion of their attempts to overcome nationalism's appeal via appeals for defensive jihad, the doctrine of *al-wala' wal-bara'* (loyalty and enmity), and the proclamation of a caliphate. Then, in the fifth section, I shift the discussion to the power of subnational identities, specifically tribalism. I explain the challenge tribal identity poses to transnational jihadi groups, which reject tribalism. Unable to eradicate tribalism, jihadis often seek to co-opt tribes.

ISLAMISTS, JIHADIS, AND NATIONALISM

Before discussing the adversarial relationship between the transnational movements—al-Qaeda and the Islamic State—and the nation-state, first, it is important to address briefly the compatibility between Islam and nationalism. Admittedly, such a framing is somewhat misleading, giving agency to Islam when, in reality, it should reside with those individual Muslims for whom Islam is a living experience. Therefore, my approach does not view religion as a given and self-evident set of rules, norms, and beliefs. Although religion often involves some fundamental tenets over which there is little to no disagreement (for example, the centrality of Islam's five pillars: declaration of faith, almsgiving, prayer, fasting, and pilgrimage), most aspects of faith require interpretation of texts and traditions. Despite the restrictions on independent interpretation in Islam, Sunni Muslims worldwide recognize the legitimacy of diverse interpretations, as manifested in the acceptance of four legitimate schools of Islamic thought (*madhahib*). The acceptance of such diversity has been one of the factors that facilitated the tremendous expansion of the Islamic faith throughout the world. Thus, exploring the compatibility of Islam and nationalism implies examining the various ways in which practicing Muslims have seen this relationship.

Muslims view the message of Islam as universal, but that does not easily translate to support for political Islam, particularly not in its transnational form. Most Muslims report that they believe the sharia should be the law of the land or at least a source of their countries' legislation. Such an attitude is particularly pronounced in states that have already witnessed some elements of sharia in their legal system, thus making it familiar, less threatening, and more palatable to these states' Muslim citizens. However, data also reveals that a majority of Muslims do not share transnational jihadis' views of the sharia. Most Muslims surveyed think that sharia law should not apply to non-Muslims, express greater support for only partial—instead of full—application of sharia, and prefer using the sharia in family and property disputes over its application in criminal cases and its use as a guide for determining criminal punishments.[4] Overall, Muslims appear to have different notions of what sharia law actually entails, requiring that observers take the data about Muslims' attachment to sharia law in perspective.

Although public opinion surveys found that religion plays an important role in the lives of most Muslims, a majority (in some cases only a small majority) of Muslims in Middle Eastern countries prefers that Islam will not play a significant role in political life.[5] There is a similar rejection of allowing religious leaders influence over government decisions. This rejection, which Mark Tessler views as an indicator for the rejection of political Islam, further increased in post-Arab Spring Egypt and Tunisia after actually experiencing life under Islamist-run governments.[6]

In fact, according to the Arab Barometer public opinion survey, an overwhelming majority of Muslims in Arab countries would like to live under a democratic regime. Perhaps surprising, among the supporters of democracy, more expressed a preference for democracy without Islam over a democratic regime that will incorporate Islam.[7] Thus, while seemingly holding contradictory positions, evidence suggests that most Muslims value their religious identity, but do not necessarily see it as a comprehensive guide for a political system, let alone for a worldwide religious order. They express sympathy for fellow Muslims in their time of need and will send donations, but their views of pan-Islam reflect solidarity among Muslims, not a desire for an all-encompassing political entity.

The rejection of Islam as a system for a global political order could be seen in Muslims' general denunciation of al-Qaeda and the Islamic State. PEW surveys found that sympathy to al-Qaeda has declined consistently throughout the Muslim world.[8] Other studies have shown that Muslims reject ISIS, too. According to the 2016 Arab Opinion Index, an overwhelming majority of Arabs in the Middle East and North Africa have a very negative view of the Islamic State.[9] The Arab Barometer survey found that a large majority of Muslim subjects expressed rejection of extremism and its manifestations such as suicide bombing.[10] This rejection of ISIS cannot be attributed simply to a rejection of its methods. A study examining the positions of Muslims in Middle Eastern countries found very little support for the Islamic State's goals as well (0.4 percent in Jordan, 6.4 percent in the Palestinian territories),[11] implying rejection of its caliphate project and lack of support for abolishing Muslim states and forming in their stead a transnational political entity based on religion.

These findings suggest that notwithstanding the sympathy Muslims may have for the ideas of Arab and Islamic unity or their attachment to their Islamic identity, they do not have a principled objection to the nation-state. In fact, studies have found that with the surprising exception of Tunisia, and less surprising of Pakistan, Muslim subjects largely identified themselves first by their nationality and only then by their Muslim identity. Moreover, despite a low starting point—reaffirming the late arrival of nationalism to the Middle East and its struggle to take hold—sense of national identity has increased dramatically in the recent decades.[12] They clearly do not believe that their religious identity precludes identification with a specific nationality or find a worldwide Islamic polity necessary for the promotion of Islamic personal and social behavior. Even when Muslims wish to see more aspects of Islamic law and morality guiding their states' policies, their views of what these aspects entail tends to focus on personal and family matters,[13] or on the application of Islamically mandated criminal punishments,[14] not on foreign policy and security affairs. Thus, while an increased role for Islam might shape (or reflect) state identity, it does not imply the eradication of the state's national identity. Some Muslims may seek an increased role for religion within their states, but that does not indicate support for a wholesale rejection of the state-based international order and conflict with all actors who subscribe to it.

The picture is more complicated when considering Islamists—those Muslims who envision Islam as the fundamental factor in shaping Muslims' social and political life and seek to promote this vision using political means. While the Islamists are, by definition, supportive of a political role for Islam, many accept the nation-state. Indeed, most Islamists view the state as a fact and seek to reconcile religious rule with nationalism. Groups identified with the Muslim Brotherhood emphasize the centrality of localized efforts to the promotion of Islamic revival. They plan to bring about the establishment of Muslim states ruled by Islamic law through a bottom-up process,[15] but, in general, they envision multiple separate Muslim states, and they accept (at least rhetorically) that these states would be nation-states embedded within the broader state-based international order. In European countries in particular, the Muslim Brotherhood generally accepts that Muslims are a minority, assume that the nation-state is going to remain the fundamental political unit, and direct their efforts toward creating more pious Muslim communities, strengthening Muslim solidarity, and carving out greater political space for Islamist politics. They do all these things while acknowledging the importance of local conditions in shaping the activities of each Brotherhood European branch.[16]

One can identify diverging attitudes towards the nation-state even among jihadi groups. In principle, the jihadi worldview underscores the superiority of Islam over all other subjects of identification, including nationalism. Moreover, jihadis' emphasis on the founding of Islamic political polities (whether the more localized emirate, or the all-encompassing caliphate) necessarily puts them in conflict with the nation-state as the fundamental form of governance. And yet, many jihadi groups have emerged locally, and while they subscribe to the same end-state of establishing a global caliphate as transnational jihadi groups do, in reality, they often pay only lip service to Islam's universal mission. They may utter a commitment to the universal spread of Islam, but such a declaration usually represents the expression of an article of faith, not a call to action. In their view, the transformation of the entire world is remote, unlikely to take place anytime soon and definitely not in the speakers' lifetime. Unperturbed by the Herculean task of transforming the whole world, many jihadi outfits can concentrate their efforts on using violence to bring about change within their own countries of origin.[17]

Ahrar al-Sham in Syria exemplifies this category of nationally focused jihadi actors. Many of its founders had fought in the insurgency in Iraq in the previous decade and were released by the Bashar al-Assad regime in 2011 as part of its successful plan to paint the revolution in religious and sectarian colors.[18] The group concentrates on fighting the Assad regime and has tailored its rhetoric accordingly, clarifying that its armed campaign has a clear and limited goal: change in Syria. In an op-ed published in the *Washington Post*, the group's spokesman Labib al-Nahhas declared Ahrar al-Sham "a mainstream Sunni Islamic group that is led by Syrians and fights for Syrians." Al-Nahhas also lamented that the group has been accused falsely of having organizational links to al-Qaeda and of espousing al-Qaeda's ideology, trying to argue that not only are the group's goals limited, but its agenda is compatible with the inclusive vision advanced by the states that support deposing Assad.[19]

Granted, political considerations could force jihadi actors to adopt conciliatory non-threatening rhetoric for instrumental reasons while still holding extreme positions. Jihadi groups also can adopt gradualism, focusing first on their home countries before pursuing the broader jihadi agenda. To some extent, the Islamic State of Iraq, the precursor to ISIS, did just that, expanding its interests from Iraq to Syria and then to the rest of the world. Either way, such actions indicate that these groups recognize the many pitfalls of adopting—or even being associated with—a transnational agenda. Even if they intend to shift their focus at some point in the future, such organizations could find that what began as a deceptive disguise can take on a life of its own and, following internal dynamics, become a genuine commitment to localize the struggle at the expense of any broad agenda. Even if local jihadi groups may shift their focus when opportunity presents itself, the international community is not powerless to thwart the transition. It has time to assure that such opportunities do not emerge and that localized jihadi threats are contained.

Jihadi groups established to promote a state-specific agenda sometimes expand their operations and carry out attacks outside their home countries. Struggling to operate inside Egypt, the *Gama'a Islamiya*—while not altering its focus on change in Egypt—made a failed attempt on the life of Egypt's President Hosni Mubarak when he visited Addis Ababa for a summit of African leaders (1995). Nationally based jihadis also have attacked states that ally with their enemies, as when the Algerian GIA (French abbreviation for Armed Islamic Group) carried out terrorist attacks in France (1995) in retaliation for the French support of the embattled Algerian regime. Although such operational expansion strengthens the international dimension of jihadi terrorism and poses a greater challenge to international peace and stability, it does not necessarily constitute expansion of a group's political objectives.

Local failures brought some jihadi groups to make more significant changes, ranging from forming alliances with transnational jihadi groups, to what Sid Tarrow calls a scale shift,[20] which in the jihadi context means reorientation of their agenda and adoption of the objectives of transnational jihadism. After failing in Egypt and in desperate need of funds, Ayman al-Zawahiri's *Egyptian Islamic Jihad* (EIJ) hitched its wagon to al-Qaeda.[21] Similarly, unable to revive the campaign against the Algerian regime and losing members to the regime's amnesty programs, the GSPC sought to join al-Qaeda.[22] In theory, such shifts may result from ideational change, not only from operational constraints and opportunities. Most cases of jihadi groups joining al-Qaeda or the Islamic State could be explained by organizational needs. Consequently, in the absence of strong and genuine attraction to transnational ideologies, states may be able to affect branches' calculations and contain the threat they pose to international order.

FOREIGN FIGHTERS

The phenomenon of jihadi foreign fighters injects additional complexity to the discussion of jihadism and nationalism. Notwithstanding the inclination of most Islamist and jihadi actors to operate locally, since the 1980s war in Afghanistan, Muslims of all strands have interpreted belonging to one *umma* as requiring them to assist fellow Muslims whenever non-Muslim forces invade their lands. Thomas Hegghammer identified 18 cases of post-1945 conflicts involving Muslim foreign fighters.[23] The war against the Soviets attracted 5,000–20,000 foreign volunteers.[24] Recently, the wars in Iraq and Syria saw the mobilization of close to 40,000 Sunni Muslims.[25] Most of this contingent joined the Islamic State's caliphate, but some (especially prior to the rise of ISIS) were not attached to transnational jihadi organizations; rather, they came to help Muslim brethren under attack.

When individuals join armed conflicts based on religious identity and convictions, often without their states' sanctioning and sometimes against the states' expressed will, they constitute a force amenable to religious transnational agendas. Although foreign fighters usually mobilize to support a limited and geographically contained campaign, the historical record indicates that jihad arenas could emerge as the engine for transnational jihadism. They facilitate interaction among Muslims from different nationalities, the exchange of ideas among them, and the creation of networks of individuals who bond over shared experiences on the battlefield.

It is not surprising that al-Qaeda rose from the war against the Soviets in Afghanistan, or that the Islamic State emerged and developed global ambitions following its predecessors' confrontation with the American forces in Iraq. Indeed, both bin Laden and al-Zawahiri argued that their experience in Afghanistan changed their lives and strengthened their commitment to the cause.[26] According to al-Zawahiri, the Afghan jihad "also gave young Muslim mujahideen—Arabs, Pakistanis, Turks, and Muslims from Central and East Asia—a great opportunity to get acquainted with each other on the land of the Afghan jihad through their comradeship-at-arms against the enemies of Islam . . . came to know each other closely, changed expertise, and learned to understand their brethren's problems."[27]

Notwithstanding the real danger that local jihad arenas would boost transnational jihadism, the threat must not be overstated. After all, the number of Muslims who actually take part in armed resistance against invading non-Muslim forces is miniscule in comparison to the worldwide Muslim population, standing currently at about 1.8 billion people. Moreover, many volunteers join what they view as a one-off conflict in a particular geographic location. They may see Muslims coming under attack, but not Islam or the entire *umma*. Once the conflict ends, many foreign fighters seek to return to their home countries and get back to their lives, not to harm these states.

Other foreign fighters may wish to continue their jihadi activities elsewhere, but not necessarily to embrace a transnational agenda. Indeed, after the war against the Soviets, the mujahideen who remained active were divided into two main groups: those who went to fight in other locations where Muslims came under clear attack (that is, in Bosnia and Chechnya), and those who wanted to return home and bring down local regimes (most notably, jihadis from Algeria and members of the Egyptian Islamic Jihad and the Gama'a Islamiya). Bin Laden's vision of transnational jihadism, focused on targeting the U.S., gained currency among jihadis only after these two alternative visions for jihad—local fights and defense of Muslims who come under non-Muslim occupation—collapsed around the mid-1990s.[28] Thus, even when jihadi foreign fighters fail to demobilize, they do not necessarily boost transnational jihadism. This is not to suggest that veteran foreign fighters are not a danger, only that such fighters may represent more localized threats to the countries they target, and the danger they pose could be contained.

In this context, it is noteworthy that Abdallah Azzam, the spiritual leader of the mujahideen in Afghanistan who constructed the religious legitimation for non-Afghan Muslims' participation in the war against the Soviets[29] and played a central role in organizing the foreign volunteers arriving at the arena, supported the institutionalization of transnational jihad. Similar to bin Laden, Azzam envisioned armed jihad as the only way to liberate Muslim lands and supported the founding of a mobile force that would reinforce defensive jihad elsewhere (with a priority to the Palestinian arena). However, in contrast to bin Laden's vision, Azzam—who kept friendly relations with the Saudi authorities—showed pragmatism, favoring some restraint by opposing the targeting of regimes in Muslim majority states. Azzam was assassinated in November 1989, possibly at the hands of jihadi rivals. One must wonder whether he would have approved of bin Laden's turn against Saudi Arabia and the United States.

It is important, then, to be cautious lest states' responses to the foreign fighters phenomenon trigger a self-fulfilling prophecy and end up heightening the threat posed by foreign fighters. After the war against the Soviets ended, substantial numbers of foreign volunteers wishing to return to their home countries and resume their normal lives found themselves trapped. The policies of apprehensive home countries thus pushed many who might have been able to reintegrate into their societies to continue their jihadi careers. While the indoctrination efforts of the Islamic State and its track record of attacks in the West makes efforts to nab the returnees justified and inevitable, the odds of successful reintegration by foreign volunteers should not be dismissed out of hand. After all, many foreign fighters immigrated to Iraq and Syria to realize utopian lives in a caliphate, only to find an immense gap between the vision that attracted them and the reality on the ground. Numerous volunteers were lured by empty promises, only to find that the Islamic State is corrupt and its brutality knows no bounds. Moreover, many foreign volunteers seduced by the Islamic State's propaganda found themselves trapped, as ISIS prohibited their return home and their home countries promised them long prison terms.[30]

TRANSNATIONAL JIHADI GROUPS' VIEW OF NATIONALISM

The apparent contradiction between jihadis' universal vision and their often much narrower operational focus disappears in transnational jihadi groups. Such actors are distinct from both the Islamists of the Muslim Brotherhood and the state-based jihadi organizations in their multinational composition, their involvement in cross-border armed struggles, and the breadth and audacity of their objectives. The superiority of Islam over nationalism shapes transnational jihadi groups' near-term objectives, not only their distant goals, and consequently puts them in direct clash with the tenets of the international order. Transnationalism is not reserved for future phases to be implemented after success is reached at the local level; it is a feature and an objective for the present. Transnational jihadi groups make the *umma* and Islam their central referents, rejecting their segmentation by states' physical borders. The composition, structure, and activities of these groups are all geared toward fighting for the worldwide protection of Islam from an alleged "crusader" conspiracy, and toward uniting the *umma* under one political and religious authority.

Transnational jihadi groups promote Islam as an alternative to nationalism. Jihadi speakers regularly praise Islam as a unifying force, while warning that nationalism is driving people apart. In their statements, jihadis juxtapose Islam and nationalism, arguing that in contrast to the exclusionary nature of nationalism, Islam is inclusive and the only system in which actors can genuinely experience equality. Under Islam, they maintain, one's race, nationality, or other identity markers have no power because all Muslims are brothers, united in their faith. Thus, al-Shabab describes Islam as

> a religion that guarantees your rights. A religion in whose sharia all are equal, and where neither the white has precedence over the black, nor the black over the white, except by virtue of faith. Islamic sharia is not based on a racist ideology nor does it endorse a social hierarchy based upon biological differences. We invite you to a religion that transcends ethnic and geographic boundaries.[31]

Transnational jihadi groups view nationalism as antithetical to Islam and as an instrument for dividing the Muslim *umma* into separate states where there should be one Islamist empire uniting Muslims worldwide. According to al-Qaeda, the division of the *umma* did not emerge organically. Rather, it resulted from purposeful and malignant efforts of the "Crusaders." In this enterprise, which began with the successful British measures to split the Ottoman caliphate into nation-states,[32] the *umma*'s enemies have used nationalism to mask the scheme's religious underpinnings. Al-Qaeda goes even further, arguing that nationalism is a scheme to pit Muslim states against each other so that they will exhaust their resources through infighting and become distracted.[33] Thus, nationalism is a tool to stop Muslim states from uniting to promote the interest of the *umma* and to prevent them from facing the real threat, that of the "Jews and Crusaders."

As a result, exposing the religious nature of the conflict and underscoring the importance of the *umma* as the reference group to which Muslims owe their allegiance are central to transnational jihadis' mission. This view has several implications: first, there are Muslim issues and Muslim interests; second, religious affiliation imposes restrictions on states' freedom of action; third, when Muslim subjects arise, all Muslims have a right to intervene, regardless of the position of the states involved; fourth, in some cases, participating in the defense of Muslims becomes a duty for all; and finally, the interests, needs, and obligations of the *umma* are best served by a caliphate.

Transnational jihadis proclaim that all issues concerning Muslims are the interest of the entire *umma*. Therefore, Muslim grievances are never the sole affair of the Muslim population that is suffering from direct repression; rather, it is a matter for the *umma*. This formulation takes away the prerogative of a Muslim community, and the state representing it, to determine its own particular interests and to design policies based on its understanding of the community's particular needs and circumstances. As members of the *umma*, Muslims are all required to promote its goals, which, according to the jihadi logic, necessitates confrontational strategies. A Muslim community may have some advantages and prerogatives derived from its greater familiarity with conditions on the ground, but, in reality, it has only very limited freedom: it must listen to fellow Muslims and follow the path dictated by universal Islamic principles (in their radical jihadi interpretation, of course).

This reasoning was prominent in al-Qaeda's discussion of the Israeli-Palestinian conflict. Al-Qaeda spokesmen have been highly critical of the Palestinian Authority and even of Hamas for their policies vis-à-vis Israel. Notwithstanding its absence from the Palestinian arena, al-Qaeda claims that it has a right, and in fact a duty, to offer advice to its Palestinian brethren and that the Palestinians have no authority to take actions that al-Qaeda views as controverting Islam. Al-Zawahiri explained that the plight of the Palestinians is not a local or regional issue that could be addressed through political means, but an "aggression against the house of Islam, as the Muslims are one nation, and their land is that of one country."³⁴

A decade later, al-Zawahiri made similar arguments regarding the Syrian arena. In his words, "Jihad in Syria is the jihad of the entire Islamic *umma*, and not the jihad of the Syrian people, or the jihad of the people of Sham, or the jihad of the people of Idlib, or Dara'a, or Damascus. . . . The land of Islam is a single town, and the Muslims are one *umma* working towards the same cause, from big to small, and they are one hand against any other."³⁵

The religious nature of the conflict and the superiority of Islam over nationalism requires, according to transnational jihadis, the adoption of a Muslim, not national, foreign policy. If religious identity trumps nationalism, the policies of Muslim states must follow a religious logic and promote religious goals and objectives shared by all Muslims. Thus, in the name of Islam, jihadis delineate clear limitations on basic state prerogatives. Viewing national identity as inherently secondary to a state's religious identity implies that national identity cannot inform Muslim states' interests. In such a perspective, Islam restricts Muslim states' freedom to design and implement independent foreign policy: Muslim states are required to ally and cooperate with fellow Muslim states, and they are prohibited from allying or keeping friendly relations with non-Muslim states. Among the specific restrictions on Muslim states' autonomy is a prohibition on approving of and legitimizing non-Muslims' continued control of territories that once came under Muslim rule (for example, Israel and East Timor).³⁶ Domestically, jihadis demand that Muslim states implement sharia law and reject democratic rule, which they view as inherently contradictory to Islam.³⁷

Jihadis' attack on the nation-state and international order even extends to the use of non-religious discourse and arguments in justifying state policy. On the face of it, jihadis should be able to engage, and perhaps even agree with, some elements of international law and prevailing international norms. However, their rejection of the legitimacy of any legal and moral argument that is not based on Islamic sources does not allow them to accept any common ground with states. Even when Islamic law and morality should lead to similar behavioral expectations to international law and norms, jihadis reject the possibility of engagement with alternative logics. Thus, in his famous *fatwa* (religious ruling) authorizing the use of weapons of mass destruction (WMD),³⁸ the radical Saudi cleric Nasir bin Hamd al-Fahd rebuked all those seeking to form a position based on international law. In his opinion, discussion of the legitimacy of WMD use must be based on Islamic rulings and interpretive rules.³⁹

Transnational jihadis' rejection of nationalism goes beyond reducing the options available to Muslim communities when they face enemies; it also creates behavioral expectations for those Muslim states that live in peace. Membership in the *umma* creates specific obligations that must govern Muslims' behavior whenever their brethren living in a different nation-state come under attack. Highlighting the solidarity among all Muslims, jihadis argue that it is imperative to assist fellow Muslims wherever they are. One's nationality must not stand in the way of one's religious obligations. But the jihadis go further, also determining the exact way in which Muslim states must react. Muslim states are prohibited from simply expressing solidarity with their suffering brethren; they must proactively assist them (particularly when their suffering is caused by non-Muslim states).

Diplomatic efforts to support suffering Muslims are viewed by jihadis as insufficient. They are associated with acceptance of an international order that is built on the primacy of state actors, the principle that states must not interfere in the domestic affairs of other states, and the acceptance of the unique role of international forums in any action taken against aggressor regimes. In jihadi eyes, a real commitment to the *umma* requires taking tangible steps, normally in the form of armed assistance. Muslim states' search for non-military solutions is viewed as the abandonment of Muslim leaders' obligations, reflecting either their betrayal or their incompetence. In this perspective, rhetoric and diplomacy are not legitimate tools, but merely instruments that Muslim rulers use to cultivate a positive, yet deceptive, image without having to take risks and incur costs.

If Muslims must be guided by Islam rather than state law, and if Muslim states are bound by Islamic rules and forbidden from following man-made domestic and international law, then the Islamic state—that is, the caliphate—is the ideal alternative framework for governance.

Ceremonially, ISIS leader Abu Bakr al-Baghdadi emphasized in a sermon he delivered days after he assumed the title "caliph" that the self-styled caliphate is based on religious affiliation that surpasses national identifications. In his words, the caliphate

> is a state where the Arabs and non-Arabs, the white man and black man, the easterner and westerner are all brothers. It is a khalifah that gathered the Caucasian, Indian, Chinese, Shami, Iraqi, Yemeni, Egyptian, Maghribi (North Africa), American, French, German, and Australian. Allah brought their hearts together, and thus, they became brothers by His grace, loving each other for the sake of Allah, standing in a single trench, defending and guarding each other, and sacrificing themselves for one another. Their blood mixed and became one, under a single flag and goal, in one pavilion, enjoying this blessing, the blessing of faithful brotherhood.[40]

Importantly, the caliphate is unlike Muslim-dominated modern states, which are first states and only then Muslim and thus submit to international rules of behavior rather than to Islamic law. It is also distinct from the option of forming a great power by uniting Muslim-majority nations, akin to the unification of the German and Italian states in the nineteenth century, or from a European Union-like confederation of Muslim states. Such an amalgam may overcome divisions within the *umma*, but it is not ruled by Islam.

The caliphate is the embodiment of Islamic order and is ultimately bound to substitute for the nation-state (Muslim and non-Muslim). It is inherently unique because it draws its legitimacy from the divine, not from other states' external recognition, or from membership in the international community and the various international organizations that support the management of global politics. Similarly, the legitimacy of the Islamic state does not stem from adherence to international norms, or from compliance with international law; rather, it derives from following religious commands and implementing the sharia.

These distinctions are important. In the jihadi view, any effort to anchor state legitimacy in secular man-based norms, rules, and institutions inherently undermines its Islamic legitimacy. A state cannot be both Islamic and a member of the international community. States cannot appeal to both religious and international legitimacy because all attempts to bring these two logics together inherently contradict a central tenet of Islam: God's authority cannot be shared! Anyone who suggests differently violates the sacred principle of *tawhid*—the unity of God—that God is unique and superior in every way. For jihadis, any efforts to reconcile Islam with the nation-state imply not only the usurpation of God's sovereignty, but also an abhorrent attempt to make people and institutions equal to God.[41]

The restoration of the caliphate is a central objective of transnational jihadis although jihadis disagree about the timetable for its founding: ISIS assigned great importance to its early announcement, whereas al-Qaeda believes that the reintroduction of the caliphate must be preceded by the demise of the United States. According to al-Zawahiri,

> Every Muslim must seek to unite [the *umma*] in a state of the caliphate that provides equality among Muslims regardless of their peoples, countries and ethnicities, and which rules by the sharia and believes in the unity of Muslim homeland, and which is not a nationalist tribal country, and in the brotherhood of Islam and not the nationalistic tribal bond.[42]

The caliphate is also required for practical reasons:

> The reality confirms that today there is no room for the small countries and small states in the midst of the savage imperialists and colonization and the large presence of parties that have the tendency to be attracted to them, either willingly or fearfully.

Hence, the need for the revolution to remain in progress until the mujahideen of the east meet the mujahideen of the west and the entire nation's people would be liberated.[43]

Transnational jihadis, thus, reject the nation-state and the state-based order in which it is embedded. Theirs is an alternative vision that cannot coexist with the existing world order. The following section focuses on the means through which al-Qaeda and ISIS have tried, and failed, to overcome the ideational barrier to their desired Islamic order.

ATTEMPTS TO OVERCOME THE POWER OF NATIONALISM

How do transnational jihadi groups translate their worldview into concrete action? The first step is to fight the predominant discourse, which puts the nation-state at the heart of world politics and consequently sees conflict in either international or intra-state terms. Thus, in an effort to tear off the "mask" al-Qaeda's enemies wear, bin Laden declared that the conflict is not between nations; rather, it is "fundamentally religious," pitting the "Zionist-Crusader alliance" against Muslims.[44] Another al-Qaeda leader, Abu Yahya al-Libi, protested attempts to frame the conflict in non-religious terms: "Misrepresentation and defeatism had reached a stage in which some have said that our fight against the Jewish occupiers and the criminal Christians is not a religious fight, but only a conflict over the lands they occupied and the homes they seized unlawfully."[45] Seeking to set the record straight, al-Qaeda maintains that, in reality, there is an orchestrated campaign aiming to eradicate Islam from the face of the earth.[46]

Transnational jihadi groups put special emphasis on promoting the doctrine of *al-wala' wal-bara'* which, in a nutshell, highlights the bond between Muslims while rejecting ties with non-Muslims. Basing interaction on religious affiliation is a way to undermine interest-based relationships and to weaken ties that are based on non-religious identity markers, primarily nationalism. Building on Quranic verses and Islamic traditions, jihadis have interpreted *al-wala' wal-bara'* very broadly, turning it into a forceful command for Muslims to work together and a comprehensive prohibition on friendly interactions across the religious divide.

In December 2002, al-Zawahiri released his book *Loyalty and Enmity: An Inherited Doctrine and a Lost Reality*, in which he argued that to neglect to fulfill God's commandments regarding Muslims' association with each other and to disavow all non-Muslims has emerged as a major threat to Islamic belief and tawhid. According to al-Zawahiri, Muslims are prohibited from befriending non-Muslims and are ordered to hate all infidels because the latter despise Muslims and will never be content with them as long as they persist in their faith. The infidels wish to return the Muslims to a state of infidelity. Thus, God forbids Muslims from showing affection to those who oppose him and his messenger Mohammad, aiding them (particularly against Muslims), confiding in them, appointing them to dignified and important posts, glorifying their religious ceremonies and customs, and encouraging—and even praising—their falsehood. Loyalty must be shown to fellow Muslims only.[47]

For al-Zawahiri, this doctrine had clear political and operational implications: Muslim states are prohibited from cooperating with the U.S. and other non-Muslim states fighting against al-Qaeda and its associates, and they apostatize (thus becoming a legitimate target for jihadi violence) when they ally with the infidels. Adopting this far-reaching interpretation of the doctrine of *al-wala' wal-bara'* also means that Muslim minorities in the West should outright reject their host countries and refuse to assimilate into non-Western societies. To the extent that Muslims are forced to keep living in the West, they must distance themselves from the corrupting influences of Western societies. Instead, they must guard their identity as Muslims, ally with the Muslim groups that fight the West, and work to undermine the stability of their host-states. Beyond its political objectives, the call for *al-wala' wal-bara'* also should be understood as an attempt to shed light on religion as the main factor dividing people and create clear distinctions between Muslims and non-Muslims, erasing in the process any gray area between these two groups.

Thus, the doctrine provides transnational jihadis with justification for intervening in conflicts involving Muslims throughout the world, leading them to offer assistance to Muslims in distress wherever they are, whether Kashmir, Chechnya, Myanmar, or elsewhere. But this assistance also implies that these communities lose their independence, as jihadis assert their right to constrain the freedom of operation of Muslim actors when they perceive their actions as violating Islamic percepts.

More prominent in the jihadis' toolkit is the doctrine of *defensive jihad*. According to Rudolph Peters, defensive jihad is, first, a mandated response to an invasion by a foreign non-Muslim state into Muslim lands; second, a means to prevent oppression and persecution of Muslims outside the territory controlled by Islam; and third, a retaliatory response to a breach of treaty by the non-Muslim enemy.[48] In recent decades, jihadis have expanded the scope of events understood as reflecting aggression against Muslims to include any obstacle to the propagation of Islam, even in its most radical interpretation.

Thus, restrictions such as the Muslim headscarf ban and limitations on speech inciting violence against non-Muslims are viewed by jihadis as legitimate justifications for defensive jihad.[49] The result is that transnational jihadism turned a very limited category of events that trigger defensive jihad into an all-encompassing one.

The defensive jihad doctrine thus includes a built-in mechanism to usurp the nation-state's most pronounced prerogatives: the use of coercive means. Whereas the international community views states as the sole legitimate wielders of violent means, transnational jihadi groups emphasize the command to assist Muslim brethren. According to the jihadis, when Muslims come under attack, their defense becomes a collective duty for all Muslims, whether or not Muslim regimes approve coming to the aid of those suffering. Therefore, if a Muslim state refuses to intervene, the Muslim *umma*— whether non-state groups or individuals—is required to step in and fight. With a broad view of what constitutes an aggression against Islam and Muslims, and a concomitant expectation that Muslim states regularly would clash with non-Muslims on a range of issues, jihadis can claim that they are legitimately appropriating the right to fight from states. In fact, when defensive jihad is in order, even local jihadi and Islamist groups are told that they have no right to prevent transnational jihadi groups from joining the fight.[50]

Predictably, the regimes in Muslim states refuse to accept that the conditions of Muslims elsewhere is their affair and that such a low bar for defining aggression should force them into an armed conflict with states that are often much more capable militarily and economically. They do not deny the importance of Muslim solidarity but, in contrast to transnational jihadi groups, see fewer causes requiring the expression of solidarity and view the mode of its expression as primarily diplomatic. Moreover, they absolutely reject the notion that their state prerogatives could be so easily appropriated by armed non-state actors for whom particular interpretations of Islamic scripture are far different from those of mainstream scholars of Islam.

Notably, whereas al-Qaeda relies heavily on the defensive jihad doctrine, ISIS has pursued an even more daring path, using its establishment of a self-styled caliphate to legitimate its calls for the mobilization of the *umma*. Because the role of a legitimate caliph gives him authority over all Muslims regardless of where they reside, by announcing the caliphate, the Islamic State has claimed the right to order all Muslims to pursue jihad. Furthermore, the purpose of mobilization does not have to be restricted to defending Muslim lands and the oppressed faithful; the caliph is entitled—even required—to call for *offensive jihad* for the purpose of expanding *dar al-Islam* (the territory under Islamic rule). Thus, by claiming the right to lead an offensive jihad, ISIS goes beyond arguing that under certain conditions Muslims' obligations trump state interests: it asserts the caliphate's supremacy over and negation of the nation-state.

In addition to its expected role in mobilizing the *umma* to jihad, the reintroduction of the caliphate was also pertinent to the Islamic State's efforts to overcome the entrenched power of nationalism. In contrast to al-Qaeda, ISIS believed that the establishment of a caliphate now—rather than after exhausting the far enemy and the local regimes—would be a more effective way to unite Muslims and elevate their Islamic identity at the expense of their national identities. Such a transformation was particularly important in the Islamic State's core areas of Syria and Iraq. ISIS wanted the Sunnis living under its control to shed their national identities and see themselves as citizens of the caliphate. Bringing in foreign fighters had the potential not only to enhance ISIS's capabilities, but also to dilute local national identities and ease the creation of a Muslim national identity.

To the Islamic State's chagrin, it found changing the way people prioritize different facets of their identities a very elusive endeavor. Locals, particularly in Syria, were upset that the foreign volunteers received special treatment.[51] As enemy forces reached ISIS-controlled population centers, many of the locals who joined the ISIS forces during the group's heydays became reluctant to fight and die for it. In places such as Mosul, foreigners from the Caucasus, who had nowhere to escape, fought to the death, while locals sought to save themselves.[52]

The power of nationalism and the complexity of engineering identity shifts should not have come as a surprise to the Islamic State. Conflicts between foreigners and locals were documented in Afghanistan, Iraq, and elsewhere. They often involved disagreements about Islamic practices. In conflicts outside the Middle East, locals often complained that Arab volunteers were looking down on them, perceiving them as less authentic Muslims, in part because many locals did not know Arabic, the language of the Quran.[53]

This challenge was not restricted to relations between jihadis and locals; it often manifested even among the jihadis themselves. Although interaction did facilitate the creation of networks of jihadis of different nationalities during the 1980s Afghan war, many jihadis still demonstrated considerable local attachments, banding together with co-nationals. Many of the guesthouses in Peshawar catered to the needs of particular nationalities. In response to this challenge, Abu Yahya al-Libi encouraged bin Laden to mix jihadis of different nationalities and spread the operations of al-Qaeda's branches throughout their designated region. He warned against forming groups based on nationality, fearing that they would focus on their home countries and neglect the big picture.[54]

Lessons from the interaction between jihadis of various nationalities during and after the war against the Soviets informed this view. According to al-Libi, many jihadi groups were organized according to their national affiliations instead of uniting their efforts under one banner. The result, he maintained, was a failure to realize the full potential of the jihadi movement. He warned against the tendency of jihadi groups to exhaust all their resources by focusing each on its front, losing sight of the jihadi movements' broad objectives. The founding of al-Qaeda as a multinational group with transnational objectives was supposed to prevent such counterproductive developments, and franchising is allegedly part of the effort to unite jihadi groups under one leadership to prevent the misdirection of jihadi resources. Moreover, al-Libi uses the cooperation between states as another justification to pursue greater unity among jihadis. In his words, he advised Libyan jihadis to unite with their Algerian brothers because they,

> must not overlook the unity of the enemies of the faith against them. They [the enemies] all come bearing their men and horses regardless of the differences in their creed, politics, and interests. They overcame all of that and agreed upon one interest, which is to annihilate jihad and the mujahideen. Their—the enemies of Allah—biggest wish is that every group or party of mujahideen separates and becomes confined within its own region and borders.[55]

The Islamic State faced similar dilemmas. At first, it founded battalions based on shared language. Many volunteers from Europe knew little Arabic and thus could not be trusted to understand commands in a foreign language. There were exceptions, though. Whereas the French-speaking fighters were deployed together, German-speaking jihadis were spread across a number of units.[56] Over time, the Islamic State decided to dissolve some language-based battalions and establish mixed ones instead. This move—prompted by problems with ISIS Libyan forces and with the overly independent Russian-speaking jihadis—reflected the organization's fear that its fighters might develop a distinct identity and become loyal to their battalions' leaders at the expense of their loyalty to the group.[57]

TRIBAL IDENTITIES

On the face of it, transnational jihadism, with its emphasis on religion as the most important identity marker, is antithetical to tribalism no less than to nationalism.[58] But in contrast to the shallow roots of nationalism, tribalism has always been a pillar of social order in Muslim societies in the Middle East and North Africa. Whereas nationalism—imported from the West—was viewed as a foreign scheme to undermine Islamic identity, and thus a clear target for jihadis seeking to cleanse the region from all forms of Western influence and penetration, the complex relations between Islam and tribalism required a difficult balancing act.

Islam emerged within the tribal society of seventh-century Arabia. The story of Islam's early days was, therefore, one of a struggle of a faith-based community to survive, expand, and ultimately break a hegemonic social and political order that was based on tribal affiliation. Muhammad promoted an alternative source of social and political identity, constructing the *umma* as the primary identity group. His efforts triggered a fight with the much stronger tribal elite of Mecca and eventually forced him to immigrate to Medina. Less than a decade later, and in a much stronger position, Mohammad returned to Mecca victorious. Yet, even then, tribalism was so deeply rooted that it could not be eradicated and fully supplanted by Islamic identity. Instead, Mohammad focused on co-opting Quraysh, Mecca's preeminent tribe. Notably, his successors adopted a similarly accommodating strategy, seeking to tie the tribes to Islam and to guarantee Islam's superiority instead of attempting to demolish tribalism as a pillar of order.

The success of the Muslims' expansion efforts increased the *umma's* attractiveness, creating a positive feedback loop and leading additional tribes to pledge allegiance to the prophet. But the Islamic identity was not internalized by many of the tribes. Immediately after his death, some tribes who viewed their pledge as limited to Mohammad sought to break away from the *umma*. The prophet's successor and Islam's first caliph, Abu Bakr, responded decisively to this existential threat to the young *umma* by beating the defecting tribes in the *Ridda Wars* (the wars of apostasy). Abu Bakr's success established that allegiance to Islam could not be retracted or renegotiated.

Over time, many tribes turned into an important force in promoting the Islamic agenda. In modern times, long before the emergence of transnational jihadism, tribal forces played a central role in the creation of the Wahhabi Saudi state and in anti-colonial jihadi rebellions. More recently, Islamic emirates emerged in tribal areas in Afghanistan, Pakistan, Yemen, and elsewhere—reflecting, according to Olivier Roy, the "Salafization" of tribes.[59] Despite the seemingly successful accommodation of Islamic and tribal identities, the tension remains. Indeed, radical Islamists have been irked by traditional tribal elders' links to secular states, pre-Islamic tribal traditions (such as celebrations around gravesites), and lax attitudes toward behaviors such as smoking and drinking, which radicals view as un-Islamic.

In principle, global jihadis' emphasis on the *umma* and their call for the *umma*'s unification contradict the segmentation manifested in tribal divisions. Similarly, tribal elders' lineage-based legitimacy stands in contrast to the jihadis' emphasis on piety and Islamic knowledge-based legitimacy. Linking tribalism to the pre-Islamic *jahiliya*,[60] jihadi ideologues warned against "foolish tribalism." According to Abu Yahya al-Libi, "[They were] societies of ignorance, barbarianism, and tribalism, built on injustice, tyranny, barbarism, oppression of the weak, corruption, and a separation from values. In general, these societies were living like animals, without any religion and without belief in God."[61] In the same vein, ISI's late leader Abu Omar al-Baghdadi expressed his belief that tribalism is incompatible with the primacy of Islam, arguing that it is one of the roots of apostasy. According to al-Baghdadi, allegiance, immigration, and jihad—which he argued are the pillars of Islam—would not have been accomplished had the Muslims not disavowed their tribal loyalties.[62]

And yet, throughout the Muslim world, jihadi groups collaborate with tribes. In fact, jihadis acknowledge that tribes have been prominent among those embracing jihad today.[63] In its *Insurgent Magazine*, al-Qaeda's branch in the Indian sub-continent declared,

> There is something intrinsically good about tribal society that everywhere it is the tribes and tribal society that have defended Islam against a global onslaught and have sheltered the Mujahideen. This is a phenomenon that we see repeating itself from Mali, Somalia, Yemen to Afghanistan and the tribal belt of Pakistan. No wonder, the biggest proponent of the Mc-culture, America—the very symbol of that artificial life that we see growing like cancer in our cities—sees the threat coming not from Karachi, Islamabad, Lahore, Riyadh or Cairo, but Waziristan, Abyan, Mali, and the tribal hinterlands of Somalia. It is the tribal areas in these Muslim countries that are the prime target of the neo-Crusaders' military and cultural onslaught.[64]

Instrumental reasons could partially explain some tribes' attraction to jihadism. Jihadis could serve as force multipliers for struggling tribes, enhancing the tribe's status and providing fighters, arms, and financial resources. Cooperation with transnational jihadis has been used to strengthen tribes fighting predatory states, to increase tribal leverage with governments, as well as to improve tribes' ability to compete with neighboring tribes. Alliances of tribe members with transnational jihadi groups often reflect internal fissures within tribes as young members—primarily from middle- or low-level clans—rebel against tribes' traditional authority structures.[65]

Like their predecessors centuries earlier, jihadis, too, recognize the difficulty of consolidating religious identities at the expense of tribal ones. They also have understood that tribal support could make an immense contribution to their cause, and the equally great costs they would incur from alienating the tribes. Tribes located in remote border areas where the state is unable to exert meaningful control are prized safe havens. Indeed, al-Qaeda operatives who escaped the American onslaught in Afghanistan would not have survived without local support in Pakistan's tribal areas. Tribal hostility toward the encroachment of the Pakistani state into the tribal areas on the Afghan border made them invaluable for the weak jihadis.[66]

Pashtunwali, the tribal code of behavior that emphasizes hospitality and the protection of guests, helped many jihadis to survive, but did not guarantee it. After the jihadis crossed the border into Pakistan in their escape from the American forces in Afghanistan, some locals handed them over for financial rewards rather than providing them shelter. In order to strengthen tribal commitment to defending their jihadi guests, fleeing al-Qaeda operatives sought to marry into tribes in Pakistan's Federally Administered Tribal Areas. Even al-Zawahiri married into a local tribe in Damadola in the remote Pakistani tribal agency of Bajaur.[67]

That did not mean that transnational jihadi groups submitted in the face of tribalism. Though al-Qaeda avoids general condemnation of the tribe as a social structure, it seeks to influence particular tribes and turn them into supporters. In many statements, al-Qaeda lauds the tribes who support jihad—and even those who remain neutral—referring to them as the key supports of the mujahideen and even as the future of the jihadi movement. The attempt to co-opt tribes is particularly pertinent to Yemen, where tribal social structure is robust, whereas the Yemeni state is perilously weak. Thus, al-Qaeda called the Yemeni tribes:

> O proud tribes, which God honored by making them support His religion, and history wrote chapters about your brilliant pictures of manhood and heroism: Your brothers in Gaza are fighting with stones, and you have seen their steadfastness and persistence in war. You have the equipment and weapons, and your zeal was never taken from you. You are known for your keenness for supporting Islam, so may God reward you for this. This is your day, so fight against them before they control you tomorrow. Fight against them as one man, fight for your religion and your good qualities, help those who seek your protection, and return these bright chapters of support and jihad. Do not turn your back on the *umma* of Islam.[68]

Eager for tribal support and fearful of tribes becoming "awakened" by "crusaders" (mostly America) or other anti-jihad groups, al-Qaeda warns its members to avoid conflict with the tribes. When asked about hostile tribes in Afghanistan, al-Zawahiri warned against generalizations. He noted that the U.S. is offering large amounts of money for those willing to betray al-Qaeda's leaders and rank-and-file, acknowledging that some tribal elements in both Afghanistan and Pakistan were blinded by greed. Nevertheless, praising the Afghan tribes, al-Zawahiri claimed that the majority supports the jihadis and upholds the Afghans' "splendid Islamic traditions" of hospitality and giving protection to guests.[69]

An al-Qaeda military leader proposed five methods—focused primarily on accommodation—for preventing conflict with tribes and avoiding the establishment of tribal anti-jihadi militias. The first requires jihadis to understand the priorities of the particular stage of their jihad. When they have only illusory control, they should focus on the parts of jihad that unite the fighters and the tribes instead of those that divide them and make them susceptible to crusader influence. The second method is "talking to people on their level of understanding, according to their school of thought" and not trying to impose doctrine they do not understand. Instead, the jihadis should slowly guide tribes toward the correct understanding of Islam as they gradually gain their respect and loyalty. The third is not to force the tribes to follow strict religious rules in which they do not yet believe, thus turning them into enemies only because they still do not accept the jihadis' views. The author warns of the negative repercussions of branding people as infidels and immoral. He urges the jihadis to bring the tribes to their side or at least keep them neutral. Fourth, the author recommends "halting the punishment from some of those who deserve it" to avoid widespread dissent, especially when it comes to punishment of respected group leaders, and to avoid people saying "Muhammad kills his companions." Finally, the fifth step is to win over (and to focus on) powerful, respected group leaders under the assumption that those who respect them will follow.[70]

Despite their cautious approach, jihadis condemn—and even brand as apostates—tribes that are either "weak" enough to be convinced by the "crusaders" or that choose to side with them. Al-Qaeda calls such tribes weak, greedy, wavering, and unreliable. It lambasts their lack of intelligence, which results in blindness to the way the "crusaders" are using them. For example, in a statement referencing the situation in Iraq, bin Laden argued that the U.S. wickedly schemes to tempt the tribes and buy their allegiance. He maintained that many "free and proud tribes" refused to form Awakening Councils and to "sell out their religion or defile their honor." At the same time,

> Some weak-hearted people have accepted this. . . . These have betrayed the religion and the nation. They have brought lowliness, scandal, and disgrace to themselves and to those who followed them. This disgrace will live with them forever unless they repent. The evilest of tradesmen are those who trade with their religion and that of their followers. They sell out their religion in return for a mortal world.[71]

Such "infidel" tribes are then warned that they must repent, lest they one day stand before God and receive punishment.

Rather than fighting the tribes to shift their identity, al-Qaeda believes in its ability to co-opt and mobilize them in service of its cause. However, because in many cases it could not count on the cautious tribal elders to support a jihadi agenda that upends the status quo, al-Qaeda has sought to support the emergence of an alternative leadership, investing in the indoctrination of young tribal figures through intensive military and religious training.[72] Al-Qaeda has supported a new generation of aggressive young tribal leaders in places such as Pakistan, Afghanistan, and Iraq, thus contributing to the erosion of the traditional tribal order. In many locations, jihadis also participated in assassination campaigns against central figures in the tribal hierarchy, intended to remove opposition to the jihadi groups forcefully and to intimidate tribal elders from resisting the jihadis and young tribal allies.

Similar to al-Qaeda's central leadership, the Islamic State of Iraq, too, recognized the need to gain the tribes' support. In an effort to portray ISI as non-threatening, inclusive, and gaining power every day, Abu Omar al-Baghdadi maintained that 70 percent of Sunni tribes were committed to ISI and that members of each large tribe received a seat on its "widened Shura council."[73] However, in contrast to al-Qaeda's position, its representative in Iraq, al-Zarqawi and his successors, often failed to heed bin Laden's warning against entering into conflict with the tribes.

The group repeatedly clashed with tribes that refused to join ISI even as they were taking part in the anti-American insurgency. Attempts to take over smuggling routes that served as primary sources of revenue for some tribes, as well as the imposition of a behavioral code that went against the habits of many tribe members (for example, smoking), backfired: angry tribes started forming "Awakening" councils to resist ISI and even allied with the U.S. to decimate the group.[74]

AQC took this experience as a cautionary tale and increased its efforts to avoid clashing with tribes. Bin Laden attributed the setbacks in Iraq to the jihadis' mistakes. In particular, he lamented the poor judgment of the Iraqi branch, which by killing hundreds of tribe members inflamed tribal sensitivities and turned the local Sunni tribes from allies to enemies.[75] Recognizing that in a tribal culture the killing of a tribe member could agitate the whole tribe against the killers, al-Qaeda urged caution in all dealings with the tribes lest misjudgment turn a potential ally into a fierce enemy.

The relationship between al-Qaeda's branch in Yemen and the local tribes following the arrival of the Arab uprisings to the country is emblematic of the limitations of the group's efforts to co-opt tribes. A study by Nadwa al-Dawsari reveals that tribe members who joined AQAP did so as individuals and against their tribes' wishes. Many of the youth who join AQAP are frustrated young people, isolated in their communities and with poor economic prospects. In AQAP, they find a sense of purpose and the potential to become influential in their communities.[76]

Overall, the tribes see AQAP as a threat, a view that weakens its ability to make significant inroads into tribal areas. According to al-Dawsari, the Yemeni tribes reject al-Qaeda's excessive violence and are reluctant to cooperate with the group because tribal laws prohibit fighting the government. Moreover, tribes often are deterred from cooperating with the jihadis because they fear the airstrikes and military incursions that follow AQAP penetration and lead to casualties among tribe members, to displacement, and to wide destruction of property, which ultimately result in the erosion of tribal authority and social order.[77]

When tribes cooperate with AQAP, it is usually due to the shared interests in the face of mutual security threat such as Houthi expansion. Even then, cooperation tends to be shallow and opportunistic. On the other hand, when tribal interests conflict with those of AQAP, tribal leaders stand up to the group. Normally, they try to resolve conflicts using peaceful means. They turn to violence only as a last resort. When a military offensive against AQAP threatens to hurt Yemeni tribes, they volunteer their mediation services in an attempt to reach an agreement for the peaceful expulsion of AQAP from their area. Only in parts of the country where the tribal structure is relatively weak did AQAP know greater success, acquiring territory and gaining greater local influence.[78]

ISI learned a different lesson from its early experience: its efforts to co-opt tribes by offering them incentives would be accompanied by the threat of an even greater punishment. The acquisition of large swaths of territory under Abu Bakr al-Baghdadi put the group in conflict with Sunni tribes that valued their independence. It bought the loyalty of some tribal leaders by funneling its largesse to cooperative sheikhs, thus giving them advantage over rival tribes. But tribes that resisted the group found it ready to inflict greater, not lesser, violence. Emboldened by its success and in a better position to coerce unsupportive tribes into compliance, ISIS meted out collective punishment on any tribe that tried to resist its domination. Brutally suppressing tribal challenges in Iraq and Syria, it ended up massacring thousands of tribe members.[79]

The Islamic State's treatment of tribes is not merely a reflection of its inclination toward greater aggressiveness, but reflects different political priorities. Al-Qaeda's emphasis on fighting the "far enemy," and its view that the establishment of emirates and ultimately the caliphate are more remote objectives, made it view conflicts with tribes (and also the Shia) as unnecessary and costly distractions. It needed the tribes as allies and saw little benefit in turning them into enemies. In contrast, ISIS prioritized governance and the establishment of its caliphate. Consequently, the independence of the tribes was understood as a more urgent problem that must be addressed immediately. The establishment of the caliphate put ISIS in direct conflict with the Sunni tribes of Iraq and Syria; it viewed them as an obstacle to the consolidation of caliphal authority and as competitors to ISIS's state-building project that must therefore be confronted head on. Under such circumstances, ISIS could not settle for dual authority structures and could not accept tribal neutrality. Tribes that did not surrender would be fought, and to the death if necessary.

ISIS's brutality has largely gained it the tribes' obedience, but fear, it soon found out, does not produce legitimacy and is not conducive to support at times of great need. ISIS's expansionism created a constant need for manpower. The need increased exponentially when the group overreached, dragging the U.S. and its tremendous airpower into the fight. The shallowness of tribal support for ISIS's ideology became evident as the war turned against ISIS, causing it to lose city after city as well as incurring numerous fatalities. As the circumstances changed, the group learned the limitations of coercion; no longer able to compel effectively tribe members to support the collapsing caliphate, ISIS found itself lacking much needed tribal support.

In nationalism and tribalism, transnational jihadi groups find competing sources of identity, which severely constrain their ability to promote the jihadi agenda. Whereas many radical groups tailor their objectives to accommodate the prominence of the state as a building block of the international system, those adhering to a transnational agenda seek to overcome these obstacles. These transnational groups, encapsulated in al-Qaeda and ISIS, emphasize the primacy of religious identity, present the nation-state as a construct that is foreign to Muslims and incompatible with Islam, attempt to "expose" the "true nature" of the conflict, and devise arguments and mechanisms to subvert states' authority.

They also view tribal attachment as incompatible with an ideal Islamic society, but given the deep roots of tribalism in the Middle East, North Africa, and South Asia, these groups usually would settle for accommodations with the tribes. Jihadis view the tribes as an important force multiplier when allied and as a strong obstacle when an enemy. Because al-Qaeda's strategic plan emphasizes confrontation with the "far enemy"—the U.S.—it generally seeks to avoid conflict with the tribes and instead works to form alliances with them. During the few times that al-Qaeda branches experimented in governance, al-Qaeda's central leadership encouraged them to learn from the bitter experience of ISI, share authority with the tribes, and avoid counterproductive clashes.

The Islamic State, on the other hand, followed a much more ambitious strategy—both in the scope of governance it sought and the accelerated timetable to its achievement. By introducing a caliphate and emphasizing governance, it ended up in direct confrontation with both the states and the tribes that stood in its way. To some extent, ISIS represents the most successful attempt by a jihadi group to implement a transnational ideology. Through the establishment of the caliphate, it appealed to Muslims worldwide to take part in a project that emphasized their religious affiliation while denouncing other identity markers. Yet, its initial success, followed by devastating losses, underscores the ideational limitations imposed by nationalism, tribalism, and ethnic identities.

Despite ISIS's social engineering efforts, the group could not even lead the people living in the territory that it controlled to abandon their tribal and national identities. Within its territory, foreign volunteers have not melded with locals to produce a robust Islamist identity. More often than not, locals have perceived the jihadis who came from abroad as foreign, resented their privileged position, and chafed under their extreme brutality. Furthermore, although the Islamic State successfully suppressed tribal rebellions, it has failed to legitimize its rule.

3

Grand Plans Collapse on the Walls of Reality

To a large extent, the limits of transnational jihadism begin with its unrealistic expectation to transform the world and its inability to present a viable operational plan. Nearly 20 years since al-Qaeda carried out its first formal operation (the bombing of the American embassies in East Africa), and after both models al-Qaeda and ISIS used for pursuing their global agenda failed, transnational jihadi groups refuse to admit defeat and alter their objectives and plans accordingly. Their public commitment to remake the world (or at the least, the Middle East and North Africa) saddles them. When they try to adjust their strategies, they fail to offer a compelling alternative because they cannot—or are unwilling to—abandon their original objectives.

In the face of an American-led global onslaught al-Qaeda turned to franchising without altering its expansive goals. This improvised response has helped the group survive, but it was not cost-free as franchising is incompatible and even undermines al-Qaeda's global agenda. As for the Islamic State, its global aspirations collapsed spectacularly after its hubris and overreach, as with its advances in Iraq and Syria, exposed it to the wrath of a broad coalition of much stronger military forces and to American air power to which it had no answer. Notwithstanding jihadis' ability to strike states all over the world, their ability to shape global politics according to their desires is very limited. Their violence, then, becomes more nihilistic than strategic.

But the grandiose plans of the main transnational jihadi groups must not obscure the fact that all transnational movements are facing material systemic constraints that make the production of cross-border political effects particularly challenging. I term the obstacles transnational actors, but particularly jihadi ones, must overcome when they seek to turn efforts in disparate locations into transnational strategic effects the "aggregation problem." This problem stems from the need to match resources to objectives and the difficulty of operating across borders. Because transnational jihadi actors seek expansive political effects, they must mobilize the Muslim masses and present an operational plan that will enable the jihadis to overcome an international community that is bent on maintaining the state-based order and working to prevent contagion effects that risk international order. The aggregation problem is complemented and exacerbated by ideational systemic forces encapsulated in the "localization trap" discussed in the previous chapter.

In the face of a punishing worldwide counterterrorism campaign, al-Qaeda was unable to create the transnational goals it intended to. Even the American invasion of Iraq, while increasing sympathy to the group's narrative of an anti-Muslim American campaign, did not lead to mass mobilization. On the face of it, branching out allowed expanding al-Qaeda's membership, but it also pushed the group into the "localization trap," shrinking the political effects it could achieve. The much more daring Islamic State's own attempts to expand forcefully across borders appeared more successful when the group erased the Syria-Iraqi border and controlled vast territory in both countries. But its expansion drive soon hit a wall, pitting the group against forces with capabilities it could not respond to. The ISIS experiment appears to confirm bin Laden's analysis and warning that efforts to form an Islamic political entity would fail if taken prior to the departure of the U.S. from the world stage.

The chapter begins with a discussion of the global aspirations of the Islamic State and al-Qaeda before presenting the concept of the aggregation question. It then turns to the various ways jihadi groups and thinkers have been trying to deal with the problem. The chapter presents bin Laden's strategic vision, which focused on bringing about systemic change through fighting the U.S. (the far enemy), and al-Qaeda's franchising strategy that emerged after al-Qaeda's predictions for the post-9/11 struggle collapsed. It, then, examines the works of two prominent jihadi strategists Abu Bakr Naji and Abu Musab al-Suri and the solutions they present to the aggregation problem. After examining these works, the discussion turns to the "master plan" associated with Sayf al-Adl and Abu Musab al-Zarqawi. This plan charted a seven-stage, twenty-year plan for jihadi victory, which had considerable impact on al-Zarqawi's successors in ISIS. After assessing the viability of the "master plan," I discuss the operational logic behind the establishment of ISIS's caliphate and its failure to produce the intended result. The chapter ends with an allusion to the two faces of religious commitment: the belief in the inevitability of victory allows jihadi groups to explain away failures and stay committed to the cause, but at the same time, it discourages serious strategic planning and learning from failures.

GLOBAL ASPIRATIONS

The Islamic State and al-Qaeda seek to overthrow the state-based order and establish an Islamic system in its stead. Such global aspirations are surprising when considering the enormity of the task compared to these groups' meager capabilities. This gap makes it easy to dismiss the objectives of transnational jihadis as no more than grandstanding. After all, even powerful men such as Napoleon and Hitler, leading the strongest militaries in pursuit of global—or at least continental—domination, were shown the limitations of their power. To expect that jihadis, with their relatively small number of followers, limited financial resources, and rudimentary arms, would achieve their grand proclamations defies logic. And if it is so unrealistic, one would be forgiven if he or she does not believe that these jihadis' grand plans are anything other than disingenuous posturing. But bin Laden and many other leaders of the jihadi movement truly believe in their cause, and all paid considerable personal price for their life choices.

Their adherence to global objectives has been genuine, even when they understood that their realization might take a very long time. In a personal letter, bin Laden's close associate and one of al-Qaeda's most important leaders Atiyatallah al-Libi states, "The entire world is waiting for us to conquer it with Islam, to invade and conquer the countries of infidels until there is no unrest, and the religion is for God, so the unbelievers don't have an overwhelming authority that deters people from entering or converting to Islam."[1] Other transnational jihadis reveal, in writing and orally, that others share this view.[2] Moreover, it fits with transnational jihadis' understanding that theirs is a cosmic battle between the forces of "truth" and the agents of "falsehood."[3] Such understanding of the nature of the conflict produced a strong conviction among some of the jihadi leaders that victory would inevitably occur and that failures are merely tests from God.

Attributing the fight's outcome to divine will allows leaders to explain away battle failures, and to some extent, it assists jihadis in coping with defeats, consequently boosting their resilience. As ISIS spokesman Abu Muhammad al-Adnani clarified, God did not promise those fighting in his name victory at all occasions. In fact, God ordained that days of victory and defeat alternate. Defeats are tests for those loyal to God. Although setbacks are inevitable, the victory of Allah's servants is predetermined.[4] However, the belief in ultimate victory also has a considerable adverse downside for the jihadis because it enables them to move ahead with their plans without presenting a realistic and fully developed causal theory of war outcomes or seriously considering the implications of material power imbalances. Such a sense of certainty undermines learning from mistakes. Jihadi actors unsurprisingly enter confrontations without a solid strategic foundation and end up unable to attain their political objectives.[5]

THE AGGREGATION PROBLEM

Transnational jihadi groups set their sights high: they seek to gain control over Muslim lands, unite them under one caliphate, and expand into non-Muslim states. To achieve these very ambitious goals, they must topple existing regimes that are almost always stronger than their challengers and that could often count on external aid to help in resisting the jihadis. When gaining control over a territory, jihadis must also overcome popular resistance to the disruption of traditional social and legal practices and to the imposition of severe restrictions on the population and harsh punishments of those violating jihadis' rules.

More relevant for this study is the immense challenge of expanding jihadi rule across borders. The obstacles to jihadis' efforts to gain control over one country are amplified manifold when they turn their sight internationally. They can succeed locally and still fail to produce broader effects. For the purposes of this book, the need to move from local successes to a favorable systemic outcome is called "the aggregation problem." It involves a two-prong challenge: first, how to garner popular support for the jihadis' all-encompassing revolutionary vision and how to mobilize a sufficient number of Muslims to join the fight; and second, how to operate across borders when such activities trigger interstate cooperation to thwart the jihadis' efforts.

Jihadi actors have long complained about "fickle" Sunni communities.[6] Sunnis engulfed in ethnic and sectarian conflicts never gave the jihadis who came to their aid more than tepid and conditional support. At times, jihadis provided much needed military assistance to distressed Sunni communities only to see that they would be out of the locals' favor once a peace agreement was negotiated or when the jihadis tried to implement their ideas for a sharia-ruled society.[7]

Public support is essential for the survival of insurgent groups, let alone to the attainment of their end state. Gaining such support is challenging enough for a local jihadi group operating within its own country, but the challenge is far greater when it involves transnational jihadi groups and a cross-border agenda. Friction between a local population and foreign jihadis who are often unaware of local traditions or intentionally disrespectful have been particularly harmful for transnational jihadi groups. In some cases, foreign jihadis treated local Sunni communities who disliked the jihadis' rigid dictates (particularly regarding dress codes and personal behavior) harshly. Even when locals in one country support the jihadis—usually for the jihadis' commitment and military prowess at a time when no other effective force exists—they may not wish to live under repressive jihadi rule when the war ends.

Al-Qaeda recognizes that "the people's support to the mujahideen is as important as the water for fish."[8] In a letter to al-Zarqawi, al-Zawahiri warned that "in the absence of this popular support, the Islamic mujahid movement would be crushed in the shadows, far from the masses who are distracted or fearful, and the struggle between the Jihadist elite and the arrogant authorities would be confined to prison dungeons far from the public and the light of day."[9]

The group's experience in Iraq has taught it that while the local Sunni population will embrace the jihadis coming from afar, such support will dissipate in the face of a jihadi overreach. Indeed, in Iraq, the transnational jihadis of al-Zarqawi saw how their treatment of local Sunnis resulted in a remarkable about-face as these local allies of al-Qaeda's Iraqi branch formed Awakening Councils to fight the jihadis. Adding insult to injury, many of these councils' members used to fight the occupying American forces, only then to seek U.S. assistance against the jihadis. Al-Qaeda also acknowledges that given the centrality of tribes in many of the states targeted by jihadis, it is imperative to understand their needs, and directly confronting them is highly counterproductive.

Inferring lessons from the debacle in Iraq, al-Qaeda came to believe that success would require reshaping underprepared Muslim societies. Interestingly, ISIS learned a similar lesson, but it adopted a radically different strategy to attain the outcome. Indeed, whereas al-Qaeda began seeking to influence society gradually and through persuasion and some service provision, the Islamic State focused on social engineering via imposition, repression, youth indoctrination, and efforts to demonstrate effective governance.

When jihadis shift from local conflicts to pursuing their transnational agenda, their mobilization efforts face even greater challenges. Being transnational implies pursuing broad objectives that are far less salient for local populations. For reasons discussed in the previous chapter, locals who are accustomed to viewing themselves as a part of a national community, an ethnic group, or a tribal society are far less likely to identify with regional and global agendas. These individuals may support jihadi groups when they emphasize local causes, but indigenous populations rarely have any interest in fighting abroad as the transnational agenda requires. Thus, even local gains do not save transnational jihadi groups from the difficult challenge of converting popular support for local causes into support for the regional and global agendas.

Severe operational constraints on cross-border activities further exacerbate transnational jihadis' mobilization challenges. In principle, the international community does not see local actors seeking regime change within their home country as inherently problematic and as requiring international intervention. After all, a decentralized international system, based on the principles of state sovereignty and non-intervention, need not respond collectively to localized conflicts, especially when they do not involve a threatening cross-border spillover. Even when armed non-state actors benefit from safe haven across the border from their main arena of operations, their local focus could keep the matter as a bilateral question between the non-state actor's target and its sponsor (whether active or passive), which does not trigger international intervention.

Transnational jihadi groups, however, have a more expansive presence and threaten a larger number of states. They violate state sovereignty not merely as a matter of necessity but also as a matter of ideological commitment. By rejecting the principle of state sovereignty, and concomitant state prerogatives, transnational jihadi groups elicit a much stronger international response than single-state actors. Their dedication to cross-border expansion puts them in direct conflict with the international community because their actions violate established norms against forceful acquisition of territory[10] and because they clash with the great powers' determination to prevent the emergence—through expansionist policies—of another great power.[11] As numerous UN Security Council Resolutions have emphasized, the expansionist efforts of transnational jihadi groups turned them, in the eyes of the international community, into a threat to international stability which requires international mobilization to thwart their plans.[12]

In the successful planning and execution of the 9/11 attack, al-Qaeda took advantage of the failure of the U.S. to understand the threat properly and devise robust policies to counter it. But in the attack's aftermath, al-Qaeda lost its advantage as the much more powerful U.S. vowed to never be caught unprepared again and launched a global campaign against the group and its associates. The "War on Terrorism" does not guarantee the thwarting of all al-Qaeda's plots, but it makes successful attacks—particularly of the 9/11 scope—far less likely. Technological innovations have enabled instantaneous cross-border communication between members of jihadi groups, as well as spreading images of their atrocities worldwide, but technological developments also made it far easier for the international community to surveil and target jihadis (primarily via drones). Furthermore, the ability to carry out terrorist attacks does not provide al-Qaeda and ISIS with guidelines for bringing about the far-reaching political changes they seek.

The international community responded to the transnational threat posed by al-Qaeda and other jihadi actors by strengthening international cooperation. Emphasizing that the struggle against the global jihadi movement must be based on respect for the principle of state sovereignty, the international community views the individual states as the first line of defense. States carry primary responsibility for preventing the use of their territories to harm other states. All states—but primarily those that lack sufficient capacity to fulfill effectively their obligations to other members of the international community—are encouraged to seek foreign assistance. And strong states are urged to provide such aid, while the UN counterterrorism subsidiary collects and distributes best practices. The result has been an uneven, yet meaningful, tightening of state borders, regulation of financial transactions to make terrorism financing more difficult, the training of large counterterrorism forces throughout the world, increased supervision over material for WMD, and extensive intelligence sharing.[13]

As a result, operating across borders has become much more difficult, even among the states in the Middle East and North Africa, where borders are relatively porous. Electronic surveillance and the ability of American drones to target jihadis practically everywhere further contributed to the segmentation of jihadi action. Consequently, leaders of transnational jihadi groups face great difficulties communicating with operatives located elsewhere. True, Islamic State assaults in Europe have shown that cross-border communication is possible, but it involves great risk to all parties involved. Such attacks contributed to a very high attrition rate within the Islamic State's external operations branch.[14] Communication has been a particularly serious problem for al-Qaeda because the U.S. sieged its leadership in the border regions of Afghanistan and Pakistan.

The difficulty of coordinating operations across borders creates fertile ground for principle-agent problems among jihadis. Leaderships must choose between reducing operational tempo and delegating authority to subordinates. But when a leader delegates authority to operatives far away, he puts the fate of the struggle in the hands of agents he cannot control and or effectively supervise. Communication challenges imply severe constraints on the ability of a transnational jihadi group's leadership to provide timely guidance when its agents struggle with tough choices. Indeed, the question of the ability of Ayman al-Zawahiri to provide timely instructions to Jabhat al-Nusra stands in the heart of the debate over the legitimacy of al-Nusra's break with al-Qaeda.[15]

Over the years, various jihadi thinkers presented several ideas for overcoming the aggregation question. Bin Laden formulated his America-first strategy as a solution to the failure of jihadis to topple "apostate" regimes. But his plan also implied that the removal of the United States from the Middle East (or the preferable option of a total collapse of the U.S.) will enable transborder gains. The Islamic State had a different plan, in which its self-styled caliphate was the vehicle for trans-border expansion. Other jihadi strategists also presented ideas for the conduct of transnational jihadi struggles, which included elements of a solution for the aggregation problem. The most important of these are Abu Bakr Naji's work *The Management of Savagery* and Abu Musab al-Suri's *The Call to Global Islamic Resistance*. Because both works received considerable scholarly attention,[16] I will focus only on their relation to the aggregation question. But first, it is necessary to answer the following question: how did al-Qaeda seek to achieve its political objectives?

AL-QAEDA'S STRATEGIC PLAN AND ITS PITFALLS

Al-Qaeda's strategy, as articulated by bin Laden, has been based on two primary convictions: first, the establishment of an Islamic state is impossible as long as the U.S.—"the head of infidelity"—spearheads a global onslaught against Muslims and Islam. Therefore, al-Qaeda must prioritize attacking the U.S. over the confrontation with the "near enemy," that is the "apostate" rulers of Muslim states. Second, given an unfavorable balance of power, al-Qaeda could not be more than a vanguard. To attain its goals, al-Qaeda needs to mobilize the *umma*. According to al-Qaeda, provoking the U.S. to fight Muslims and Muslim states openly and exposing its weakness would lead the Muslim masses to unite behind al-Qaeda.

The first argument has been based on the view that the U.S. is invested in the existing international order that serves its hegemony and consequently, it values keeping the regimes that support it in power. Thus, although deposing the rulers of Muslim countries is an objective of utmost importance, it could not materialize as long as the U.S. protects them. Given the overwhelming advantage of the U.S in material capabilities, fighting the near enemy would be futile: the United States will not let its allied regimes fall, and it definitely will not allow jihadis to capture these states and supplant the ruling regimes. Fighting "apostate" regimes would only lead to the waste of essential resources.

Thus, the only solution, according to al-Qaeda's grand strategy, is to focus on targeting the United States. Attacks on the U.S. would force it to pursue countermeasures that will fail to achieve their objectives, but will exhaust its resources and weaken its morale. Al-Qaeda does not envision winning a direct confrontation with the United States. "The difference between the West and us in the field of technology—and therefore the military field as well—has become immense, and if we continue to use what was imposed on us from weapons and methods and fields of fighting, we will stay slaves to the West."[17] Thus, the victory al-Qaeda seeks would be attained through the use of creative methods (such as the 9/11 turning of American civilian airplanes into guided missiles) and the attrition of enemy forces: "In this stage, if we cannot manufacture weapons like the weapons of the Crusader West, we can destroy its complicated industrial and economic system, and exhaust its forces."[18] Ultimately, al-Qaeda believed that it will establish a "balance of horror" with the United States as the costs of America's alleged domination of the Muslim world will outweigh its benefit. Exhausted, the U.S. will acquiesce, abandon the hated regimes, and cease to support Israel.[19]

In drawing this strategy, bin Laden was influenced heavily by a vivid analogy: the disintegration of the Soviet Union. In a rosy self-serving reading of the collapse of the Soviet Union, bin Laden found a model for the Herculean task of overcoming entrenched order that is dominated by great powers hostile to challengers, and particularly to Muslim challengers. According to bin Laden, the defeat of the Soviet Union in Afghanistan led to its disintegration. With the Soviets unable to exercise their domination anymore, all their proxy regimes in Eastern Europe lost their shield and collapsed.[20] Al-Qaeda's grand strategy is, thus, based on repeating this scenario with the United States.

Seizing on the Soviet case cannot be dismissed as merely a disingenuous attempt to gain support among Muslims; al-Qaeda senior leaders discussed it repeatedly—and uncritically—in internal communications.[21] Astonishingly, the assumptions underpinning the analogy are not a subject of debate. Bin Laden attributed the collapse of the Soviet Union to the Afghanistan quagmire only, ignoring multiple structural and political causes. Consequently, al-Qaeda did not stop to examine how other factors beyond the clash between the U.S. and the jihadis could affect the resilience of the U.S. and prevent its collapse and the anticipated withdrawal of its support from the Arab regimes. Bin Laden's view that the failure of the Soviets was an expression of God's will strengthens the inclination to avoid critically examining the war against the Soviet Union and its disintegration. Trust in God thus substituted realistic strategic analysis.

The second conviction, according to which the American reaction to al-Qaeda's attacks would lead to the mobilization of the Muslim masses, was based on exaggerated sense of self-importance and a baseless belief that Muslims will accept al-Qaeda's atrocities as legitimate, will view the group as their champion, and will seek to join the cause willingly. The masses were supposed to draw inspiration from al-Qaeda's success in carrying out the

9/11 attack, grasp that their preconceptions of the invincibility of the U.S. were based on a myth, and begin believing their ability to win the war against Islam's "enemies." But the group was astonishingly naïve to assume that its target audience would prioritize religious identification over national identity. It did not only exaggerate Muslims' interest in living under Islamic rule within their various states, but also it incredibly believed that Muslims are interested in abolishing the states in which they live and replacing them with one transnational Muslim polity.

Al-Qaeda misperceived how the Muslim masses would react to its actions and to the American response. Contrary to al-Qaeda's hopes, most Muslims did not view 9/11 favorably.[22] Instead of cheering, Muslim leaders and groups throughout the world harshly condemned the attack. Moreover, the masses whom al-Qaeda wished to awaken did not view the American invasion of Afghanistan as an anti-Muslim campaign, pitting the unbelievers against the *umma*, and consequently they did not heed al-Qaeda's call to arms. There is also no indication that 9/11 brought about a radical change in Muslims' view of U.S. power and resolve. Although the subsequent Iraq war generated much greater opposition than the war in Afghanistan, and even translated to the mobilization of thousands of foreign fighters from across the Muslim world, the overwhelming majority of the *umma* still remained passive.

Al-Qaeda's emphasis on the role of American hegemony in thwarting the Islamic renaissance informs the group's attitude toward one of its primary end states: the establishment of the caliphate. In al-Qaeda's view, the U.S. will invest tremendous resources in resisting the caliphate, thus crippling the U.S. must precede the caliphate's restoration. A premature emphasis on the caliphate would constitute a misuse of scarce Muslim resources and threaten the whole enterprise.

Al-Qaeda's central leadership also rejected the introduction of Islamic emirates as premature and fought their seductive power. In letters to its branch in the Arabian Peninsula, bin Laden and his lieutenants repeatedly warned against forming an emirate in Yemen. According to AQC, taking power is only the first step; the emerging emirate will need to provide security and other services to the people under its control. Al-Qaeda understands that the demands of governance might conflict with the needs of fighting. It sees a necessary balancing act:

> The matter of strengthening to set the rule of Allah and managing the areas required a big capability of taming, gentle care and assimilating the society while combating the foe, which also requires rigor and vigilance; these methods can be contradictory at times, but at others it would be sacrificing one side on the account of the other.[23]

Worse, although jihadi efforts have weakened the United States, it is still powerful enough to topple any emirate. The negative implications of such collapse have enormous consequences; it will demoralize jihadis while undermining their position among the people. Bin Laden warned that if the jihadis fail, the Muslim population may not trust them again.[24]

A letter from the leader of al-Qaeda in the Arabian Peninsula (AQAP) to his counterpart at al-Qaeda in the Islamic Maghreb (AQIM) echoes these dilemmas. In the letter, Nasir al-Wuhayshi sought to impart on his colleague lessons from AQAP's experience governing a small territory in Southern Yemen for a few months during 2011–2012 before the group was driven away.[25] Al-Wuhayshi noted that by assuming governance responsibilities, AQAP took on itself an expensive project that often required a trade-off between services to the governed and weapons. Furthermore, when the governed territory was attacked by overwhelming force, the group found that instead of gaining the support of the locals in defending the area, it felt compelled to retreat in order to safeguard the people's lives.[26]

Thus, rather than a strategy for gradually building the caliphate, al-Qaeda's leadership largely viewed the founding of emirates before the U.S. is weakened sufficiently as counterproductive. As a result, al-Qaeda decided that the best way to avoid the dilemma of whether to spend resources on local governance or on the group's external operations is to avoid establishing emirates. If circumstances lead it to capture territory, it should transfer governance to local leaders and try to work behind the scenes (as al-Qaeda tried to do in the Yemen port city of Mukalla[27]).

After failing to capture the imagination of the *umma*, al-Qaeda struggled to acclimate to its new reality. The devastation it experienced following the American invasion of Afghanistan even led prominent al-Qaeda figures to demand re-thinking of the group's strategy.[28] By 2003, around the time of the U.S. invasion of Iraq, al-Qaeda embarked on organizational expansion through the establishment of branches, some comprised of al-Qaeda's cadres, and others formed through mergers with other jihadi outfits.

This gradual expansion was compatible with al-Qaeda's understanding that it could not succeed alone. It also signified al-Qaeda's need to create beachheads in Middle Eastern and North African countries after the hopes for quick rallying of other jihadi groups and the Muslim masses around al-Qaeda due to its success in targeting the U.S. were frustrated. By announcing its expansion, al-Qaeda also was able to push forward a narrative of success, even as it struggled to renew its operations against the United States and its allies.[29]

Decentralization may have been a necessary response of an armed non-state actor struggling to survive an onslaught it was hardly prepared for. In the form of establishment of local branches—each relying primarily on local forces operating in their familiar environment—decentralization was also a reasonable response to improved interstate cooperation that hindered the group's ability to operate across borders. Portraying each merger as the continuation of al-Qaeda's efforts to unite the *umma* and to fight its enemies, al-Qaeda has not backed down from its declared anti-American program.

Forming branches, each focused on a region rather than one particular state, was viewed as a way to achieve success across borders and to mold together jihadis from different countries. But the group still has to overcome the problem of aggregating disparate efforts into systemic effects. Indeed, until the Arab uprisings upended regional order, brought down regimes, and dismantled borders (or at least made crossing them much easier), each of al-Qaeda's branches tended to focus on one country. Nowhere was the change in opportunities more pronounced than in al-Qaeda's branch in the Islamic Maghreb. In a letter to the leader of AQAP, signed at the end of March 2011, an upbeat Atiyatallah al-Libi declared that "Libya is now ready for the jihad, and because of its important location, it will be a jihadist battlefield opening on Algeria and the Sahara, Sudan, Darfur, Chad, the depth of Africa. In addition, it is an opening onto Tunisia and Egypt."[30]

The founding of branches is viewed as means to conduct a struggle that must be fought on multiple fronts. Yet, al-Qaeda's leadership understands the necessity of not losing sight of the broader objective. Branch activities must align to promote the strategy dictated by AQC, instead of succumbing to the temptation to establish small emirates. The jihadis cannot settle for controlling only part of the region. Given the immense power of those fighting it, all branches must prioritize the overall strategy as AQC dictates and avoid local measures that are bound to fail and that will end up weakening the general efforts. The idea that all branches must serve the broader strategy and limit their actions to their designated arenas is central in AQC's critique of Abu Musab al-Zarqawi. After al-Zarqawi sent suicide bombers to strike in Amman (2005), he was harshly scolded by Atiyatallah. The latter reminded him that he is merely a leader of a branch; therefore, he lacks the ability to see the broader picture. Thus, he must not overstep and begin a terror campaign outside his arena without the direct instructions coming from AQC.[31]

Franchising might have been a necessary solution to the aggressive counterterrorism campaign that followed the 9/11 attack, but it risked undermining the coherence of al-Qaeda's transnational agenda. As explained in chapter 2, local attachments tend to be stronger and more deeply rooted than non-territorial religious solidarity. As a result, branches tend to focus on their local arenas, at times, at the expense of the broader agenda. Segmentation also diminishes multinational composition. Multinationalism remains in the aggregate, but the membership at the branch level is based on local forces.

Despite clear instructions from bin Laden and al-Zawahiri to focus on Western targets,[32] over time, AQC accepted ever-widening exceptions that only strengthened the franchises' inclination for localism. Exceptions made to allow branches to act in self-defense against the local regimes tended to divert attention from the "far enemy" to the "near enemy," particularly as under al-Zawahiri, al-Qaeda adopted an expansive view of what kind of actions could legitimately trigger self-defense. The result was further emphasis on local struggles at the expense of the global one. Because al-Qaeda could not abandon the fight against the U.S.—its *raison d'etre*—but its branches have been pursuing local agendas, it ended up promoting a muddied strategy. The Islamic State's caliphate-based model (and its collapse) certainly made al-Qaeda's rhetorical commitment to its U.S.-first strategy necessary for distinguishing the two groups. But in practice, even al-Zawahiri gave ground and underscored the importance of local conflicts.[33]

MANAGEMENT OF SAVAGERY

In 2004, a jihadi using the pseudonym Abu Bakr Naji, posted online a book titled *The Management of Savagery*, in which he offered a formula for the expansion of a Muslim state. Later, Naji was identified Muhammad Khalil al-Hakaymah,[34] a mid-level operative in the Egyptian Gama'a Islamiya, with strong ties to al-Qaeda's central leadership. In 2006, al-Hakaymah announced that Gama'a Islamiya had merged with al-Qaeda, a claim that was rejected by the Egyptian group's leadership.[35]

Naji's vision of expansion involves the creation of islands of disorder that are soon filled by rudimentary jihadi rule—"the management of savagery"—based on the provision of security and basic services to the local population. These islands serve as launching pads for expansion to neighboring lands and the gradual consolidation of an Islamic state. Naji draws inspiration from historical precedents; he argues that Islamic history shows that in the gaps between the fall of one caliphate and the emergence of another, Islamic rule emerged in various locations, gradually evolving into very small states, before uniting to form a caliphate.[36] He expects that the formation of the restored caliphate would follow a similar process.

Jihadi targets are separated into primary and secondary countries. Primary countries—Naji lists Jordan, the Arabian Peninsula, the Maghreb states, Pakistan, and Nigeria—are selected based on geographic considerations, weakness of the ruling regimes, their inability to control the country's periphery, weak sense of nationalism, availability of weapons, presence of jihadi cadre, and intrinsic characteristics of the country's population. On the other hand, secondary states are those neighboring primary states, and while they may also be targets for attacks, their main role is to serve as a logistics base.

Ideally, success in establishing states in the primary locations will enable the jihadis' expansion, through direct intervention, to the secondary countries.[37]

The central features of the current international system make the founding and expansion of a caliphate particularly complicated. Naji notes that the consolidation of the state-based order in the Middle East during the 20th century through the creation of nationalist regimes and erection of state borders as one such limiting factor. He also suggests that popular consent of a region's population is necessary for expansion to succeed.[38] The resistance of the great powers is another constraining factor.

However, neither challenge is insurmountable. There are locations in the periphery—Afghanistan, for example—where states' descent into disorder (or "savagery"), combined with particular geographic and living conditions, makes them viable places for jihadi administration.[39] Moreover, the tendency of great powers to overextend would assist jihadis' expansion efforts. Overextension exposes the great powers to jihadi strikes though these countries—overly confident in their power—often fail to see their own limitations. Another factor that contributes to a superpower's decline and thus works on behalf of the jihadis' plans is the absence of social cohesion among such large states. Jihadi groups could build on the existence of social cleavages and, through terrorist attacks, deepen them.

Thus, the 9/11 attack is central to the ability of the jihadis to win. The attack undermined the prestige of the U.S. among both the masses and the global elites, while simultaneously increasing the jihadis' numbers and geographical reach. It also weakened the United States' social cohesion. Naji presents the attack as an escalatory move that drew the U.S. into a trap: needing to recover its prestige, the U.S. sent military forces to intervene abroad and attack Muslims directly, rather than via proxies. But for all its capabilities, he argues, the U.S. is unable to establish order in countries where it intervenes. Jihadi operations expose the American weakness while enhancing the jihadis' prestige. Additionally, the American failure and the direct targeting of Muslims boost jihadi recruitment as enraged Muslims—persuaded that resistance could succeed because God ordained the ultimate victory of the true believers—join the jihadi "caravan" and contribute to the exhaustion of the United States.[40]

In *The Management of Savagery*, Naji advocates terrorist attacks throughout the Muslim world and beyond. In this way, the U.S. would have to spread its efforts and invest greater resources. The American response to jihadi attacks would lead it to escalate its efforts until they reach unsustainable levels. Moreover, Washington's pressure on local regimes will force them to use scarce resources, resulting in the regimes' further weakening.[41]

The problem of aggregation does not seem to preoccupy Naji. He is confident that the caliphate could materialize. For that purpose, he seeks to drag the masses, as well as all parties and movements into the battle, and to unify everybody into a single force.[42] Specifically, Naji's response to the aggregation problem is that victory in one jihad arena will lead the jihadi forces to invade neighboring states. Naji is optimistic about the prospects of such expansion in part due to his very low estimation of U.S. resilience. He argues that following its retreat from Iraq, the U.S. defensive shield for the apostate regimes is being lifted which would lead to the collapse of such regimes.[43]

Behind this logic are the unsubstantiated assumptions that Muslims see the brotherhood in religion as their primary political identity and that they reject the institution of the nation-state. These assumptions lead Naji to anticipate popular support for the jihadis and willingness to abandon the nation-state for an Islamic state.[44] But he does not entertain the possibility that most Muslims do not want to give up on their national identities and may not want the sharia, especially in its extreme jihadi interpretation, to determine all state action. He also does not consider the possibility that Muslims will view jihadis as foreigners trying to impose foreign order on the locals, rather than as part of the collective.

The book proposes that jihadi groups and emirates should follow a policy of exacting costs from their enemies in order to deter them from resisting the jihadis. As a result of repeated attacks, the enemy would feel helpless and retreat. Naji believes that the ability of the jihadis to exact a price from its enemies will allow their survival even after they have established "administration of savagery." By carrying out such attacks, jihadis can either deter enemy attack from the air or coerce the enemy to stop the airstrikes. Central to this idea is the spread of attacks to locations throughout the world and their execution by other jihadi groups. Not only will the enemy be frustrated by the jihadis' ability to make it pay the price in any location, if the attacks take place in states that are friendly to the U.S., Washington's ability to respond forcefully will be curtailed.[45]

One reason for Naji's optimism regarding jihadis' ability to hurt their enemies and to sow divisions among an alliance of enemy states is that despite their shared animosity to Islam, self-interest drives their actions. Consequently, these states emphasize their security and survival and will prefer to postpone costly conflict until more convenient circumstances emerge. Such an instrumental view makes breaking treaties a regular feature of international life. Thus, carefully tailored attacks would lead targeted states to reconsider whether the benefits expected from continuing to fight the jihadis are worthwhile and lead them to withdraw from the anti-jihadi alliance.[46] Another factor assisting the jihadis is the nature and the psychology of the apostate regimes and the armed forces which constrain their ability to endure pressure and intimidation over extended periods of time.[47]

The strategy proposed—as the author clarifies—assumes a self-conscious jihadi movement, in which groups feel mutual obligation to support each other, even if they differ in "intellectual and operational matters."[48] Naji argues that such commonality exists among all those who follow al-Qaeda. As for other actors who do not follow al-Qaeda, spreading awareness among the *umma* regarding the obligation to unite their goals and methods, and to help each other, would lead them to embrace the required level of solidarity.[49] This view is a naïve one at best: experience has shown that most Muslims reject the jihadi vision and their methods. In fact, even the notion of the *umma* may find very limited appeal among Muslims, leading only a few to mobilize to assist their fellow Muslims elsewhere, while the rest are unlikely to go beyond registering their support without taking any meaningful action.

THE CALL TO GLOBAL ISLAMIC RESISTANCE

The Syrian jihadi Mustafa bin Abd al-Qadir Setmariam Nasar, commonly known as Abu Musab al-Suri, presented an alternative to the strategy discussed in Abu Bakr Naji's *The Management of Savagery*. Al-Suri developed his ideas over decades of experience in several jihad arenas, primarily in Syria, Algeria, and Afghanistan. He articulated his thinking in a 1,600-page volume (published online in 2005), titled *The Call to Global Islamic Resistance*. Notwithstanding al-Suri's independent status, and consequently, lack of a power base, this *magnum opus* gained wide attention among jihadis worldwide.[50] Scholars agree that al-Qaeda after 2001 adopted some of al-Suri's ideas.[51]

Al-Suri offers a strategy for a global insurrection, carried out by multiple independent perpetrators and small cells throughout the world. It is described as "the popular uprising of an entire nation, across the Islamic world and in places where Islamic diaspora communities of various nationalities are present."[52] Associated with "lone-wolf" terrorism, this work focuses on creating systemic effects from numerous uncoordinated terrorist attacks. This plan calls for a global uprising taking place at a time when jihadi organizations—under siege from the U.S.—are crippled and cannot spearhead the resistance.

Al-Suri characterizes the global Islamic resistance as one of a system, not an organization (*nizam la tanzim*). It is a "system of action," and as such, it differs from the common emphasis on centralized clandestine organizations. It is built on bonds created between individuals, cells, and small groups. These bonds are not organizational, but reflect shared beliefs, system of action, shared name, and mutual goal of resisting the U.S. and its allies through jihad. In al-Suri's words, "The idea is to transform the individual jihad into a phenomenon which embraces the efforts of everyone under a single name, for a single goal, with a single slogan, regulated by a single educational politico-judicial program."[53] Noting the potential of this resistance, al-Suri optimistically assesses that it could produce "tens of operations or more daily."[54] Interestingly, operations in Muslim states are identified as the primary mission of the Islamic call. In contrast, attacks in Western countries serve primarily to produce deterrence and to retaliate against these nations.[55]

The age of the nation-based jihadi organizations—hierarchical with a central decision-making authority determining policy—has come to its end. This process, which began in earnest with the emergence of the post-Cold War American-led international order, was completed with the aggressive response of the international community to the 9/11 attacks. With the U.S. facilitating coordination on the international level and complementing individual regimes' measures to suppress jihadi organizations, the structured organization which seeks to topple local regimes can no longer be the preferred vehicle for resistance. A new thinking is required.[56]

In contrast to the diminishing value of state-based jihadi organizations, al-Suri judges jihad in "open fronts"—overt and enduring military campaigns—as beneficial, bringing success on the battlefield while also serving as an effective instrument for garnering Muslims' support (manifested in a boost to recruitment and fundraising). The "open fronts" also enable a more comprehensive indoctrination of the volunteers than jihadi organizations fighting local regimes have been able to carry out. Notwithstanding these contributions, al-Suri admits that thus far the "open fronts" largely failed to bring the desired political objectives (except for the case of the Taliban's Afghanistan).[57]

Importantly, despite the great value of "open fronts," their viability depends on particular enabling conditions. Arenas appropriate for "open front" jihad must have a large land mass, long borders, terrain that makes fighting easier for the guerillas and difficult for their foes, sufficient resources to withstand a siege, population with military skills, access to weaponry, and political conditions conducive to jihad.[58] But, in the post-9/11 environment, the United States' overwhelming military advantage and its determination to fight the jihadi movement openly made fighting on such fronts largely an exercise in futility.[59]

As a result, al-Suri emphasizes a third element: the terrorism-based global uprising carried out by individuals and small cells. Terrorism by disconnected perpetrators strikes fear among the civilian population. And because it is so difficult to prevent, such a scheme could produce a larger number of attacks than terrorist organizations could, resulting in greater impact. Moreover, states' responses in the aftermath of such attacks do not diminish the strength of the jihadi movement in the way attacks by hierarchical organizations do because the attackers operate independently and thus security services cannot reach beyond the perpetrators and dismantle terrorist networks.

The advent of the internet and satellite TV are essential for such independent jihad because they enhance attacks' value. The primary responsibilities of the jihadi movement with regard to this type of jihad is to popularize it, call Muslims to carry out terrorist attacks, provide vital instructional information to potential perpetrators (preferably through experience on the open fronts), and when attacks take place, to contextualize them and give them meaning beyond the particular incident.[60] Notably, al-Suri wrote this book prior to the emergence of social media, which produced new means of communication and expands public exposure to reports and images from such terrorist attacks, thus increasing their impact.

Al-Suri envisions a radical change in the functioning of existing transnational jihadi groups (at the time he wrote the book that implied al-Qaeda Central) as the "Central Circle" of the Islamic resistance. Rather than maintain a command-and-control relationship with other elements of the Islamic resistance, the Central Circle's primary responsibility is to provide ideological, strategic, and tactical guidance, communicated without direct contact. In his early thinking, al-Suri assigned the Central Circle with responsibility for building a centralized military capability for the "open fronts." But, he temporarily abandoned this objective after concluding that following 9/11 U.S. power undermined the ability to engage in "open front" fighting.[61] Although jihadis who gain experience on an "open front" would be a great instructional asset for the independent cells of the global resistance, al-Suri maintains that such fronts cannot emerge at that point. These cells (when not comprised of experienced jihadis) would need to rely on indirect training.[62]

While the spread of terrorist attacks by "lone wolves" and small self-starting cells has demonstrated this work's relevance to the fight waged by transnational jihadis, one must not exaggerate al-Suri's ability to formulate solutions to the aggregation question. *The Global Islamic Resistance Call* offers a path for continued jihadi activity, but it does not provide viable mechanisms for the production of political effects. Al-Suri himself admits that in order to achieve political success individual jihad must be part of a program that would turn such acts from isolated events into a phenomenon.[63]

The success of individual jihad depends on instilling the sense of belonging to the *umma* among Muslims and adopting a global perspective for the jihadi enterprise. As discussed in the previous chapter, such ideational transformation is challenging given the strength of competing identity markers such as nationalism and tribalism. Moreover, since many of the operations of the jihadis would impose costs on Muslim states and their populations, the jihadis must persuade Muslims that they are paying a necessary price for their liberation from the control of the West and the apostate regimes (though to reduce potential hostility of local Muslims against the jihadis, the latter should direct their attacks first at primary targets like U.S. and its allies, and to the extent possible, avoid inflicting direct pain on Muslims).[64]

The author himself notes that most Muslims internalized the Sykes-Picot borders and self-identify with their nation-state. However, he suggests that the breadth of the American assault on the jihadi movement brought jihadis of different nationalities to view themselves as operating against the same enemy (the U.S.) in one encompassing global arena, implying that the U.S.-led War on Terrorism bolstered jihadis' cross-border, a-national Muslim identity.[65]

Moreover, al-Suri overstates the ability of independent small groups of jihadis who were not groomed by experienced unit "builders" to follow his instructions for targeting. Experience suggests that rank and file often do not understand how their attacks are connected to broader political objectives. Therefore, it is likely that some jihadi operations will be counterproductive. Different jihadi actors likely have dissimilar views regarding preferred and legitimate targets, producing, as a result, incoherence.

Finally, individual jihad by itself cannot bring the *umma*'s desired results. The global insurgency requires the re-opening of "open fronts" in order to seize territory and establish Islamic rule. Implicitly, this idea suggests, at the least, undermining the resolve of the U.S. to fight in order to free the "open fronts" from Washington's debilitating hold. But if the U.S. hostility to Islam and Muslims is as deep as al-Suri believes, it is a big question whether fear would trump hatred. Furthermore, if the U.S. views the jihadis as a security threat now, why would it succumb to pressure when such a retreat will only magnify the perceived threat to the U.S.?

Al-Qaeda and the Islamic State both encouraged lone-wolf terrorism though—in contrast to al-Suri's view—they have viewed lone-wolf attacks as an addition to organization-based actions. Al-Qaeda has begun disseminating instructional material online as early as 2003 when its Saudi branch published the online magazine *Mu'askar al-Battar* as a virtual training camp. Later, its branch in Yemen dedicated considerable space in its *Inspire* magazine to instructional articles such as "How to make a bomb in the kitchen of your mom."[66] But given al-Qaeda's wishes to avoid counterproductive operations, it needed sympathizers who would heed its call for violence to understand accurately the desired target selection and the restrictions on violence.

Burned by its experience with undisciplined agents (primarily al-Zarqawi), it did not go far in incorporating independent jihad into its strategy.

ISIS, on the other hand, has been less apprehensive of agents' overreach because it has little qualms about the use of indiscriminate violence. It encourages extreme and indiscriminate brutality against the West, Shia, and even other Sunni jihadi groups. If inflicting pain is the only thing that matters and all action would be legitimized by ISIS's ultra-radical clerics, then the group need not ask for more than the perpetrators of independent jihad to leave behind a message (such as a Facebook status update or YouTube video) paying homage to the group and its self-styled caliph Abu Bakr al-Baghdadi.

The Islamic State's emphasis on independent jihad reflects its dire need to compensate for its own reduced ability to operate. In encouraging such attacks, it seeks to produce a self-sustaining dynamic in which one lone-wolf attack inspires other individuals to carry out their own operations. For that purpose, ISIS even sought to present attacks by individuals and small groups that were directed by ISIS operatives as case of lone-wolf attacks of awakened Muslims.[67] Ultimately, although ISIS-inspired attacks throughout the globe (including in the United States, Germany, France, Australia, and Canada), they failed to generate momentum that would turn them from isolated events into a strategic threat.

THE MASTER PLAN

Although Naji's work is largely a statement of guiding principles for a jihadi strategy, rather than a concrete action plan, it received considerable attention from both al-Qaeda and the Islamic State and had a clear influence on ISIS. In a 2005 book about Abu Musab al-Zarqawi, the Jordanian author Fu'ad Husayn presented a detailed 20-year, seven-stage action plan that would ultimately end with the establishment of the caliphate and the victory of the Muslims. According to Brian Fishman, this "master plan" was the result of an effort by the al-Qaeda leader Sayf al-Adl, aided by members of the al-Zarqawi network in Iraq, to bring together al-Qaeda's strategic vision with al-Zarqawi's action-based, near-term focus.[68] The plan was hatched in Iran where al-Adl spent most of the last 17 years under house arrest. Although the Iranians limited al-Adl's freedom, he was still able to coordinate al-Qaeda's operations in Saudi Arabia and continue his efforts to strengthen al-Qaeda's relationship with al-Zarqawi's group.[69]

There is little evidence to suggest that bin Laden approved the plan, and according to Fishman, this strategic plan was not the only one linked to al-Qaeda.[70] Moreover, not only there is no indication that al-Qaeda Central had a specific timetable for establishing the caliphate, but it is also clear that the group did not plan on restoring the caliphate as quickly as the plan suggests. As a matter of fact, the focus on fighting within the Middle East (that is against the "near enemy") and on the establishment of the caliphate in Iraq conflicts with bin Laden's strategic view.

Although Husayn's book is written in a manner suggesting shared strategic understanding between AQC and al-Zarqawi, in reality, al-Qaeda's leadership rejected many of his actions and even maintained that they reflected an inability to grasp the broader picture.[71] The part dealing with this overarching plan reads as if it reflected al-Zarqawi's analysis, with al-Qaeda's name added primarily to increase credibility and bolster al-Zarqawi's standing within the organization. The plan emphasizes countries that are central to al-Zarqawi's agenda (Iraq and the Levant states of Syria, Jordan, and Lebanon), but is suspiciously ambiguous on bin Laden and al-Zawahiri's home countries of Saudi Arabia and Egypt.

Al-Qaeda's strategic thinking, as portrayed in Husayn's book, sees a war between the United States and Iran that would weaken both considerably and serve al-Qaeda's objectives as practically inevitable. But despite a substantial number of al-Qaeda documents and internal communications coming to light in recent years, there is surprisingly little to confirm that AQC ever shared al-Zarqawi's intense hostility to Iran, or even that it viewed Iran as playing a vital role in the defeat of the United States (as the master plan predicts). In contrast, judging by ISIS's actions (in particular its attempt to restore the caliphate), the plan falls more in line with the perspective of al-Zarqawi and his successors in the Islamic State.

Nevertheless, Fishman's argument that the master plan was designed to link al-Qaeda's grand strategy to al-Zarqawi's operational plans receives some support in al-Zawahiri's 2005 letter to al-Zarqawi. The letter includes a short discussion of al-Zawahiri's view regarding the jihadi plan for Iraq. His plan is divided into four stages. In the first stage, the jihadis expel the U.S. from Iraq; in the second stage, they would establish an emirate (which could over time develop into a caliphate) in the Sunni areas from which the U.S. departed. In the third stage, the jihadis will expand their operations to Iraq's neighboring countries before turning their sights to Israel in the fourth stage.[72] The letter is designed to constrain the operations of al-Qaeda's Iraqi branch, so it is difficult to judge whether it represents a shift in al-Zawahiri's view of al-Qaeda's strategic plan. It is possible that for a while, the belief in the impending American defeat led al-Zawahiri optimistically to think that following its failure in Iraq, the U.S. would abandon the Middle East and consequently enable the anticipated jihadi expansion.

The master plan views two interlinked factors that would allow al-Qaeda to overcome U.S. resistance. The first involves expanding the battlefield by targeting the U.S. everywhere. Doing so would expose the inability of the U.S. to shield its allies. The U.S. would have to spread its forces, thus expanding the resources required to invest in the fight. Additionally, such expansion would make it easier for the jihadis to exact further costs from the United States, and more broadly, to exhaust its forces.[73]

The second factor focuses on the opportunistic use of existing conflicts—primarily the conflict between the U.S. and Israel on one side, and Iran on other—to advance the jihadi agenda. Jihadis believe that this conflict will produce valuable opportunities for their advances. For example, an American attack on Iran intended to curtail its nuclear program should reduce Iran's capabilities and distract Tehran, allowing jihadis' crossing from Afghanistan and Pakistan to pass through Iran to join the jihadi forces in Iraq. Along similar lines, the plan anticipates that the U.S.-Iran conflict will lead Washington to undermine Iran's allies in Syria and allow jihadis to cross the long border between Iraq and Syria and join the fight against the United States. Moreover, jihadis will have an easier time infiltrating Lebanon and attacking Israel from Lebanese territory. Iranian retaliation against Gulf states also will be beneficial for the jihadi efforts in the Arabian Peninsula.

As for a solution to the mobilization challenge, the master plan envisions a positive feedback loop in which every success by al-Qaeda will strengthen it:

> Every victory, large or small, achieved by al-Qaeda will open the door to large numbers of the *umma*'s young men to join its ranks and various fields all over the world. Someone who cannot join directly will embark on forming his own group that feeds on the same ideology in an endeavor to achieve the goal by using the same means and approaches.[74]

The first of the master plan's seven stages is "the awakening stage" that began when al-Qaeda attacked the "head of the snake" (the United States) and, allegedly, led that nation to "act chaotically." As a result, the Muslim *umma* has awakened and finally realized the true nature of the war. Another alleged effect of the successful attack on the U.S. was a considerable expansion of al-Qaeda from an organization with limited resources and capabilities to a vast network with considerable and ever increasing resources. Supposedly, the attack also gave jihadis the right to lead the *umma*. The stage ended with the American occupation of Baghdad.

In the following three-year stage, dubbed the "eye-opening" stage, the *umma* wakes up to the reality of "occupation" and builds a jihadi army in Iraq. During this period, it would begin attacking Israel, burn oil fields to deprive the West and their proxy regimes of oil revenues, begin establishing power bases in vital areas in the Muslim world, and prepare instructional religious studies and infrastructure for "electronic jihad." In the third stage, "the stage of standing upright" (2007–2010), the jihadi army built in Iraq would deploy forces to neighboring countries, at first focusing on the Levant. With a presence on Israel's borders, al-Qaeda would intensify its attacks on Israel, which, in turn, would increase the group's standing and resources.

The fourth stage, "the stage of recuperation" (2010–2013), focuses on overthrowing the "subservient" regimes as the expanded battlefield makes it difficult for the United States to defend its allies, exposing the regimes to jihadi attacks. Economic warfare results in the dollar's drop and eventual collapse; the country's economic decline—due in part to the "schemes of the Jewish economists"—results in public pressure on American leaders to abandon Israel. Although this stage seems to be compatible with al-Qaeda's notion that only the defeat of the U.S. will enable the toppling of the Arab regimes, one must note that it envisions parallel efforts to both continue to weaken the U.S. and to wrestle control from the apostate regimes of the Middle East.

In the fifth stage, "the stage of declaring the state" (2013–2016), the regimes' hold loosens further, and Israel weakens. The U.S. decline is accompanied by China's rise as a superpower less hostile to Islam. The following stage, "the stage of absolute confrontation," sees the onset of an all-out confrontation between the forces of faith, led by a strong al-Qaeda, and forces of global atheism. This fight starts immediately after the establishment of caliphate that would provide leadership, effective use of the *umma*'s resources, reconstruction, and the dissemination of "rights, justice, freedom, and equality on earth." The caliphate will also create a new international balance of power with the caliphate rising, while forces hostile to Islam retreat. In the final stage, the war ends with the Muslims victorious.

There are limitations to what one could infer from a blueprint, but with caution, it is possible to identify some of the plan's shortcomings. Al-Qaeda's expectation that the U.S. will come to blows with Iran, which would destabilize the region and allow jihadis to take advantage of the weakening regional actors, failed to materialize. As a result, the jihadis could not bring into Iraq the numbers they were hoping for. Even with the cooperation of the Assad regime, which enabled the arrival of foreign fighters to Iraq through Syria, the jihadis were unable to bring a sufficiently large number of volunteers to Iraq. Al-Zarqawi lamented what he viewed as insufficient commitment by Iraqi Sunnis and the low numbers of foreign volunteers. For this reason, fomenting civil war between Iraq's Sunnis and Shia became all the more important as al-Zarqawi expected that it would increase the number of fighters amongst Iraq's Sunnis and would bolster their commitment to fighting.[75]

Similarly, the promise of clashes with Israel did not match jihadis' capabilities. Notwithstanding jihadi efforts, their attempts to target Israel were few and unsuccessful. And they failed to motivate the *umma* to join the struggle. They were so insignificant that the jihadis were criticized that while they carry out massacres in markets in Muslims states, leading to large number of civilian casualties, the jihadis are absent from the Palestinian arena.[76] The plan also underestimated the strength of the American-Israeli alliance; the prediction that the U.S. would disengage from Israel under the pressure of jihadi challenges and economic crisis proved incorrect. The plan also overestimated the jihadis' ability to carry out large-scale debilitating cyber-attacks on the United States and to manipulate the gold market in order to bring about the dollar's collapse.

Second, some of the assumptions underpinning the "master plan" were dubious. The plan assumes that there are only two forces in Muslim states, the corrupt regimes and the jihadis, neglecting the existence of other actors and ignoring common divisions between different jihadi groups (primarily between those pursuing transnational jihad and the establishment of the caliphate in Iraq and those seeking a national Iraqi jihad and a struggle to regain Sunni rule in the country). Furthermore, the jihadis ignored the possibility that Muslim publics might rebel against the regimes in order to install a more democratic regime that will create economic opportunities, not to form a jihadi state.

The plan also assumes that Muslims do not need to be won over, only awakened and injected with confidence. Reality never matched these expectations. Evidently, the international community did not see 1.8 billion Muslims uniting behind the jihadis as a real danger that should force external actors to give up and abandon the Muslim-majority regions. Notwithstanding the efforts of some Islamophobes to portray all Muslims as enemies, governments understood the great diversity of Muslim voices, traditions, and interests, as well as the very limited—though clearly worrying—appeal of jihadism. Even when ISIS announced the caliphate and expanded throughout the Middle East and North Africa, it never reached the capabilities that would turn it into a major power with impact on the global balance of power. It failed to attract large numbers of followers and undermine states that were not already weak and divided. And after initial success facing relatively weak forces, ISIS forces were defeated by a combination of local forces and foreign airpower, not even requiring the Islamic State's Western enemies to mobilize large forces.

Furthermore, accepting Fishman's argument that in the eyes of the Islamic

State most Muslims are apostates implies that the group's recruitment potential is far lower than the number of Muslims worldwide. That means ISIS was expecting to achieve more with a significantly smaller number. Fishman maintains that the Islamic State's radical view contributed to its inability to form a globe-spanning caliphate because instead of mobilizing the entire world's Muslims to fight for the caliphate, the ISIS vision implies considerably fewer forces having to confront a much larger enemy comprised not only of infidels, but also numerous "apostates."[77]

Finally, the plan's view of Syria's potential for jihad rests on a shaky analysis. According to the blueprint, American hostility to Assad would allow the jihadis to bring down the Syrian regime because in contrast to U.S. policy supporting its ally regimes in the region, in the case of Assad, the U.S. would not attempt to rescue him. Such a reading makes Syria an exception to al-Qaeda's argument that the jihadis must attack the "far enemy" before it will be able to tackle the local regimes. Fishman maintains that this exception bridged the gap between al-Qaeda's strategic vision and al-Zarqawi's plans.[78] While Syria did end up as a jihad arena six years after the master plan became public, it was not caused by a jihadi initiative, but in response to the brutal response of the regime to the popular uprising in Syria. Moreover, the plan's assumption that the U.S. will make an exception to its commitment to prevent jihadi advances conflicts with bin Laden's conviction that the U.S. is inherently and permanently hostile to the jihadi movement and Islam. Such alleged enmity suggests that Washington should be willing to form an alliance with Assad against the greater threat posed by the jihadis. Lastly, the U.S. response to the threat posed by ISIS demonstrated that it could fight the jihadis in Syria even without siding and cooperating with the Assad regime.

THE ISIS CALIPHATE

The examination of ISIS's actions reveals its inability to overcome the aggregation problem despite what on the face of it appears as much more comfortable conditions. A few developments contributed to the Islamic State's remarkable success in 2014 before it started losing territory: a corrupt Iraqi government that alienated the country's Sunni community while simultaneously weakening the Iraqi armed forces; the civil war in Syria; the availability of weaponry (including American-made weapons given to the Iraqi military only to become ISIS's loot); and American reluctance to re-enter the Middle East shortly after its forces left Iraq. Under these conditions, ISIS was able to launch a blitzkrieg attack and capture Mosul and other Sunni-dominated

Iraqi cities before quickly turning its attention to expanding its territory in war-torn Syria.

It is difficult to tell whether the Islamic State's gambit would have succeeded had the group avoided committing war crimes against the Yazidis or beheading American and British journalists and aid workers with great fanfare. It is likely that even had the U.S. tolerated a jihadi state in parts of Iraq and Syria, any move on Jordan or Saudi Arabia would have brought American forces back to the region. But ISIS did not really give its state a chance to consolidate because of its leadership's offensive orientation. Rather than dedicating itself to state-building, ISIS sought to both build a caliphate and to expand worldwide. As a result, it pushed forward without the ability to sustain its campaign, and its push only generated more enemies who became more willing to confront the group.

Foolishly, the Islamic state had no viable economic plan for its caliphate. It focused on extracting resources through "taxation" and conquest. At first, ISIS relied on the appropriation of the property of Christians, Yazidi, and Shia who had lived in the areas it conquered and the looting of Iraqi banks to fund its expansion. But these were finite resources. Taxation of Sunni citizens of the self-styled caliphate generated additional income, but its potential was limited because ISIS did not have a plan for growing the ISIS economy to increase revenues. The group controlled the limited cross-border trade, and its determination to control the lives of the people living in its territory and to prevent any foreign influence meant that whatever international trade it engaged in was very limited. Such trade involved primarily basic staples, which is hardly useful for sufficient revenue growth. Taxation of salaries paid by the Iraqi central government to its employees in Mosul was an important funding source at first, but it vanished when the government stopped making such payments.[79]

With funding from trade considerably restricted, ISIS leaders focused on fighting as a way to generate much needed revenue. Hailing the loot its fighters pillage, the Islamic State dismissed the need to develop agriculture (development of industry, especially privately owned, was of an even lower priority). Instead, they emphasized the economic benefits of conquest.[80] Emboldened by its initial military success, ISIS appeared to believe that it could continue its winning streak and use it to strengthen its caliphate. But the Islamic State's initial success was in a large part the result of the weakness of its enemies, and notwithstanding the group's military prowess, it was not enough to defeat stronger actors. ISIS's continued belligerence soon put it in conflict with much more robust forces, the most important of which was the United States. Moreover, it found out that it had no solution to its enemies' airpower. Thus, the entry of the U.S. into the fight made ISIS advances less likely because it could not move in large formations, or American airpower would decimate their forces from above. ISIS learned this lesson the hard way after losing thousands of fighters in the battle for Kobani.[81] Unable to continue its conquests in its main arena of operations, ISIS could have hoped to expand elsewhere, but by that point, there was an already strong international coalition lined up against it in any of the *willayas* (provinces) it established. Even in locations in which it managed to capture territory, its progress was slow. Far from a financial bonanza, expansion was costly and far from sufficient to sustain an aspiring empire. Small islands of ISIS controlled-territory, such as the city of Sirte in Libya, could perhaps fit into Naji's "management of savagery" plan, but after forming a caliphate, they reflected a reversal in the group's fortune. Moreover, the level of hostility that the Islamic State generated implied that even such islands would come under attack and that its forces would be dislodged.[82]

Although the Islamic State presented its attempt to restore the caliphate as the fulfilment of a religious commitment,[83] the caliphate also was designed to serve the group's grand strategy. ISIS believed that the establishment of the caliphate would catch the imagination of the *umma* and encourage the group's sympathizers across the world to travel to the territory it controlled and strengthen its forces and state-building efforts. Later, as ISIS faced increased pressure in Iraq and Syria, it called on its followers to commit terrorist attacks in their countries.[84]

But in introducing the caliphate, ISIS had additional objectives: delegitimizing its competitors and mobilizing the Muslim masses. By declaring al-Baghdadi a caliph and demanding that all Muslims pledge him their allegiance, the Islamic State claimed that he has authority over all Muslims regardless of where they reside. Such authority lends additional force to the call to join the Islamic State by presenting it as a religious obligation. Moreover, relying on the expansive authority of the caliph, ISIS sought to force its competitors to join it as subordinates. In the words of its late spokesman al-Adnani: "The legality of all emirates, groups, states, and organizations, becomes null by the expansion of the khilāfah's authority and arrival of its troops to their areas."[85]

Enthusiastic response to the declaration from the masses and other jihadi groups could have mitigated the Islamic State's aggregation problem, but it was a gamble without a solid foundation. The group incorrectly assumed that Muslims are more attached to the idea of the caliphate and are willing to make great sacrifices for it. It also assumed that Muslims would accept the authority of an individual whom they do not know or did not choose and individual who promoted a version of Islam that is foreign to and rejected by the overwhelming majority of Muslims worldwide. ISIS was also overly optimistic to believe that jihadi groups would line up behind it simply because it announced itself as a caliphate. Soon, ISIS illusions crashed against the walls of reality.

Whereas the previous chapter examined the ideational obstacles standing in the way of transnational jihadi groups, this chapter focused on the material shortcomings of the global jihadi project. Looking at the works of Abu Bakr Naji and Abu Musab al-Suri, and analyzing bin Laden's strategic plan for al-Qaeda, al-Zarqawi and al-Adl's "master plan," and Abu Bakr al-Baghdadi's strategic logic for re-establishing the caliphate, the chapter highlighted the shortcomings of the various jihadi strategies for confronting the U.S. and the "apostate" regimes. It determined that all of these grand strategies fail to overcome the aggregation problem: they exaggerate the ability of transnational jihadi actors to motivate the masses to join their cause, and they overestimate jihadis' ability to produce political effects that will give rise to a sustainable transnational Islamic state capable of overcoming the considerably stronger forces of its enemies.

The failure to produce a viable solution to the aggregation question is not surprising given the gravity of the task and the meager abilities of the jihadis. But it also must be noted that the plans presented above relied on dubious assumptions about Muslims' attachment to their religious identity; its superiority in the political realm over other identity markers (such as nationalism); the ability to reach a consensus about how to implement Islam within an Islamic state; the ability of the different jihadi groups (national and transnational) to agree on achievable goals and the strategy to attain them; and the ability of the jihadis to mobilize the masses.

But these false assumptions also expose a deeper problem: over-reliance on divine help. All transnational movements that use violence to promote their objectives face the aggregation problem, but jihadi groups are in an even more disadvantageous position because their religious beliefs render them particularly susceptible to unrealistic expectation and less capable of critical analysis of their enterprise. Even Naji, whose work focuses on strategic analysis, discusses close to the end of his book the many miracles God has performed on the battlefield throughout history. He thus suggests that the balance of power between the jihadis and their much stronger enemies will similarly change at "rates that the mind cannot perceive."[86]

Sometimes, terrorist leaders' own beliefs about the inevitability of victory cripple terrorist efforts. Because religious terrorist groups attribute the fight's outcome to the will of God, leaders easily can explain away failure in battle. Such an attitude could boost actors' resilience by assisting them in coping with defeats. However, the belief in ultimate victory is counterproductive when it leads jihadis to move ahead with their plans without presenting a fully developed causal theory of war outcomes or seriously considering the implications of material power imbalances. Additionally, a sense of certainty is likely to undermine actors' interest in learning from mistakes. Thus, jihadi terrorists are particularly prone to enter confrontations without a solid strategic foundation. In such cases, states are likely to be surprised by the initiation of terror campaigns, but also able to thwart the terrorists' goals.

4

Intra-Jihadi Conflicts

Internal conflicts have plagued the jihadi movement since its emergence during the 1980s war against the Soviets. At the end of the war, Egyptian jihadis, determined to return home to fight the Mubarak regime, fought over resources with Abdallah Azzam, who rejected the Egyptians' revolutionary agenda and believed that donors' money should be used to support struggles of Muslims who came under occupation.[1] The veteran jihadi Mustafa Hamid (also known as Abu Walid al-Misri) argued with bin Laden on military affairs.[2] And together with Abu Musab al-Suri and another prominent Syrian jihadi, Abu Khaled al-Suri, denounced bin Laden's disregard for the interests of the Taliban, and specifically for disobeying its leader Mullah Omar's instruction not to give interviews to Western media.[3] These incidents are just the tip of the iceberg, reflecting a movement embroiled in constant acrimony even as—and perhaps because—it retains a sense of shared identity.

Internal conflicts within the jihadi movement have been a fixture even when other variables changed. Disputes continued at times of expansion as well as contraction, before 9/11 and after, and in the Middle East as well as in North Africa and Central Asia. They took place between different groups within the movement: between nation-based jihadi groups such as the Egyptian Islamic Jihad (EIJ) and their co-nationals in the Gama'a Islamiya; between groups of different national origins such as when the Algerian GIA killed members of the Libyan Islamic Fighting Group (LIFG) who came to Algeria to explore ways to assist their fellow jihadis in the fight against the Algerian regime;[4] and between transnational jihadi groups and local jihadi organizations, as when the Islamic State of Iraq confronted local Iraqi groups (al-Qaeda's Iraqi branch was criticized strongly even by al-Qaeda's closest associate in the country *Ansar al-Sunna*).[5] Intra-jihadi conflicts also have taken place between transnational jihadi groups as in the case of al-Qaeda and the Islamic State, as well as within a transnational group. Internal conflicts reached a peak with the 2013 breakout of fratricidal violence in Syria between the Islamic State and Jabhat al-Nusra (JN), and later between the Islamic State and all other jihadi groups that refused to accept Abu Bakr al-Baghdadi's authority as a caliph.

Schism is often the result of preference divergence. State-focused jihadis argue over objectives and strategy with jihadis supportive of a transnational agenda. Sometimes, such conflicts also involve turf wars as transnational and local jihadi groups compete over scarce resources. But there is also plenty of schism taking place within organizations when a group's central leadership holds different objectives and priorities than its agents; rank-and file do not understand how violence is expected to advance particular political objectives; and group leaders fail to impose their authority on rouge agents.[6]

Transnational jihadi groups are particularly vulnerable to the adverse effects of preference divergence. As they expand across borders, they often take under their wings branches that previously subscribed to localized agendas. The central leadership's ability to engage in effective oversight is weaker when it is separated from its agents by international borders and must rely on couriers. The ability of a transnational group's leadership to prevent local leaders from abusing their relationship with the group in pursuit of their own self-interests is limited as well. Indeed, al-Qaeda leaders expressed their frustration with al-Zarqawi's actions, such as his independent initiative to carry out a suicide bombing operation in Jordan.[7] A few years later, still believing that the Islamic State of Iraq is subordinate to AQC, al-Qaeda's leadership saw Abu Bakr al-Baghdadi adopting a distinct agenda of his own. Not only did ISI ignore al-Qaeda's strategy (for example, by repeatedly targeting Shia[8]), it sought to use the declaration of al-Baghdadi as a caliph to force al-Qaeda to accept his authority.[9]

Given the schisms within the jihadi movement, evaluating the threat it poses by aggregating the numbers and capabilities of its components would result in an exaggerated threat assessment. Such an assessment, in turn, is likely to have considerable negative effects; it boosts the image of the jihadis and thus, plays into their narrative of prowess. Another result is the misallocation of funds as the fight against the jihadis leads the U.S. to invest resources it could otherwise use for its other urgent priorities, without achieving the results it is hoping for. But perhaps the most important implication of acknowledging the prevalence and severity of internal disputes is that it allows identifying points of disagreement among jihadis and consequently, the tailoring of policies to deepen these divides. After all, transnational jihadis' inability to prevent or mitigate diverging preferences could be used to expose the leadership's lack of control, while the agents' overreach could be used to taint the reputation of the whole group.[10]

Because jihadis' internal conflicts have been the subject of numerous works,[11] in this chapter, I examine only those aspects with particular relevance to transnational jihadi groups' ability to operate and expand across borders and to attain trans-border political objectives. I begin the chapter with a discussion of the strategic disagreements, clashes between foreign fighters and locals, and intra-personal hostility that plague the jihadi movement. In the next two sections, I turn to the role of religious narratives and arguments in heightening internal conflicts. First, I examine the divisive role of the practice of *takfir*, in which Muslims declare others as apostates deserving of punishment of death. Internal conflicts over questions of authority and the obligations actors take on themselves when they give an Islamic pledge of fealty (*bay'a*) receive an elaborate treatment in the following section. To illustrate the role of *bay'a* in intra-jihadi conflicts, I discuss the conflict between AQC and ISIS following the latter's declaration of its expansion to Syria and its attempt to appropriate JN, al-Qaeda's use of the Taliban as a foil to ISIS's caliphate's claims and allegiance demands, and the defection of JN from al-Qaeda. Ultimately, I argue that viewing themselves as religious actors who operate to attain religious objectives using only Islamically permissible action, jihadis often find that their radical religious ideology becomes a source of division, not unity.

STRATEGIC DIFFERENCES

Disagreements over strategy are perhaps the most obvious hindrance for unity among jihadis, transnational or locally focused. Such disagreements could derail collective action among jihadis. Although jihadis repeatedly declare that their struggle is part of an eternal fight between the forces of truth (the jihadis) and the forces of falsehood (the "Jewish-Crusader alliance" and the "apostate regimes")[12]—what Mark Juergensmeyer calls a "cosmic war"[13]—the long-time horizons such a view involves failed to prevent jihadis from arguing over immediate issues such as the choice of a strategy. On the face of it, the enormity of the jihadi enterprise, the power of their sworn enemies, and jihadis' belief in God's promise of an eventual victory, all should have allowed jihadis to smooth over their strategic differences and postpone a self-defeating conflict. But especially after the emergence of the Islamic State and its push to establish a caliphate, it has become evident that many jihadis expect to see quicker results, therefore making their disagreements more urgent. The friction created when transnational jihadis operate in the same arena as local jihadis also brings intra-jihadi clashes over strategy.

Heated debates over strategic priorities could be observed as early as the end of the 1980s. With the war against the Soviets winding down, Arab-Afghans bitterly argued about the future of the jihadi movement. Reluctant to let the spirit of jihad fade away and see the emergent jihadi movement—that for the first time brought together jihadis and jihadi groups from all over the world—disintegrate, the multitude of jihadi actors contemplated their next moves. At first, two main ideas dominated jihadi plans for the post-Afghanistan era. Abdallah Azzam advocated for continued fight in defense of Muslims who came under attack by non-Muslim nations. By contrast, members of state-based jihadi groups pushed to focus on toppling the "near enemy"—the regimes ruling their home countries. These two paths coexisted throughout much of the decade as jihadis brought their fight back to their home countries of Egypt, Algeria, and Libya, while others joined jihad arenas in Bosnia, Kashmir, and Chechnya.

As the two options resulted in disappointing results, a third option, emphasizing the U.S. as the primary target began taking hold. In the early 1990s, bin Laden was still not strongly attached to any one direction. He was supportive of both efforts to fight foreign "occupiers" and "apostate" regimes. However, after the Saudi regime rejected his offer to use veterans of the war in Afghanistan to protect Saudi Arabia from a potential Iraqi attack, and instead invited American forces, bin Laden was outraged.[14] Already hostile to the U.S., this episode led bin Laden to advocate a third path for jihad that emphasized fighting the world's sole remaining superpower. Bin Laden's strategic analysis, which emphasized attacking the American "far enemy" in order to facilitate a confrontation with the "near enemy" in a later stage, was discussed in the previous chapter. Bin Laden's analysis was controversial. Far from uniting all jihadi groups behind his America-first strategy, bin Laden found that many within the movement rejected his actions. After 9/11, some jihadi groups and leaders were furious that in his actions bin Laden destroyed their safe haven in Afghanistan, ended the Taliban regime, and made all jihadi groups a target of the U.S.-led War on Terrorism.[15]

The debate over strategic priorities continued even as the American invasions of Afghanistan (2001) and Iraq (2003) brought the "far enemy" to Muslim lands. Some jihadi groups chose to join al-Qaeda as branches, which meant a re-orientation of their strategies to align with al-Qaeda's emphasis on the "far enemy." Elsewhere, jihadi groups such as the Egyptian Gama'a Islamiya and the Libyan Islamic Fighting Group not only critiqued al-Qaeda,[16] but also sought to reach accommodations with ruling regimes.[17]

Disagreements over strategy were not limited to interaction between al-

Qaeda and locally based jihadi groups. They existed within al-Qaeda as well, as the group's franchises in Muslim countries often failed to move beyond paying lip service to the "far enemy" agenda, focusing, instead, their efforts locally against near enemies. The rise of ISIS brought with it a competing strategy for the attainment of cross-border strategic effects and exacerbated debates over strategy. These two main transnational jihadi groups share the end goal of restoring the caliphate, but they differ on how to reach that goal. Whereas al-Qaeda elected to emphasize attacking the United States, the strategy of the Islamic State—despite its global aspirations—emphasized attacking the "near enemy." Whereas al-Qaeda viewed the collapse of the United States as a precondition for sustainable success in the Middle East and the reintroduction of the caliphate, ISIS viewed the restoration of the caliphate not only as an end-state, but also as central to the fight to bring Muslim rule and the implementation of the sharia. These diverging priorities have resulted in the underutilization of jihadi resources, which were insufficient to begin with.

Although disagreements over strategy have hurt the jihadi movement, it must be noted that they did not have to result in particularly damaging violent confrontations. Disagreements could have been limited to verbal critique. In reality, in the case of al-Qaeda's rivalry with the Islamic State, the latter's belligerence prevented the containment of the conflict and resulted in vicious fratricidal violence that further weakened the jihadi movement. Wrangling over strategy, each group criticized the other for failing to understand the strategic circumstances, for misidentifying who should be viewed as part of the enemy camp, and, of course, for misunderstanding the proper way to bring about change.

In al-Qaeda's view, ISIS failed to act strategically. Instead, it was "blinded by temporary tactical gains."[18] According to al-Qaeda, ISIS's strategy led it to waist energy and resources on a distraction—fighting local "puppets" of the U.S. who are "cheaply bought and easily replaced." Al-Qaeda maintained that in doing so, the Islamic State played into the hands of the United States by allowing it to avoid direct confrontation with the jihadis and, instead, turn to proxies to fight on Washington's behalf. Moreover, unable to understand its limited capabilities, ISIS is seeking frontal confrontations it cannot sustain. As a result, it sacrificed thousands of fighters in pointless battles such as the fight to capture Kobani, which offered no strategic gains.[19]

Al-Qaeda lamented what it viewed as ISIS's counterproductive tendency to refuse any cooperation with other Islamist movements who wish to address the crisis that the *umma* is experiencing. Although al-Qaeda believes that these groups' policy prescriptions are wrong, it does not reject automatically the possibility of cooperating with them under the right circumstances.[20] In contrast, not only did ISIS reject any cooperation with other groups, it actively sought to dominate them. Such an attitude led ISIS to assault other Muslim groups, including jihadi groups that were bent on fighting the *umma*'s enemies but, instead, fought for their lives. This fratricidal violence, al-Qaeda argued, distracted the Islamic State from the *umma*'s main enemies, undercut efforts to unite the opposition against these enemies, and led to the loss of numerous fighters from all groups.

Al-Qaeda also criticized what it saw as ISIS's narrow-minded focus on violent means in its relations with other local actors, when there are additional tool, such as proselytizing. ISIS turned jihad from a means to attaining the *umma*'s goals into an end. Moreover, it sought to fight wars of annihilation against an ever expanding list of enemies. Summarizing ISIS faults, an al-Qaeda insider asserted that "ISIS, in their illusionary self-glorification wants to wage a conventional offensive elitist-exclusive jihad without any popular base." In comparison, he maintained, al-Qaeda is focused on a defensive effort, backed by popular support, in which it is implementing a modern view of asymmetric warfare while trying to minimize the burden on the *umma*.[21]

Although much of al-Qaeda's criticism of the Islamic State's effort to restore the caliphate focused on theological aspects, it also had a strategic dimension. Al-Qaeda argued that because of the jihadis' military weakness it should avoid the premature announcement of the caliphate. The introduction of a caliphate requires first the liberation of Syria and the building of a strong military that would be able to confront the strongest actors in the international system. Because al-Qaeda preferred to build a strong force that would be able to affect the global balance of power, the group even decided not to use Syria as a launching pad for terrorist attacks in the West.[22]

ISIS, on the other hand, viewed al-Qaeda's strategy as an unnecessary delay. It saw the introduction of the caliphate as necessary for overcoming division within the *umma* in general and the jihadi movement in particular. Seeing the failure of al-Qaeda to bring about change, the Islamic State saw the caliphate as an important difference-maker. It was destined to become a focal point around which Muslims worldwide would unite and move to action. The caliphate would also remind fellow jihadis of their ultimate objectives (caliphate and establishing God's rule) and thus, lead them to overcome their differences and bring them together. ISIS also insisted on prioritizing the fight against the Shia, which al-Qaeda understood as an undesirable distraction.

Contrary to ISIS's hopes, assigning such a central role for the caliphate created a zero-sum game between the organization and fellow jihadi groups in which the success of ISIS was detrimental to other jihadis' wishes to maintain their independence. Thus, the self-styled caliphate ended up in direct conflict with fellow jihadi groups that did not share ISIS's vision, rejected its strategic priorities, resented its coercive means and brutality, and valued their own freedom.

FOREIGNERS MEET LOCALS

Transnational jihadi groups seek to produce cross-border effects and to expand throughout the Muslim world. But when deploying fighters to foreign countries—supposedly in support of local Muslims fighting oppressive regimes and foreign occupiers—jihadi groups repeatedly have undercut their missions by falling into conflicts with the locals. Jihadis' attempts to impose their radical interpretation of Islam on indigenous Muslim communities did not go well with the locals, whether they were located in the Middle East or in the periphery of the Muslim world. Chapter 2 discussed transnational jihadis' failure to overcome the nationalism trap as most Muslims maintained primary allegiance to their nation-state or tribe. In this section, the focus shifts to the struggle of transnational jihadis to form strong alliances with local jihadi groups.

It must be noted first that the Arab jihadis who formed and dominated the jihadi movement had an inherent bias, leading them to view the Middle East as the most important region and its Muslim inhabitants as superior to non-Arab Muslims. The region has a unique place in jihadis' heart because it is the birthplace of Islam and the Prophet, the home of Sunni Islam's three holiest sites (in Mecca, Medina, and Jerusalem), and the seat of the ancient Umayyad and Abbasid caliphates. Arabs and Arabic similarly are viewed as superior to non-Arabs and non-Arabic speakers because the first Muslims were Arabs and the Quran's language is Arabic. Notably, this bias exists despite jihadis' attachment to the concept of the *umma* and the belief that faith surpasses any ethnic, tribal, and national identities.

A dismissive view of non-Arab regions' direct significance for the jihadi movement's objectives has accompanied the jihadi emphasis on the Middle East and its Arab Muslims. Despite the centrality of Afghanistan to the emergence of a transnational jihadi movement, al-Qaeda viewed the country as merely an instrument. The main battle, according to al-Zawahiri, was to take place in the Middle East: "The victory of Islam will never take place until a Muslim state is established in the manner of the Prophet in the heart of the Islamic world, specifically in the Levant, Egypt, and the neighboring states of the Peninsula and Iraq; however, the center would be in the Levant and Egypt."[23] According to al-Zawahiri, battles in the Muslim periphery, in places such as Afghanistan, Bosnia, Chechnya, and Kashmir, serve a bigger purpose of building capacity for the major battles that will take place elsewhere, that is, in the Middle East.[24]

This worldview produced conflicts between Arab jihadis and their non-Arab hosts. As Vahid Brown argued based on documents recovered in Afghanistan, Arab chauvinism led al-Qaeda and other "Arab-Afghans" to look down at non-Arab locals whether they are Somalis, Uzbeks, or Afghanis.[25] It poisoned Arab jihadis' relationships with potential allies outside the Middle East, and weakened their ability to mobilize non-Arab Muslims in pursuit of any transnational agenda. Because the dismissive attitude to non-Arabs often was based on cultural differences and diverging political goals, it was not limited to non-jihadis but extended to local jihadi and Islamist groups. Mustafa Hamid reports a pre-9/11 meeting with al-Qaeda leaders in which they described the Afghans as "thieves and liars" unqualified for the difficult undertakings required from the group's allies.[26] Al-Qaeda operatives in Somalia similarly held negative opinions of their potential local partners, seeing them as corrupt, disorganized and ineffectual.[27]

Some jihadis in Afghanistan (though rarely al-Qaeda itself) refused to support the Taliban regime because the Taliban emerged from the Hanafi school of thought of Islam and were not Salafis. Some justified their refusal to side with the Taliban by claiming that the group is fighting fellow Muslims—the Northern Alliance—and thus, that their fight represents a *fitna* (civil war among Muslims), which is reviled in Islam. Some justified their opposition to the Taliban by claiming that the group did not do enough to eradicate local Sufi traditions such as grave-worshiping and polytheism that jihadis abhor.[28] Jihadis in Afghanistan also engaged in fierce arguments about how to treat jihadis who supported the Taliban, with the most radical jihadis even denouncing al-Qaeda and others for their support for the Taliban.

Negative views of the Afghan people in general and the Taliban in particular led many jihadis to consider the Islamic state it established not as a genuine emirate that could serve as the nucleus of the caliphate, but rather as another temporary safe haven.[29] This dismissive view of the Islamic Emirate of Afghanistan was prevalent even among the Taliban's Arab supporters. Most notably, al-Qaeda's support for the Taliban was instrumental and based on pragmatic needs rather than genuine support for the Taliban's right to rule and respect to its authority.[30] Indeed, by defying Mullah Omar's instructions to al-Qaeda not to provoke the U.S. and to bin Laden specifically to stop giving interviews to foreign media, al-Qaeda exposed its disrespect for the authority of the Taliban and its leader. Biased against non-Arabs, al-Qaeda leaders viewed Afghanistan indifferently, as a place that is good only for training before the Arab jihadis return to their home countries to fight their local regimes,[31] and that is secondary in its importance compared to the Middle East.[32] Ayman al-Zawahiri's EIJ (prior to merging with al-Qaeda) did not believe anything could be expected from Afghanistan due to ideological and doctrinal shortcomings.[33] Ultimately, despite declaring its loyalty to the Taliban, al-Qaeda did not mind sacrificing its ally and protector. The 9/11 operation, carried out without the Taliban's prior knowledge and approval, brought destruction to Afghanistan and led to the removal of the Taliban regime, dispatching its leaders to exile in Pakistan. A non-Arab country, Afghanistan was easy for bin Laden to sacrifice in pursuit of al-Qaeda's war on the United States.

Transnational jihadis also find themselves arguing—and sometimes, as in Iraq and Syria, even fighting—with local groups in the Arab Middle East. An early sign for the conflict between the transnational jihadis and local Sunni insurgents in Iraq (Iraqi jihadis included) was evident in al-Zarqawi's assessment of Iraq's Sunnis, conveyed in a letter to bin Laden and al-Zawahiri. Al-Zarqawi criticized Iraq's Sunni fighters for what he viewed as a lack of jihadi spirit. He complained that they are risk-averse, willing to forgo a victory for a safe return to their homes. Al-Zarqawi also accused the local Sunni groups of pursuing ineffective fighting methods, resulting, in his view, from their inability to appreciate the importance of martyrdom. He also lamented Sunni groups' slowness to see the need of uniting the efforts of all jihadi forces.[34]

Al-Zarqawi's view was compatible with other foreign fighters' sense of moral superiority over local Sunni groups—including Islamists ones—who were deemed by the foreigners as less ideologically motivated and focused on a nationalist agenda. But an internal document written by an anonymous ISI leader, in which he reflected on the group's difficulties, laid part of the blame at the foreigners' door. The author was critical of the locals, arguing that because they never studied al-Qaeda's ideology, they failed to understand the foreign volunteers' priorities. He also critiqued the locals' only partial commitment, contrasting it with the foreign fighters who were seeking martyrdom. But the author also maintained that because the foreign fighters arrived at the arena ignorant of Iraq's people, culture, terrain, and dialect, their ability to operate was limited. The foreigners were unable to blend in among the local population, creating as a result security hazards to the locals, who were also disgruntled that the foreigners' inability to do things on their own. The clash between the foreigners' lofty expectations and the local fighters more realistic and methodical approach further contributed to the friction between locals and foreigners.[35]

In the following decade, similar trends affected the Islamic State both in Iraq and in Syria. Foreign fighters accounted for the overwhelming majority of the suicide bombers.[36] Uprooted, they also were deemed more reliable by the group's leadership because in contrast to local members they did not need to negotiate competing allegiances.[37] Moreover, given ISIS imperialist objectives and willingness to use extreme violence against all who stood in its way, it came to rely on foreign volunteers, who were less hesitant than the group's local members about using violence against rival rebel groups. Obviously, turning to foreigners to fight locals exacerbated the latter's hostility to ISIS's foreign fighters. Local Iraqis and Syrians, including ISIS members, were further chafed by privileges afforded to the group's foreign members, such as a better apartment and higher pay, which did not correspond to their contribution to the caliphate.[38] And as ISIS expanded, absorbing thousands of outsiders more attracted to the utopian caliphate than to the ongoing war, local members of the group in Syria also complained that some foreign volunteers do not want to fight or demonstrated poor fighting skills.[39] And with military defeats, local members of ISIS began suspecting that there were spies among the foreigners who undermine its war effort. In Deir al-Zor, dozens of Syrian fighters defected from IS after accusing their foreign commanders of using them as cannon fodder.[40]

INTER-PERSONAL CONFLICTS

Inter-personal rivalries join differences over strategy and clashes between foreign fighters and local jihadis in bolstering competition (and conflict) between jihadi organizations. These rivalries within the highly opinionated jihadi elite involve leaders of jihadi organizations, as well as some unaffiliated personalities. Among the unaffiliated figures, one can find strategists such as Abu Musab al-Suri (whose work was discussed in the previous chapter) and Mustafa Hamid, the Egyptian journalist turned jihadi, known as a fervently independent thinker who never shied from expressing his own opinions, including criticism of bin Laden's management of al-Qaeda. Religious scholars such as the Jordanians Abu Muhammad al-Maqdisi and Abu Qatada al-Filistini, who both completed a short stint in Afghanistan, are two other examples of prominent figures who, despite their close relations with al-Qaeda, maintained their independence.

Inter-personal rivalries among the jihadi elite reflect, to some extent, the legacy of the war against the Soviets. The actions of individual jihad entrepreneurs, the most important of which was Abdallah Azzam, shaped the emergence of the anti-Soviet jihad, its institutionalization, and the emergence of a multinational jihadi movement. At times, inter-personal conflicts reflected struggle for power, even when presented as arguments over religious doctrine and personal piety. But one should not dismiss the importance of ideological differences. After all, as Nelly Lahoud persuasively argues, the nature of modern jihadism underscores its function as an individual enterprise in which each jihadi could interpret Islam for himself,[41] naturally leading to disagreements of grand proportions because they are presented as conflicts over principles that cannot be compromised.

One need not go further than the personal stories of Azzam, bin Laden, and al-Zawahiri to see how individuals came to Afghanistan, responding to requests and job offers from contact people in the area rather than as a part of an organized mobilization drive. Of these three, only al-Zawahiri had a clear organizational affiliation when he first arrived at Afghanistan in the early 1980s, yet his arrival, too, was in response to a personal request by acquaintances in the Afghan theater that al-Zawahiri would lend his professional expertise as a physician to aid the cause.[42] Although over time, the Afghan-Arabs formed organizations and created an infrastructure for bringing volunteers to the arena, opening guest houses to host them, providing them with training, and keeping tabs on their whereabouts, the role of individual unaffiliated jihadis remained strong. Even the arrival of Middle Eastern members of jihadi groups to Afghanistan in the middle of the 1980s did not eliminate the prominence of some independent members of the jihadi elite.

While members of the unaffiliated elite did not pledge allegiance to bin Laden or any other jihadi group,[43] they were privy to many consultations at al-Qaeda's highest levels and even participated for a time in the group's counselling body (the Shura Council). The quest for such elite members' advice and support underscores the embeddedness of a group such as al-Qaeda within the jihadi movement and its search for legitimacy outside of the group's own ranks.

Members of this jihadi elite have developed complicated relationships, which involve ideological affinity and disagreements, debates over strategy, and, at times, conflicting personal interests. Such relationships could change in response to new circumstances and changing personal interests. Hamid was a vocal critic of bin Laden,[44] yet collaborated with the group in running training camps and courses for foreign volunteers and was central to bin Laden's pledge of allegiance to the Taliban's leader Mullah Omar.[45] Abu Musab al-Suri was critical of bin Laden, particularly over his insubordination to Mullah Omar and his responsibility to the end of the Taliban regime,[46] yet he coordinated some of the interviews bin Laden gave to foreign media, was a member of al-Qaeda's Shura Council for a while, and after the 9/11 attack offered bin Laden support.[47] In a final example, Abu Muhammad al-Maqdisi was al-Zarqawi's mentor during the 1990s before turning into a critic of the latter's methods in Iraq. Al-Zarqawi responded with scathing critique of his former teacher in which he rejected al-Maqdisi's words as coming from a scholar that renders religious judgment while being far from the battlefield and without understanding the conditions that jihadis on the ground face.[48]

The severity of these inter-personal conflicts was magnified as ultra-radical jihadis such as al-Zarqawi and later his successors, Abu Hamza al-Muhajir, Abu Omar al-Baghdadi, and Abu Bakr al-Baghdadi, emerged as powerful actors on the jihadi scene. Unperturbed by the jihadi etiquette that had constrained internal fights within the jihadi movement from escalating, these leaders aggressively pursued their rivals, resulting in fratricidal violence in Iraq and Syria. Although it is difficult to separate these individuals from the radical ideology of their groups, this ideology pushed for governance structures and territorial possessions. It, thus, brought to fore claims for overarching authority by these self-styled rulers and to clashes with other personalities who refused to accept the authority of the leaders of ISI and later ISIS.

The death of bin Laden, whose post-9/11 stature within the jihadi movement limited personal attacks on him, was the harbinger of intense personal rivalry between the Islamic State's leader al-Baghdadi and bin Laden's successor al-Zawahiri. In contrast to bin Laden's mythical status, al-Zawahiri was much more controversial and far less charismatic and thus an easier target for ISIS's criticism. Seeking to present ISIS and its leadership as the true successors of bin Laden, the group accused al-Zawahiri of causing sedition by choosing to accept the *bay'a* of the "traitorous" Jabhat al-Nusra leader Abu Muhammad al-Joulani: "You [al-Zawahiri] made yourself and your al-Qaeda a joke and a toy in the hands of an arrogant traitor-boy who broke the pledge of allegiance that you did not see. You left him to play with you like a child plays with a ball, thus ruining your reputation and losing your history and glory."[49] In a separate statement, ISIS spokesman al-Adnani declared that al-Qaeda under al-Zawahiri "deviated from the correct method. . . . Al-Qaeda today is not the al-Qaeda of jihad. It is praised by the most despicable, the tyrants flirt with it, and the deviated and misguided come close to it. . . . Its command became a pickaxe to demolish the project of the Islamic State and the coming Caliphate, Allah permitting."[50]

It is important to note that inter-personal conflicts are not merely an artifact of inter-organizational rivalry and that they have a lasting impact on the ability of jihadis to unite and to use more effectively the jihadi movement's resources. As actors turn from arguments over doctrine and strategy to personal attacks, playing out in the media for everybody to see, they create further barriers to cooperation. Suffice to view the evolution of the conflict between al-Qaeda and the Islamic State that featured disparaging comments about group leaders and heightened the personal rivalry between al-Zawahiri and al-Baghdadi. Consequently, even observers who envision potential reunification qualify it in the need for at least one of these leaders to be removed before rapprochement could become possible.[51]

The disagreements discussed above—that is the inter-personal conflicts, divergent strategies, and the clash of cultures between locals and foreigners— are bitter. But they reach higher levels due to jihadis' tendency to frame their disagreements in religious terms and to portray rivals' refusal to accept another's religious claims as authoritative as indicative of Islamic shortcomings make intra-jihadi conflict particularly common. The manner in which debates over Islamic precepts magnifies intra-jihadi conflicts is the focus of this chapter's remaining sections.

TAKFIR (EXCOMMUNICATION)

Conflicts within the jihadi camp are almost always couched in religious terms. The dominance of the religious discourse among jihadis is natural. After all, they identify themselves as ideological actors, guided by religious imperatives and bent on advancing religious objectives, the most important of which are the restoration of the caliphate and the implementation of the sharia. Even if at times religion is used instrumentally by jihadi actors, one should not dismiss religious ideology's importance. It is a genuine commitment for most jihadi leaders, not simply a tool used by power-hungry individuals.[52] That does not mean, however, that ego conflicts and other mundane personal interests play no role in intra-jihadi dynamics and that religious claims are not used to mask power struggles.

Whether genuinely religious or merely steeped in religious terminology, disagreements among jihadis are particularly difficult to resolve. After all, they involve allegations of major violations of central Islamic tenets. In this way, they further weaken the ability of the jihadi movement to demonstrate its power in its fullest. Deferring judgment regarding the true weight of religious beliefs in intra-jihadi dynamics, it must still be recognized that the religious discourse presents two major subjects that magnify intra-jihadi contestation. The first, *takfir*—the labeling of rivals as apostates—is the focus of this section. The second, allegiance to the leader (*bay'a*) and the conditions under which such a pledge could be revoked are discussed in the following.

Apostasy is punishable by death. Consequently, the pronouncement of *takfir* legitimizes the shedding of fellow Muslims' blood. As such, disputes that deteriorate to allegations of infidelity go beyond any "normal" disagreements that could be resolved peacefully through negotiations, persuasion, and compromise. Even when the use of *takfir* does not result in blood shedding, reconciliation between the makers of *takfiri* claims and their targets is unlikely.

The conditions under which it is permissible to declare the apostasy of a Muslim is the subject of a theological debate among Muslims in general, and jihadis in particular. The practice of *takfir* is uncommon outside radical circles with most Islamic streams rejecting the proclamation of co-religionists' apostasy. Even ultra-orthodox Salafis, while not denying the legitimacy of the concept of *takfir*, are reluctant to embrace it beyond particular and very narrow set of conditions.[53] Yet, the intellectual history at the root of jihadism suggests that *takfir* is, and will remain, central to the movement.

Takfir is a fundamental element in the thinking of two of the most important sources of jihadi thought: Wahhabism and Qutbism. Muhammad Ibn Abd al-Wahhab, Wahhabism's forefather and a founder of the Saudi state, formulated ten nullifiers of Islam that essentially excommunicated all Muslims who did not join his movement. Sayyid Qutb, the radical Muslim Brotherhood luminary from Egypt, never went that far, but the logical conclusion of his teachings—such as the determination that Muslims are currently living in what he characterized as a modern *jahiliya* and are led by apostate regimes—point in the direction of expansive excommunication. Therefore, this problem will not be easily circumvented. Debates over *takfir* in all likelihood will remain a major constraint on jihadis.[54]

Beyond its theological aspects—and more relevant to this discussion—the use of *takfir* has operational implications. It not only diverts jihadis' attention from the "crusaders" to internal enemies, but it also hinders the unification of the jihadi camp and legitimizes fratricidal violence: those issuing *takfir* seek to eliminate their rivals whereas the latter must take defensive measures. Moreover, in the absence of central religious authority in Islam, or of one religious figure who would serve as the ultimate authority for the jihadis, resolving disputes regarding the apostasy of actors becomes much harder. Thus, instead of expanding the jihadi force, the use of *takfir* among jihadis weakens the movement.

Whether jihadis pronounce the apostasy of a broad category of Muslims or lobbing such accusations at fellow jihadis, the use of *takfir* undermines their ability to attain political objectives. If mobilizing the masses is a prerequisite for the success of transnational jihadi groups, then the labeling of Muslims as apostates hinders these groups' growth and even puts them in direct confrontation with these same masses. Jihadi groups bent on the use of *takfir* (and thus called derogatively *"takfiri"* groups by other Muslims, including rival jihadis) end up envisioning an *umma* that is significantly reduced in size, while boosting with their accusations the ranks of those opposing them. Moreover, by seizing on *takfir*, jihadi groups undermine one of the greatest strengths of the *umma*—its pluralism (as manifested, for example, in the acceptance of four different Sunni Islamic schools of thought as legitimate and in the absence of a central religious authority for all Muslims). The result is an agenda that reconfigures the boundaries of Islam and the *umma*.

Worried about the adverse effects of *takfir*, several jihadi figures warned against its loose use.[55] The prominent jihadi insider Ahmed al-Hamdan stated that "extremism in takfir is the filthy germ which is found in every jihadi group because of ignorance and impulsiveness and due to feeling oppressed," among other reasons.[56] Critics have dismissed the permissibility of labeling whole groups as apostates instead of designating specific individuals based on concrete evidence of infidelity. These critics also argued that the expansive use of *takfir* undermines jihad. Instead of making jihad the project of the entire *umma*, the prevalence of *takfiri* thought among some jihadi groups makes jihad a project of a small jihadi elite. Instead of fighting the *umma*'s enemies, excessive use of *takfir* separates the masses from the jihadis and turns a vast number of Muslims into targets.[57]

The Algerian GIA is the poster child of the devastating ramifications of uncontrollable *takfirism*. Emerging as the most powerful group in Algeria's 1990s civil war, it sought to compel Algerian society and all anti-regime forces to accept its dominance and to forcefully crush any opposition to its dominance. Under the leadership of zealots, the group gradually expanded its list of targets for *takfir*. The list started with the heads of the regime and members of the security forces before expanding to include all government employees, intellectuals, and journalists. Eventually, under the leadership of Antar Zoubari, the group declared all of Algerian society apostates whose blood is permissible. Other Algerian rebel groups were not spared either. The GIA maintained that they apostatized in their willingness to negotiate with the regime, acceptance of political solutions to the civil war, and rejection of armed jihad as the sole means to bring about change. GIA offered the people a stark choice: accept the GIA's authority, which meant abandoning any dialogue with the regime, or face the group's wrath.[58]

The GIA's position was too extreme even for other jihadis and was denounced by astonished prominent jihadi groups outside Algeria. The LIFG was particularly outraged after learning that a group of fighters it had sent to assist the GIA were executed by the group.[59] Even Abu Qatada al-Filistini and Abu Musab al-Suri, editors of the London-based journal *al-Ansar*, which was a central source of external legitimacy for the GIA, broke away from the group.[60] Thus, the broad application of *takfir* not only hurts the accusing group's ability to mobilize support among the masses, but also pits it against other jihadi groups that are appalled by what they see as severe religious transgressions and as a measure that is counter to jihadis' interests.

Except for the Algerian case, during the 1990s, *takfiris* were a relatively marginal fringe group within the jihadi movement. But their potential menace was demonstrated elsewhere as well. In Afghanistan, ultra-radical jihadis who opposed the Taliban and any jihadi who supported it pronounced *takfir* on the group. Bin Laden himself was worried about the adverse consequences of *takfirism*. Alarmed by events in Algeria and likely influenced by *takfiris*' attempts on his life, bin Laden warned that declaring *takfir* "on the people" is a major sin. Instead, he called on jihadis to stay away from *takfir* and leave it to the knowledgeable scholars.[61] His lieutenant Atiyatallah, attempting to delineate limits to Islamically legitimate violence, similarly declared that only qualified scholars can declare an individual as an apostate. Notably, as a first-hand witness to GIA's atrocities, Atiyatallah al-Libi rejected the excommunication of whole communities.[62] The Egyptian Gama'a Islamiya, in one of its recantation books, also warned of overly enthusiastic youth who make rash judgments on *takfir*, though in comparison to al-Qaeda the group's leadership expressed greater skepticism of the practice of excommunication, noting that it is based on human judgment that is by nature fallible.[63]

But *takfiri* tendencies among jihadis became more prevalent with the rise of Abu Musab al-Zarqawi in Iraq. Not only did he turn to *takfir* regularly, using his infamy to normalize it, he broached the idea that all Shia can be labeled apostates and thus targeted indiscriminately. A worried al-Zawahiri warned him that his position is counterproductive to the objectives of al-Qaeda. Al-Zawahiri doubted the wisdom of shifting the focus from fighting the U.S. and its allies to direct attacks on the Shia. But his objection went beyond instrumental considerations; al-Zawahiri argued that al-Zarqawi's actions lay on weak theological foundations. According to the al-Zawahiri, Sunnis never sought the extermination of all Shia and besides, the overwhelming majority of the Shia should be spared based on their ignorance of true Islam.[64] Al-Hamdan suggests that bin Laden too believed that ignorance is a legitimate defense from accusations of *takfir*.[65]

The *takfiri* mentality shown in al-Zarqawi's actions only gained strength under his successors, particularly when the Islamic State, attempting to bolster its position, labeled its Muslim foes, including jihadis, as apostates. Already as ISI, al-Zarqawi's successors employed violent means against fellow rebels and flouted around accusations of infidelity not only against Shia, but against all Sunnis who participate in democratic political processes, as well as against the rulers of Muslim countries and the armies supporting them.[66] These accusations mounted when Iraqi Sunnis who only a short time before fought alongside al-Qaeda asked for American support to save themselves from ISI domination. In response, ISI then viewed those resisting it as violating the principle of *al-wala' wal-bara'* (loyalty and disavowal) because not only did these Sunnis failed to ally with ISI and accept the authority of their emirate, the Sunnis also allied with the "infidel" forces. Abu Bakr al-Baghdadi further boosted ISIS's inclination toward *takfirism*, particularly after ISIS unilaterally announced that it has become a caliphate and named its leader "Caliph Ibrahim." The Islamic State determined that it is mandatory to accept its authority and those refusing, let alone fighting the "caliphate," are committing a grave sin.

Thus, the use of *takfir* escalates conflict between those pronouncing it and their targets, whether segments of the *umma* or fellow jihadis. It divides the jihadi movement, pitting its members against each other. And it complicates efforts to mitigate internal conflict by turning disagreements into fights over faith in which the reversal of actors' positions and even compromise are practically impossible to reach.

Ironically, the debate over *takfir* railed the leadership of the Islamic State too as its extremism did not save it from such labeling, including from the group's own ranks. Although ISIS leaders often were referred to as *takfiris* by many of the group's opponents, they became targets for allegations of *takfir* themselves. A particularly radical faction of the group known as "the Hazimis," which adhered to extreme interpretations of *takfir* even came to dominate its Delegated Committee charged with oversight over all sharia-related issues. The Hazimis advocated a position that amounted to a chain of *takfir*. Interpreting the Wahhabi doctrine of the nullifiers of Islam, it argued that Muslims are obligated to declare the apostasy of others and that exceptions made for ignorance of the sharia are inadmissible. Consequently, those failing to excommunicate apostates must become a target for *takfir* themselves.[67]

Such a view marks jihadi leaders such as al-Zawahiri as apostates, but, in the context of ISIS, it also threatened to devour the group from within. Opponents of the ultra-radicals warned that this doctrine implies excommunication in infinite regress. One of ISIS's scholars, critical of the limitless expansion of *takfir*, accused the Delegated Committee of ideological terrorism against the group's scholars.[68] Although the Committee did not suggest that al-Baghdadi is an apostate, such a determination was a logical conclusion of its positions. With claims about the apostasy of jihadi leaders and scholars expanding among the Hazimis, the self-styled caliph's own faith would become a subject of debate if he avoids labeling prominent jihadi figures such as the much revered jihadi scholar al-Maqdisi as an apostate. Even if the chain of *takfir* was to be limited by the Hazimis to three circles beyond the original target of *takfir*,[69] it would still remove the bulk of the *umma*, and the jihadi movement, from Islam.

BAY'A (ALLEGIANCE)

The need for unity is a regular theme among transnational jihadis. Unity has an intrinsic value reflecting the ideal of the *umma*. But from a practical point of view, the number of jihadis is simply far too small for the movement's broad objectives to afford division. Acknowledging the challenge, jihadi leaders repeatedly have proclaimed the virtues of unity, the benefits of unifying the movement's components organizationally and the drawbacks of fragmentation.[70] At times they moved beyond words to active unification attempts, usually with limited success. When jihadi groups do manage to move beyond cooperation and coordination to integration, the organizational transformation normally is marked by a ceremonial declaration involving the introduction of and a *bay'a*—the Islamic oath of allegiance—to the outfit's leader.

Beyond its direct role in signifying a contract between a leader and his followers, *bay'a* is an instrument for maintaining order. The Islamic custom of collecting pledges of fealty started with the Prophet (though it should be noted that it had its roots in a local pre-Islamic costume). But it gained particular importance in the aftermath of his death. In the absence of anyone with the qualifications and authority of the Prophet, Muhammad's successors, assuming the title of a caliph (the successor of the messenger of God), needed a religious boost to bolster their authority. Moreover, they had to reduce the threat that unmitigated struggle for power would undermine order and ultimately harm the nascent *umma*. *Bay'a* had the potential to assist. Islamic jurisprudence determined that once given, *bay'a* could not be easily retracted; the pledge required one to retain his allegiance to the caliph (and in later days to any ruler viewed as Islamically legitimate) even when the giver of the *bay'a* disagrees with the caliph's actions. In fact, obedience must be maintained even when a leader sins because order is in the public interest and benefits the *umma* more. Unless the caliph failed to uphold the sharia, violating one's *bay'a* is a grave sin, punishable by death.[71]

The willingness to tolerate a ruler even when he does not behave as a model Muslim could be seen, to some extent, as a necessary measure to prevent repeating the traumas of civil war among Muslims. It also complements the pluralism within Islam and reduces the danger that in the absence of clear hierarchy among the clergy, religious challenges would become all too common and harm the *umma*'s interests. Thus, by tying followers to their rulers, the institution of the *bay'a* seeks to assure that unless the ruler committed grave violations of Islam, dissent would stop short of challenging a ruler's legitimacy.

The practice of *bay'a*-giving is, of course, not reserved only to situations involving a caliph. Primarily among jihadis, *bay'a* is understood as a pledge of fealty to individuals in positions of authority, including emirs ruling territories and group leaders.[72] As such, the *bay'a* is a prominent mechanism for binding jihadis together, encouraging unity and deterring splits. It is only natural that jihadis conceptualize hierarchy and authority through an Islamic prism and that they turn to Islamic symbols to cement their relationships.[73] A jihadi subordinate does not simply accept the authority of his group's leader because this is one of the tenets of effective bureaucracy; rather, through the *bay'a*, loyalty to a superior is infused with religious meaning, and its violation is tantamount to a religious offense.

On the face of it, the religious content of *bay'a*-giving bolsters the commitment of group members to their leaders. *Bay'a* should also—at least in theory—make breaking ties more costly; the strict conditions against breaking one's oath turn the *bay'a* into a mechanism for maintaining the status-quo. It complicates attempts by emerging jihadi forces to capture and expand the "market share" within the jihadi movement: groups who pledged their allegiance are prohibited from breaking their oath and new outfits cannot easily tempt groups who had already pledged their fealty to an emir to defect and join the upstart group. Actors are deterred from breaking ties because it is impermissible. But perhaps as important are the reputational costs for violating an Islamic oath. Respecting one's own religious oath has a value of its own, and negating it marks one as an unreliable partner whose commitment to Islam is dubious. Thus, a vow to follow a leader provides ideational disincentives to insubordination and defection.

And yet, despite the intended function of the *bay'a*, jihadis—like non-religious rebels—regularly split and shift organizational ties. But in contrast to cases of non-religious actors, when jihadis defect, they cannot simply justify their actions using instrumental arguments (even when mundane conflicts over power, interests, and resources are the true reasons for their actions). Due to their *bay'a* and the centrality of Islam to their identity, they must explain their action using religious justifications, thereby minimizing damage to their reputation. The jihadi group that has suffered departures similarly would turn to the sharia to condemn the defection as a violation of the pledge.

Turning conflict over affiliation into a religious question raises the stakes for all sides involved and often leads to exacerbation of the conflict. Thus, at times, the *bay'a* turns from a source of unity into a cause for increased conflict. In fact, given jihadis penchant for radicalism and their tendency to hold an expansive view of what constitute serious religious infractions, they are more likely to challenge a leader's legitimacy and seek ways to withdraw their pledge, suggesting greater difficulty to use the *bay'a* as a source of stability and unity.

Not unlike other aspects of Islam, the scope of the *ba'ya*'s applicability and the conditions under which it could be abandoned are a matter of controversy among Muslim jurists. But as the conflict between al-Qaeda and ISIS revealed, these questions are particularly contentious among jihadis. Jihadis agree on several points: first, a pledge is given from an individual to another, thus personifying the *bay'a*. It is not a pledge to an institution or a group, but to its leader. Second, the *bay'a*-giver could be a leader of a group and pledge on its behalf. Third, after the death or removal of a leader, his successor cannot simply rely on the *bay'a* given to his predecessor. Instead, he needs to collect pledges of allegiance anew. Fourth, when a subordinate emir is replaced, his successor could reconsider the pledge and transfer his allegiance—and thus his group's—to another leader. Fifth, while a leader remains in his position of authority, his subordinates are required to respect their pledge unless he committed a grave violation of Islamic law. Six, a leader could release subordinates from their pledge.

These elements of agreement point to specific points in which the unity of a jihadi group could be shattered. The death or imprisonment of a leader of a jihadi group potentially could lead to its disintegration if no agreed upon successor who can obtain group members' pledges emerges. In a two-tier organization such as al-Qaeda, the death of the group's leader or of a branch's leader creates opportunities to reconsider and upend the relationship between the parent organization and its franchise. Perhaps puzzling, while al-Qaeda has known branch defections, none followed leadership change.[74] Following bin Laden's death, all of its franchises, including—according to al-Qaeda's leadership[75]—ISI, reaffirmed their loyalty to his successor al-Zawahiri. Similarly, after the death of al-Shabab's leader Ahmed Abdi Godane (2014), and AQAP's Nasir al-Wuhayshi (2015), their successors each renewed his group's allegiance to al-Zawahiri instead of using this opportunity to reorient their groups away from al-Qaeda.[76] This loyalty stands out because it took place while the Islamic State—at the peak of its power, when it seemed invincible—was collecting pledges and particularly was motivated to break al-Qaeda, its main competitor. On the other hand, al-Qaeda branches experienced some defections by factions that decided to abandon their pledge and transfer it to the Islamic State.[77]

Notwithstanding the general points of agreement between jihadi groups regarding the mechanics of the *bay'a*, the question of its breaking looms large over the relationship between jihadi groups, producing and strengthening intra-jihadi consternation. After seeing two of its branches (ISIS and JN) reneging on their *bay'a*, a frustrated al-Qaeda announced that "the oath of allegiance is a shari' undertaking; binding in its nature, its violation forbidden."[78] Naturally, in the absence of necessary capabilities in Iraq and Syria, al-Qaeda could not prevent these defections, but it did spend considerable energy trying to delegitimize them by arguing that the defecting outfits violated their Islamic oath. ISIS too found itself embroiled in the debate over *bay'a* when it justified abandoning al-Qaeda, asserted the mandatory nature of giving a pledge of allegiance to its leader al-Baghdadi, and harshly attacked JN for allegedly reneging on its oath.

In what follows, I use the lens of allegiance to discuss intra-jihadi conflicts that have regularly weakened transnational jihadism. I begin with the conflict between AQC and JN on one side and the Islamic State on the other after the State announced its expansion to Syria and the absorption of JN. Next, I turn to al-Qaeda's attempt to use the authority of the Taliban's leader Mullah Omar as a foil against ISIS schemes. I conclude with the case of the break between al-Qaeda and JN.

THE ISLAMIC STATE VS. AL-QAEDA CENTRAL AND JABHAT AL-NUSRA

In its rise, ISIS had to overcome the status-quo bias that benefitted al-Qaeda—the dominant transnational jihadi group of the time. The Islamic State faced a double challenge: first, it needed to justify breaking with al-Qaeda. Then, it needed to assure that the abandonment of its pledge to al-Qaeda's leadership did not undercut its own efforts to collect (and importantly, to preserve) pledges for itself. ISIS's solution was two-pronged. First, it maintained that it was never a branch of al-Qaeda and that in any case, al-Qaeda lost its way under the leadership of al-Zawahiri and was no longer worthy of allegiance. And second, by distinguishing organizations from Islamic emirates and caliphates, it denied that it broke its pledge to al-Qaeda and justified its own demand of fealty to Abu Bakr al-Baghdadi from jihadi groups.

ISIS's justification for acting as an independent actor was based on refuting the claim that authority relations existed between the group and al-Qaeda. If there was no such relationship, then no *bay'a* was broken. ISIS's argument began with the determination that not all pledges are equal. A caliph's authority is encompassing and de-territorialized, and he has authority over all Muslims no matter where they reside. In contrast, the authority of a leader of an emirate is territorial, covering only those living in the emirate-controlled area. Thus, allegiance to a leader could be restricted to the subordinate's presence in the emirate and invalid outside its borders. The scope of an allegiance to an organization's leader is even narrower, encompassing only group members.

According to ISIS, the relationship of authority between al-Qaeda and its Iraqi branch ceased to exist when ISI was announced in the fall of 2006.[79] As Aaron Zelin reminds us, after al-Zarqawi was assassinated in June 2006, his successor, Abu Hamza al-Muhajir, released an audio message in which he called bin Laden emir, but did not actually pledge allegiance to al-Qaeda.[80] If al-Muhajir did not give bin Laden the *bay'a*, then he was free to transfer his fealty (and thus, his group's as well) to a new organization: ISI. And in the absence of a formal pledge of allegiance, ISI could not be deemed an al-Qaeda subordinate. Moreover, statements from both ISI and AQC declared that al-Qaeda in Iraq disbanded when it integrated with other jihadi factions under the leadership of ISI emir Abu Umar al-Baghdadi.[81]

ISIS's argument goes further. It maintained that the introduction of ISI was more than a name change; rather, it resulted in an entity of a different nature. Instead of an organization, ISI (and after its expansion to Syria, ISIS) represented a superior entity—a state—that reflected the advancement of the jihad in Iraq.[82] The Islamic State maintained that a state is superior to an organization, and since ISI constituted a state, it could no longer be deemed an al-Qaeda subordinate. The implication, it argued, is that the group could not violate any pledge. It even reminded al-Qaeda that bin Laden himself followed that same logic when he gave his oath to Mullah Omar in his role as the leader of the Islamic Emirate of Afghanistan.[83]

The elevation of ISI's status to a state (controversial among jihadis[84]) was also instrumental to the group's relationship with other jihadi groups. Declaring itself the sole legitimate ruling party, ISI demanded allegiance from all other Sunni groups. It even killed members of other jihadi groups for refusing to pledge their allegiance.[85] According to Fishman, the establishment of ISI, coming on the heels of brewing Sunni dissatisfaction with the group, was in part an attempt to prevent rival Sunni actors from rebelling against its dictates.[86] But such coercive acts only escalated the conflict between ISI and the rest of Iraq's Sunni actors.

In 2013, when ISI announced its presence in the Syrian arena, it had a choice: ISI could act as an organization or, as it ended up doing, it could claim that its statehood expanded across the border. Whereas the first option would have been more conducive to intra-jihadi cooperation against the Assad regime, the second was in line with the group's much more ambitious aspirations. Newly named as ISIS, it was looking to lead, and was ready to impose its authority—given the reluctance of the other rebel groups to join it. The group also relied on its claims for Islamic statehood (and later as a caliphate) to stifle debate among jihadis about the religious legitimacy of its actions and to reject calls for turning to a sharia court to resolve its differences with fellow groups.[87] Its prominent scholar Turki al-Bin'ali even went against his former mentor al-Maqdisi; rejecting al-Maqdisi's call for an independent sharia court to arbitrate between ISIS and its foes, al-Bin'ali declared, "We are a state, so how would you compel us to submit to the judgment of an independent court? . . . Don't you know that an independent court means a different state?"[88]

Al-Qaeda rejected ISIS expansion to Syria, as well as its claims of independence from al-Qaeda. Al-Zawahiri argued that even after the announcement of ISI, the group continued to assure AQC of its allegiance to al-Qaeda's leadership.[89] In the spirit of the Arab uprisings, al-Qaeda also criticized ISIS's attempts to raise its status at the expense of the *umma*. Al-Qaeda argued that by unilaterally announcing itself as an Islamic state rather than simply an organization, ISIS appropriated the *umma*'s right to be consulted and participate in its own governance.[90] Al-Qaeda was also critical of what it viewed as ISIS's unpersuasive attempt to change the meaning of its pledge to al-Qaeda's leader and to limit its scope. In particular, it rejected claims that the *bay'a* can be seen as merely a form of respect and appreciation,[91] that a *bay'a* could be limited to certain affairs but not others, and that it holds in certain jurisdictions only. And yet, al-Qaeda's statements also made it clear that AQC often was left in the dark about the actions of its Iraqi branch. In fact, AQC never heard about ISI leaders Abu Bakr al-Baghdadi or his predecessor Abu Umar al-Baghdadi before the branch's shura council nominated them to their positions. Indeed, al-Qaeda's central leadership had to send ISI requests for information about the Baghdadis.[92]

Since ISIS held global ambitions, it did not settle for Iraq and Syria and was looking to also establish its authority elsewhere. Thus, it needed to identify a way to expand its authority. It could have followed al-Qaeda's path and bring under its wings unaffiliated groups attracted to the group, its ideology, or its success and resources. But this solution did not satisfy the group's ambitions. Seeking to lead the jihadi camp and ultimately, the whole *umma*, it turned to announcing a caliphate and proclaimed that al-Baghdadi has assumed the position of the caliph. Elsewhere, I discuss the reasons behind the declaration of ISIS's caliphate;[93] here, I will limit myself to its role in support of the group's authority claims.

The declaration of a caliphate and a caliph were central to ISIS's expansion plan. As before, it relied on the hierarchy between a caliphate, an emirate, and an organization to maintain that it is holding a position superior to all of its competitors and detractors. Instead of the common practice whereby allegiance is given freely after negotiations between jihadi groups, by claiming to form a caliphate, the group attempted to impose its authority on the whole movement. Since the caliph's authority expands to all Muslims regardless of their place of residence or whether the caliphate has established control over the territory where Muslims live, the caliphate proclamation served as a tool for mobilizing the Muslim masses outside ISIS's main arenas of operation. This was not a request: utilizing the caliph's claimed authority, al-Baghdadi declared immigration to the caliphate an individual duty, one that all able Muslims must obey.[94] He summoned—rather than merely encouraged—Muslims to join the Islamic State.

The Islamic State's coercive demands were not directed at the masses and unaffiliated groups only; the group also demanded *bay'a* from al-Qaeda and its branches. As the State's spokesman al-Adnani maintained:

> With this declaration of khilāfah [caliphate], it is incumbent upon all Muslims to pledge allegiance to the khalīfah Ibrāhīm [Abu Bakr al-Baghdadi] and support him (may Allah preserve him). The legality of all emirates, groups, states, and organizations, becomes null by the expansion of the khilāfah's authority and arrival of its troops to their areas.[95]

Thus, according to ISIS, by restoring the caliphate, it invalidated the legitimacy of jihadi groups. All groups, wherever they are located and regardless of any pledge they have given to other leaders of organizations, are required to pledge a *bay'a* to al-Baghdadi. Furthermore, because all groups are subordinate to the caliph, their prior allegiances become null and void. In al-Adnani's words: "We—by Allah—do not find any shar'i excuse for you justifying your holding back from supporting this state. . . . It is time for you to end this abhorrent partisanship, dispersion, and division."[96]

Al-Adnani's announcement was unlikely to persuade groups that rejected ISIS's worldview and strategy or that were attached to their independence. But it aimed at influencing them indirectly by appealing to their operatives:

> O soldiers of the platoons and organizations, know that after this consolidation and the establishment of the khilāfah, the legality of your groups and organizations has become invalid. It is not permissible for a single person of you who believes in Allah to sleep without having wala' to the khalīfah [caliph] . . . And know that nothing has delayed victory and delays it now more than these organizations, because they are the cause of division and disagreements that ruin strength . . . So let those leaders be ruined.[97]

To reinforce its claims that its break with al-Qaeda was justified, ISIS also listed what it viewed as severe ideological transgressions committed by al-Zawahiri's al-Qaeda. Among those transgressions: the abandonment of jihad, flirtation with tyrants, cooperation with secularists, and the "traitorous awakening groups." ISIS also accused al-Qaeda of splitting the ranks of the jihadis by supporting the "rebellious defectors" of JN, portraying their members as noble and honorable, and even rewarding their bad behavior by accepting their pledge of allegiance.[98]

ISIS also framed its rejection of al-Zawahiri's call (when he tried to arbitrate between al-Baghdadi and al-Joulani on the question of ISIS's decision to expand formally into Syria and absorb JN) on ISIS to leave the Syrian arena to JN and return to Iraq as a moral obligation in the face of a fundamental injustice. Distorting al-Zawahiri's message, ISIS spokesman al-Adnani stated that at a time when Shia are slaughtering and oppressing Muslims in Syria, and while Sunnis all over the world seek to assist their suffering brethren and call for unifying the ranks, al-Zawahiri's verdict was unforgivably unjust. ISIS simply could not comply: "No one will prevent us from helping our people in the Levant! No one will prevent us from fighting the Nusayris [Alawaites] and doing jihad in the Levant! No one will prevent us from staying in the Levant." Al-Adnani also asserted that al-Zawahiri diverted from the "true path" because he was seeking to impose a division that is based on the illegitimate World War I-era Sykes-Picot borders, which jihadis are ordained to dismantle, not reinforce.[99] Notwithstanding ISIS's penchant for *takfirism*, it even accused al-Qaeda of labeling the State's operatives as *khawarij*, supposedly making the spilling of their blood permissible.[100]

Interestingly, ISIS associated al-Qaeda's ideological violations with al-Zawahiri only even though in many senses there has been considerable continuity between bin Laden and his successor. While bin Laden remained a mythical revered figure and condemning him, especially after his martyrdom, could result in a backlash, his successor was an easier target. At times, ISIS presented itself as the genuine heir to al-Qaeda, loyal to the principles that al-Qaeda's current leadership abandoned under al-Zawahiri's leadership.[101]

Ironically, at the same time that it defended the claim that the *bay'a* al-Zarqawi pledged to bin Laden (and thus, to al-Qaeda) became invalid, ISIS furiously attacked Jabhat al-Nusra for allegedly violating its own oath to al-Baghdadi. Viewing itself as an independent actor at the time when JN was formed in Syria, ISIS maintained that JN and its leader al-Joulani were subordinate to al-Baghdadi. Therefore, al-Joulani transgressed because he could not legitimately abandon his oath.[102] Al-Joulani's response rejected the ISIS claim that it had no organizational connection to al-Qaeda, which implied that there was no formal relations between JN and al-Qaeda, only between JN and ISIS. He claimed that JN was affiliated with al-Qaeda and publically renewed his *bay'a* to its leader al-Zawahiri.[103] Thus, in the al-Qaeda-ISIS-JN triangle, the question of allegiance did not increase unity, but rather amplified intra-jihadi conflict.

AL-QAEDA CENTRAL AND THE TALIBAN VERSUS THE ISLAMIC STATE

The question of allegiance becomes particularly complicated when the establishment of groups, emirates, and caliphates produces cross-cutting lines of authority. In 1999, bin Laden pledged allegiance to Mullah Omar, reluctantly and via proxy rather than in person, in an effort to assuage Taliban anger that al-Qaeda defied Omar's instructions to lower the group's profile and avoid taking actions that would harm the Taliban's interests.[104] In that move, bin Laden subordinated al-Qaeda—a transnational organization—to a state leader. Al-Qaeda's flexible use of the *bay'a* over the next 20 years indicates that it did not take this pledge too seriously, adjusting its position based on changing utilitarian considerations.[105] Moreover, al-Qaeda maintained a level of ambiguity regarding the nature of its allegiance. Though, over time, it came very close to endorsing the Taliban's leader as a caliph, it stopped short of such an explicit statement. Instead, it portrayed the Taliban as guardians of the caliphate, but never really determined that the Taliban's leader was a caliph to whom all Muslims must—instead of just should—pledge allegiance. Nevertheless, because bin Laden gave a *bay'a* to the Taliban, it supposedly affected all members of al-Qaeda, including those present outside Afghanistan.

Al-Qaeda's move in 2003 to constitute itself as a two-tier organization by beginning to establish franchises outside of Afghanistan, including through mergers with other jihadi groups, complicated the lines of allegiance. Since the leaders of these branches gave an oath of allegiance to bin Laden and he pledged his allegiance to Mullah Omar, the implication was that al-Qaeda's branches were indirectly subordinate to the Taliban even as they operated in arenas far from Afghanistan and recruit local operatives who cared about their locale and perhaps about global jihad, but felt little to no attachment to the Taliban.

After the ascendance of the Islamic State, bin Laden's pledge to Mullah Omar became central to al-Qaeda's attempts to thwart the self-styled caliphate's imperialistic tendencies. Unable to stop ISIS on the ground, AQC attempted to weaken al-Baghdadi's group by playing up the role of the Mullah Omar, essentially presenting him as a quasi-caliph and arguing that not being a descent from the Prophet's tribe of Quraysh (in contrast to al-Baghdadi's alleged Qurayshi lineage) does not disqualify him from assuming the caliph role.[106] AQC emphasized that al-Qaeda's branches are subordinate to the Taliban by virtue of bin Laden's "greater pledge" to the Taliban leader, implying that al-Baghdadi violated both his oath to bin Laden and his indirect pledge to Mullah Omar.[107] Al-Qaeda even opened the first issue of its new newsletter *al-Nafir* (July 2014) with a restatement of its pledge to Mullah Omar:

> [Al-Nafir] begins its first issue with the renewal of the *bay'a* to the Commander of the Believers Mullah Muhammad 'Omar, the jihad warrior (may God protect him), and it affirms that al-Qaeda and its branches in all locales are soldiers in his army, acting under his victorious banner, by God's help and His grant of success, until the shari'a prevails . . . until every part of the land of Islam is liberated . . . until the Islamic conquests again take place . . . and return all the violated lands of Islam to the coming caliphal state, God willing.[108]

In recalling al-Qaeda's pledge to Mullah Omar, the group wished to challenge the Islamic State's narrative that it is the only legitimate representative of the *umma* by reminding jihadis and their sympathizers around the world that Mullah Omar assumed the title of the "Emir of the Faithful" years before al-Baghdadi. Reiterating its ties to the Taliban, al-Qaeda also sought to fend off the demands of ISIS that al-Qaeda submit to its authority. Finally, al-Qaeda tried to distinguish itself from ISIS by signaling that in contrast to al-Baghdadi al-Qaeda's leaders adhere to their commitments and that while al-Qaeda is only trying to please God, al-Baghdadi is seeking personal power.[109] Al-Qaeda also used the Taliban's leader for another line of attack on the Islamic State: if Mullah Omar (and his successors after him) is viewed as a caliph, then the formation of ISIS's self-styled caliphate years after Omar adopted the "Emir of the Faithful" title goes against the view that there cannot be two legitimate caliphs simultaneously.

The seeming elevation of al-Qaeda's pledge to the leader of the Taliban could be also linked to the question of the relationship between al-Qaeda branches that were considering declaring emirates in their areas of operation (primarily in Somalia and Yemen). This question goes beyond whether a branch of an organization that transformed into an emirate remains subordinate to the parent organization (the heart of the debate between the Islamic State and al-Qaeda); indeed, the issue also turns into the possibility that a newly established emirate (i.e., a transformed al-Qaeda branch) would be subordinate to another emirate (i.e., the Taliban). Al-Qaeda dealt with this problem by dissuading its branches from turning themselves into emirates and by elevating the status of the Taliban so that it could be superior to emirates as well.

Al-Qaeda's claims concerning the authority of the Taliban leader suffered a grave hit when in the summer of 2015 it became known that al-Qaeda continued to claim its allegiance to Mullah Omar, and even publically reaffirmed it, without knowing that he had died in secret two years earlier.[110] Although al-Zawahiri quickly pledged his allegiance to Omar's successor

Mullah Mansour[111] (notably, al-Qaeda's branches did not[112]), it became harder to defend a decision to stick with the Taliban after its revered leader was replaced by a considerably less regarded leader or use the Taliban as a counterweight to the Islamic State.

Furthermore, the Taliban's reputation suffered from the revelation that it lied about Omar's state and even released messages in Omar's name after his death. The lie strengthened claims about the Taliban's religious shortcomings; after all, for over two years, it was led by a figure that was not nominated to the role through a legitimate Islamic procedure and that deceptively issued statements on behalf of the dead "Emir of the Faithful." The succession crisis that ensued after the revelation of Omar's death contrasted with the Islamic State's unity behind its leader and caliph al-Baghdadi, further weakening the appeal of al-Qaeda's continued loyalty to the Taliban.[113] The episode put al-Zawahiri in poor light, looking as either out of touch or as suffering from poor judgment: if al-Zawahiri knew that Mullah Omar was dead, then he repeatedly lied about it, and if he was not aware of Omar's death, then it implies that al-Zawahiri was uninformed and that al-Qaeda's influence in Afghanistan and Pakistan has been diminished greatly.[114]

JABHAT AL-NUSRA VERSUS AL-QAEDA CENTRAL

In the summer of 2016, AQC learned once again how fragile the oaths it collected could be in the face of its affiliates' shifting strategic needs. After AQC took Jabhat al-Nusra's side in the latter's conflict with ISIS, it found that JN's loyalty to al-Qaeda was also fleeting. Acknowledging that its relationship with al-Qaeda was becoming a liability—making JN a target for the American airpower and deterring fellow rebel groups in Syria from strengthening their ties with the branch for fear of becoming targets to aerial attacks and of losing much needed foreign support—JN's leader al-Joulani decided to break with his superiors in AQC.

After receiving conditional support from Abu al-Khayr al-Masri, one of al-Zawahiri's deputies,[115] JN rebranded as *Jabhat Fatah al-Sham* (JFS).[116] This move was a controversial one that led to the defection of several prominent JN leaders who protested the dissociation from al-Qaeda.[117] Soon, it became apparent that al-Joulani's gambit failed to break his group's political isolation. Prominent rebel groups—primarily Ahrar al-Sham—still declined a merger. Moreover, al-Zawahiri and his deputies in Iran rejected al-Joulani's move and demanded JN's return to al-Qaeda's fold. But al-Joulani did not relent; despite opposition from hawks within JFS, he insisted on maintaining the group's independence. In January 2017, al-Joulani moved one step further from al-Qaeda by announcing a merger between JFS and smaller rebel groups, including the hawkish wing of Ahrar al-Sham, under the name *Hay'at Tahrir al-Sham* (HTS).[118] In this formation, he took a step back, leaving the leadership position to Hashim al-Sheikh, a former Ahrar leader. Al-Joulani settled for the position of HTS's minister of war,[119] though in reality he retained his authority over the group.

HTS, much like its predecessor JFS, failed to improve intra-rebel dynamics. Despite initial success in bringing *Nour al-Din Zinki* and a considerable segment of Ahrar al-Sham into the new organization, the unification of all Islamic groups was out of reach. Rather than bolstering rebel unity, HTS became engulfed in the escalating rivalry with Ahrar al-Sham and the alliance it formed. If HTS sought to bolster its legitimacy, then it failed miserably. Soon, HTS found itself in a violent conflict with fellow rebels while suffering defections from within, including by former JN leaders who disagreed with the decision to move farther away from al-Qaeda.[120] HTS was left exposed to critique from more moderate Syrian rebel groups as well as from al-Qaeda loyalists, while witnessing growing popular backlash. Less than a year later, most actors who joined JFS to form HTS left it, and al-Joulani assumed the role of the group's emir.[121]

Interestingly, al-Joulani critics in al-Qaeda began alleging that there is no real difference between al-Baghdadi's abandonment of his allegiance to al-Qaeda and al-Joulani's actions.[122] In an online exchange, HTS argued that it was released from its *bay'a*,[123] whereas AQC denied that claim and urged al-Joulani to reverse his actions and respect his oath of allegiance to al-Zawahiri. Criticizing HTS's move, one of al-Qaeda's leaders in Syria noted that pledges of allegiance can be withdrawn only with legal foundation. They "are not to be invalidated or broken on account of fancies, illusions, whims, suppositions, legal tricks, deception, and misleading."[124] Al-Qaeda's leader al-Zawahiri indicated that his refusal to release JN from its oath is not the result of his personal interests. He would be glad to release JN in one of two scenarios: for the unification of all jihadis in Syria or after the people of the region have chosen themselves an Islamic government. Since neither of these conditions held, al-Joulani's abandonment of his pledge was impermissible.[125]

The conflict between HTS and al-Qaeda deteriorated, leading HTS to arrest prominent al-Qaeda figures in Syria and their families. Notably, in contrast to the violence that erupted between JN and ISIS after the latter's expansion to Syria, HTS quickly succumb to internal and external pressures to release the detainees.[126] Eventually, giving up on HTS, al-Qaeda has recently begun forming a new branch in Syria.[127]

Despite (and perhaps because of) the enormity of the enterprise that transnational jihadi groups took on themselves, they remarkably have been prone to fall into internal disagreements. Jihadi groups regularly emphasize the virtues of cooperation and call for unity, but when they try to achieve this unity, they find that despite their ideological affinity there is a lot that separates them. At times, intra-jihadi squabbling even turns violent. The conflicts between jihadis—leaders and groups—are exacerbated by the religious discourse they use. Turning to Islamic precepts may make all jihadi groups declare their support for unity, but it does not necessarily lead to the unification of the jihadi forces under one banner. Instead, religious discourse magnifies the conflict among jihadis and makes compromise and reconciliation much less likely. As long as jihadis are unable to come together, overcoming in the process their strategic differences, personal rivalries, cultural differences, and Arab chauvinism, they will not be able to move beyond short-lived and geographically limited success.

5

The Way Forward

Seventeen years after al-Qaeda carried out the 9/11 attacks, many countries around the world still view terrorism as a central security threat. Despite limited ability to carry out attacks, the threat al-Qaeda and the Islamic State—the two main transnational components of the jihadi movement—pose to innocent lives in the Middle East, the West, and elsewhere still looms large. While counterintuitive, jihadi violence actually has spread since the U.S. launched its "War on Terrorism" and is now directly affecting more countries than ever. Al-Qaeda, which has been the target of a global manhunt, not only did not disappear, but also its membership has grown through the establishment of formal branches in the heart of the Muslim world. Additionally, instead of one safe haven—Afghanistan—for jihadis on the eve of the attack on New York and Washington, jihadis today find safe havens in many additional locations, including Syria, Somalia, Libya, Mali, and Yemen, among others. Finally, though transnational jihadis have failed to produce a sustained campaign of large-scale terror attacks, they have seen their sporadic and small-scale attacks receiving disproportional public attention and often sufficing to produce fear among their enemies' populations. One, therefore, would be forgiven if he or she thinks that the "War on Terrorism" has been an abject failure.

Given their demonstrated dedication to the cause and remarkable resilience, the threat that these transnational jihadi organizations pose is unlikely to end anytime soon. However, as I argued in this book, the presence and spread of jihadi terrorism does not necessarily reflect the threat level. Since 2001, jihadis failed to produce any major attack coming even close to the scale of 9/11. Moreover, their efforts to establish sharia-governed territories in Mali, Libya, and Yemen collapsed in the face of fierce American- and French-led military campaigns. Even the Islamic State, undoubtedly the jihadi outfit which made the greatest strides, controlling large swaths of territory in Iraq and Syria, and proudly sporting affiliates throughout the Middle East, Central and South Asia, and the African continent, was unable to hold on to its possessions and was stripped from much of its power.

What are we to make of this confusing picture? In this book, I attempted to present a nuanced and critical view of the transnational jihadism, with an emphasis of the danger posed by al-Qaeda and the Islamic State. I argued that not only are transnational jihadi actors pursuing unrealistic end-states, but they also lack the means to attain even much narrower objectives.

Transnational jihadi actors struggle to persuade their target audience of Muslims worldwide of the absolute supremacy and comprehensiveness of their religious affiliation. In their ideology, Islam is not merely a guide for personal behavior, but it is a system to manage all aspects of life, politics included. They also maintain that Muslims, regardless of their place of residence, are part of a political community, the *umma*, and as such, they must labor to live under one political entity governed by the sharia. These views point to rejection of nationalism, tribalism, and ethnicity as sources of political identification and bring transnational jihadis to seek the replacement of these pillars of global and local orders with an Islamic one, epitomized in a unique polity: a global caliphate.

Transnational jihadis' rejection of the existing order and of the legitimacy of nation-state means that they cannot settle for a space within the state-based order, an option state-based jihadi groups do accept. But to the chagrin of al-Qaeda and the Islamic State, the power of competing identities frustrates their aspirations to transform world politics. Most Muslims want to see religion playing a part in their daily life, but they are entrenched in their national and sub-national identities and ultimately reject the religious-based world order that al-Qaeda and ISIS are trying to establish.

The enormous scope of transnational jihadis' objectives also means that such groups have very few potential allies but many likely opponents with far superior capabilities. Consequently, success requires resources far beyond what any jihadi organization could typically marshal. But ISIS and al-Qaeda cannot even bring the full potential of the jihadi movement to bear. They have both failed to unite a jihadi movement behind one vision and one strategy because the movement is fragmented and engulfed by internal strife, ideological divisions, and personal conflicts. At times, these groups fell into different types of conflicts with other jihadi actors, some of which even deteriorate to fratricidal violence.

Intra-jihadi strife weakens transnational jihadi groups from within while their actions and vision simultaneously generate strong external resistance among non-Muslims and nation-states. Members of the international community have come together to confront ISIS, al-Qaeda, and similar groups, underscoring the immense capabilities gap between states and their non-state enemies. Interstate cooperation—deepened considerably since the 9/11 attacks—poses insurmountable obstacle for the jihadis and often forces them to localize their efforts, further weakening in this way the ability of transnational jihadis to realize their transformative ideas.

The need to turn to local struggles while maintaining a transnational agenda exposes internal contradictions within transnational jihadi groups; immediate operational needs that are necessary for group survival undermine its ideology and consequently reduce the prospects of long-term success. Localization of jihadi fights also exposes the inability of the movement's strategists to come up with an operational plan to realize their vision. Transnational jihadis must turn military success into political effects. This task is highly challenging even to armed non-state actors that focus on one country only; producing political effects across borders is much more complicated. But transnational jihadis cannot overcome their material weakness, particularly because they fail to gain significant popular support and attract a sufficient—that is, very large—number of volunteers to join the cause. As a result, even in the few cases in which jihadi groups registered some successes, it is usually narrow geographically and short-lived.

RECONSIDERING TERRORISM

The identification of the systemic barriers to success is a prerequisite for a more accurate understanding of transnational jihadism (and other armed transnational movements) and for designing a comprehensive confrontation strategy. States should promote policies that strengthen jihadi barriers to success and further deepen internal cleavages within the jihadi movement. But first, it would be useful to make some adjustments to the way people think about jihadi groups and terrorism.

Transnational jihadi actors are commonly discussed as terrorist organizations, but this label is problematic. While jihadi actors use terrorism, it is only one tool in their arsenal. Jihadis diversify their efforts; they can use different modes of operations simultaneously in the same arena or deploy different tactics in different locations. At times, the prevalence of terrorism reflects the stage of the fight the jihadi group wages. According to Steven Metz, terrorism is often the method used by weak insurgents, unable to hit better defended targets, operate in larger units, or capture and hold ground.[1]

Rejecting the distinction between terrorist and insurgent groups, some scholars even recommend not using mutually exclusive definitions and instead view terrorist groups as insurgent groups.[2]

ISIS provides an example of a group that has shifted its focus between terrorism, insurgency, and conventional fighting, corresponding to changing military conditions. Terrorism has been its fallback position at times of great weakness, such as after it lost its main territorial possessions or when its predecessors in ISI had to back down in the face of the military efforts of the U.S. and the Awakening Councils. Thus, the term terrorism is inaccurate, and its use obfuscates the threat jihadi actors pose.

States may find using the term terrorism beneficial for shaping public opinion against jihadi actors. The term focuses attention to the acts of terrorism that a group carries out and in this way shapes and reinforces public perception of the jihadis as bloodthirsty radicals who care little about human life and accept no limits on violence. It thus delegitimizes jihadi actors in the eyes of many. States exclusive rights to use coercive means and to determine who could become a legitimate target for state power strengthens their ability to convince their residents to reject armed non-state actors as illegitimate and to view states' counterterrorism excesses as permissible. To the jihadis' dismay, the label terrorism is hurting their image, highlighting the excessive and indiscriminate violence they pursue while allowing states to turn in the name of security to exceptional and repressive means with little public qualms, oversight, or resistance.

Unfortunately, despite the benefits states accrue from using the term terrorism, there is no guarantee that the language used for galvanizing resistance to jihadism would not have adverse consequences in other respects. For example, affected by their own framing of their foes as terrorists, states might internalize this misconception of the nature of the threat they face, resulting in distorted operational planning for countering the jihadi threat. Echoing this worry, Audrey Cronin warned that viewing ISIS as a terrorist group misses much of its attributes as "a pseudo-state led by a conventional army" and leads to overreliance on counterterrorism and counterinsurgency strategies.[3] Highlighting terrorism also might foreclose some policy options that states should be considering because the negative connotations of terrorism render consideration of solutions short of efforts to eradicate the threat completely less likely. If terrorists—as opposed to insurgent groups—must not be negotiated with, violent means become the only available course of action.

Moreover, because decision makers recognize the potency of the term terrorism, they often are tempted to abuse it for their own political gains, whether to win elections or to repress and vilify legitimate non-violent opposition. The danger is that in the name of fighting terrorism policymakers improperly would assume special rights and curtail civil liberties to promote unrelated objectives, resulting in a much greater harm to their countries' populations than any terrorist group would manage to. Suffice to see how the leaders of Turkey and Russia abuse counterterrorism laws to cement their authoritarian rule and to repress minorities, political opponents, as well as democracy and human rights activists.[4]

Note that I am not making a moral argument about the downsides of using such value-laden language (a valid concern to be sure), rather I express practical concern that the use of the terrorism discourse undermines the fight against jihadism. This discourse may be invoked for utilitarian reasons, but, in their policy planning, states would be better off to abandon the terrorism frame and instead consider jihadis as armed non-state actors, an alternative view that would give states greater flexibility in finding the most effective way to address jihadi threats.

Bringing politics back into the discussion of terrorism is another necessary change. Notwithstanding the inherently political nature of terrorism, scholars and practitioners alike have been focusing on terrorist groups' ability to cause harm at the expense of discussing their political objectives and strategies to attain these objectives. Because states are committed to protecting their publics from attacks on their lives, it is not surprising that they would put a very high premium of thwarting terrorist attacks. But attacks are only means to a goal. Terrorist groups are seeking to achieve political objectives. Thus, terrorists' success does not hinge merely on the ability to destroy, kill, and maim; whether they are successful or not depends primarily on their ability to use these acts of violence to compel target states to comply with the terrorists' political demands made in the service of a political agenda.[5]

The emphasis on terrorist attacks has important repercussions for the way states assess the threat. It practically sets up states for failure as even the most successful nation will never be able to prevent all terrorist plots. Therefore, no matter how successful a state's security services are, their failures are likely to loom larger than their success and generate public pressure for escalation even though sometimes such a direction would be counterproductive. Moreover, the focus on terrorist attacks creates insatiable demands for additional resources for counterterrorism without offering a plan to deal with the political foundations of each terrorist challenge. The likely result: anxiety as a natural state and a never-ending war on terrorism.

In reality, however, terrorism (and jihadi terrorism perhaps more than other forms of terrorism) rarely produces the political effects its perpetrators hope for. Terrorists are hardly the masterminds that politicians' statements and news headlines would have us think they are. Even when they succeed in wreaking havoc, they usually fail to leverage their attacks in a manner that would bring their rivals to compliance. Naturally, terrorists' odds of success are linked to the scope of the enterprise they pursue. The greater the demands terrorists make, the more reluctant states are to comply and the greater the capabilities terrorists will have to bring to bear. Demanding a state to release imprisoned members of a terrorist organization is generally easier than bringing down a regime, or persuading the target state to allow a region to secede from it. Nowhere is this gap between terrorists' wishes and actual abilities wider than in the case of transnational jihadi groups that seek to overthrow the existing state-based order and establish an alternative world order that is based on their extreme interpretation of Islam.

Transnational jihadi groups face particular challenges that locally focused terrorist organization could potentially overcome. Terrorist actors who focus on bringing about change in only one state could design a strategy that would keep other states out of the conflict. Limited objectives also might make some terrorist demands more palatable to their state enemies. But transnational organizations constitute a more encompassing threat. Those who seek to take over several existing states and become a regional power upend existing norms against the changing of borders through violent means. But their task is easier still than that of jihadi groups that reject the existing order, and, instead of seeking to be incorporated into this order, wish to overturn it.

In the rest of this concluding chapter, I will discuss the implications of each of the barriers to jihadi success. Proposing a concrete strategy for countering transnational jihadi groups is beyond the scope of this book. Instead, I sketch in rough terms some ideas for increasing the difficulties groups such as the Islamic State and al-Qaeda face: strengthen national identity and bolster sub-national identities where national identity is too weak; pursue a containment strategy that hinders the ability of jihadis to operate across borders and that would prevent them from linking disparate arenas under one jihadi polity; and finally, take advantage of schism within the jihadi movement and seek to deepen existing cleavages.

THE IDEATIONAL BARRIER

Groups such as al-Qaeda and the Islamic State are seeking to transform international politics. They wish to overthrow the state-based order and establish a religious world order on the ruins of nation-states in which the source of an individual's political identity is religious rather than nationality, ethnic, or tribal affiliation. Success, therefore, depends on the jihadis' ability to bring about monumental change in the way people are connected to each other. The challenge is even greater because the jihadis do not operate in a vacuum;

they must overcome entrenched forces that are more powerful than the jihadis and enjoy much greater popular appeal.

Transnational jihadis do not have a solution for the power of national and sub-national identities. Only a few Muslims truly buy into the jihadi framing of a war as a cosmic fight between a "Zionist-Crusader alliance" and Islam. Many of the Muslims who take arms against their countries' regimes are motivated primarily by local grievances, not an eternal fight between the "righteous" and the "forces of falsehood." Muslims may support fighting a non-Muslim state when the latter invades their country, but such fights usually reflect self-defense considerations within a state-based order, not wars of religion. Some Muslims may show greater solidarity with co-religionists whose country and communities have come under attack, but most of these foreign fighters would see their role ending once their fellow Muslims are saved, not when a radical Islamic order is imposed within that country, let alone worldwide.

A transnational jihadi organization that controls a territory has better opportunities for instilling the idea of the *umma* among the region's Muslims. But social engineering—whether by means of indoctrination or by diluting non-religious identities with the infusion of foreign supporters coming from abroad—is extremely hard to implement successfully. Seeing adult Muslims as largely compromised by years of living under non-Islamist regimes and exposure to Western influences, transnational jihadis put their hopes in the indoctrination of youth. ISIS in particular attempted to build a loyal—that is, captive—support base by indoctrinating children.[6] But for such a strategy to succeed, one needs time, which ISIS did not have. The group lost the territories it had controlled before it managed to build a strong and disciplined force with everlasting commitment to the caliphate. The Islamic State's efforts still might turn some of its "cubs of the caliphate" into a jihadi threat, but by driving the group out of the cities, its state enemies liberated the youth from continued indoctrination and opened the door for their rehabilitation.

A response to the attempts of transnational jihadis to transform world politics radically should highlight the centrality of alternative identity markers. The sense of national identity is still weaker in Muslim states compared to the West, where the idea originated, making them more vulnerable to transnational jihadis. Therefore, strengthening national identity is a key for resisting al-Qaeda and ISIS. The more people view themselves as members of a particular state, the more likely they also are to buy into the notion of a state-based—rather than religion-based—order and to reject the revolutionary frame of the jihadis. Moreover, strong national identity is likely to deter external infiltration by foreign jihadi actors, and if undeterred, lead local jihadi groups to resist actively the hijacking of their anti-regime struggle, thus serving as a counterintuitive bulwark against al-Qaeda and ISIS expansion.

Strengthening national identity could also contribute to reducing the jihadi threat to non-Muslim states. The more Muslims identify with their countries, the less likely they are to follow an ideology that portrays these countries and their populations as enemies. Ideally, states would not attempt to suppress all expressions of religiosity. Such measures carry the risk of alienating members of a religious community and increase the sense of threat to a central part of their identity. On the other hand, states should be careful to avoid unconstrained multiculturalism. They should prevent the strengthening of communities' religious identities at the expense of the nation-state. Encouraging—but not forcing—more tolerant versions of Islam also would help in preventing jihadi penetration into non-Muslim states.

Keeping Muslims away from the jihadis requires that the non-Muslim states be careful not to push Muslims into jihadi arms. In order to feel greater identification with their nation-states, Muslims must feel included, accepted, and respected, not perpetually suspected or discriminated against. Responsible, level-headed leaders are central for creating an atmosphere of inclusion; instead of generalizing from the actions of some Muslims that all hate and threaten one's state, decision makers and politicians must stand clear against Islamophobic tendencies and avoid blaming whole Muslim communities for terrorism.

Non-Muslim states should address the problem of alienation among Muslim youth primarily as a social, not security, problem. Authorities should cooperate with prominent figures within Muslim communities to deal with the problem of radicalization, but they must do so without diminishing the agency of each individual. The help of community leaders could be invaluable for counterterrorism purposes, but states should be careful not to view all Muslims as part of a religious community or seek to work with community leaders as representatives of all of the country's Muslims. Muslim citizens must be treated as individuals whose connection to their state does not have to be mediated through a religious community. Muslims in the West do not have special responsibilities to their states that other citizens lack, and they must not be held accountable (formally or informally) for the actions of a co-religionist. The responsibility of Muslim citizens to assist in thwarting terrorist attacks when they come upon relevant information about a particular threat stems from their relationship to the state (that is, their citizenship). It is a civic duty, not one derived from any confessional affiliation. In this same vein, after terrorist attacks, states should make a space for Muslims to mourn co-national victims, too.

Politicians must resist the temptation to gain political capital through Islam and Muslim-bashing; they should refrain from playing into the jihadis' hands by irresponsibly inciting against Muslims. Recall that transnational jihadis seek to erase "the grey zone" by persuading Muslims in Muslim-dominated countries, but primarily in Muslim-minority states, that they cannot trust non-Muslims and must always side with their co-religionists.[7] Islamophobia, then, is not only morally abhorrent, but it is also very counterproductive as it leads to the exclusion of people based on their religion. Such exclusion could bring alienated Muslims to accept the claims of both jihadis and the Islamophobs that Islam is their defining identity and that joining jihadi groups is the obvious choice for Muslims in non-Muslim states.

In Muslim-majority countries, the international community should take measures that would deepen the divergence of interests between local and transnational jihadis and avoid measures that would lead to convergence of their interests. Local regimes should emphasize that transnational jihadis are foreign to their countries' cultures, traditions, and norms. In contrast, they should be clear that while they strongly reject the methods of indigenous jihadis, they recognize the legitimacy of their voice. By emphasizing differences between locals and foreigner, states may be able to prevent both types of groups from deep cooperation and even integration. They even might succeed in exacerbating intra-jihadi divisions. Separating local from transnational jihadis would also reduce the likelihood that the jihadi threat would spill over to neighboring countries—the main concern of the international community.

Local jihadis still would constitute a threat to their countries' regimes, but it would be more limited than when local and transnational jihadis come together. Embedded within their own societies, local jihadis are also more sensitive to public opinion and would thus be more attentive to the need to avoid measures that would alienate the public. Their relationships with the general public as well as different local actors, such as the tribes some jihadis originate from, could add to the constraints they experience. One just needs to look at the manner in which al-Zawahiri lamented the devastating effects that the killing of a young Egyptian girl in one of the EIJ's attacks had on the group to appreciate state-focused jihadis' constraints. The event led Egyptians to reject jihadi terrorism more clearly and contributed to the group's collapse.[8]

Separating local from transnational jihadi groups could allow regimes to explore more policy responses, including non-violent measures, to divide and weaken their local jihadi opposition. The international campaign against transnational jihadi actors gives states few options for taking non-coercive measures. States have a responsibility to each other to prevent the use of their territories to attack fellow states. When facing a local threat, states would not have to rely solely on suppression, which could bring short-term positive results, but tends to sow the seeds of future grievances. Instead, regimes could adopt accommodationist moves alongside coercive means. They could even be responsive to the grievances of local actors who are less committed to the jihadi ideology and peel them off the group.

In the case of branches of a transnational jihadi group, states should explore the roots of affiliation and assess the strength of the relationship between the parent organization and its franchises. Whereas some branches might adhere to the objectives of their parent organization, for others, the relationship could be instrumental and therefore conditional. Indeed, a group may choose to become an Islamic State affiliate not because it subscribes to al-Baghdadi's ideology but because it needs resources, seeks to benefit from the prestige of the parent organization, or reflects the position of a particular leader at a particular point in time. These considerations could change, leading the branch to abandon its parent organization, or to pursue a local agenda even as it declares its support for the transnational agenda.

Although branching out could extend the lives of transnational jihadi groups, it is important to recognize that the process of localization jeopardizes jihadis' broad transnational agenda by shifting group resources to local targets and attempting to achieve local objectives at the expense of transnationalism. Moreover, localization is likely to further socialize branch members to the nation-state. In this way, instead of bringing state-based jihadis to adopt the transnational jihadi agenda and strengthen their attachment to the idea of the *umma*, it would underscore the power of national, ethnic, and tribal groupings.

Moreover, automatically equating local branches with the transnational leadership carries the risk of overstating the capabilities and appeal of a jihadi group. Such a view would lead to greater emphasis on the use of force when cheaper and more effective policy responses are available. Additionally, if each affiliate would be viewed as an extension of its parent organization, external powers (particularly the U.S.) would be pressured to increase their military role when local efforts would suffice to contain the threat. Unnecessary external involvement carries additional costs: it might confirm the jihadi narrative regarding the foreign occupation of Muslim lands and the loyalty of apostate regimes to foreign backers, resulting in increased hostility to both the regimes and the foreign interveners.

Looking at the case of al-Qaeda, it becomes evident that even though its branches helped AQC stay in the headlines and fostered image of prowess, these affiliates did little to promote al-Qaeda's systemic challenge to the state-based order or its anti-U.S. agenda. Not only do these franchises distort bin Laden's strategy, but they also show its limitations as branches reconsider their allegiance to AQC. The success of ISI prompted it to abandon al-Qaeda in pursuit of the branch's independent agenda, while Jabhat al-Nusra decided that continuing its subordination to al-Zawahiri brought it to a dead-end and that if it seeks to achieve its objectives for Syria it must dissociate itself from transnationalism.[9]

THE OPERATIONAL BARRIER

Armed transnational movements also face extreme operational constraints, exacerbated by the ideational barriers noted above. Al-Qaeda and the Islamic State do not settle for bringing about limited change in one particular location; their agendas require a system-wide change. Thus, they must be able to operate in many places simultaneously, and importantly, produce a strategy to turn operational success in several disparate locations into synergic cross-borders political effects. In reality, they often fail to beat entrenched regimes, let alone link arenas. Rarely do they have the opportunity to link separate efforts together in the way the Islamic State did in Iraq and Syria.

Jihadi success in one location is often enough to provoke international mobilization to roll back the jihadis' progress. Whether in Yemen or in Mali, once jihadi forces affiliated with the global jihadi movement have made strides, they soon saw a coalition of international forces rising to set them back. ISIS's initial success in Iraq and the Levant demonstrates the enormity of the challenge. It was the result of extraordinary circumstances that created a power vacuum the group could fill. The retreat of the American forces from Iraq, high levels of corruption that crippled the Iraqi military, initially supportive Sunni Iraqi populace willing to accept ISIS as their champion, and a civil war in Syria that distracted and weakened many of the group's opponents created a unique opening for al-Baghdadi's loyalists to beat weak foes, conquer territories its opponents held, and expand on both sides of the Iraqi-Syrian border. But even that was not enough. ISIS overreach awakened the international community to address the threat, thwarting the group's efforts to further expand and take root in new locations and dislodging it from all but a few small population centers.

Jihadi thinkers have been trying to cope with the operational difficulties, but none managed to offer a viable plan for creating and expanding an Islamic state. Convinced that their victory was preordained by God, and is thus inevitable, jihadis are resilient enough to continue to fight despite forbidding odds. However, they are still searching for a magic solution that is not forthcoming. For bin Laden, the focus on fighting the "far enemy" was necessary for a systemic change because he believed that bringing down the U.S.

was a prerequisite for toppling the Muslim regimes and the establishment of a caliphate in their stead. Bin Laden overestimated al-Qaeda's capabilities and appeal and underestimated U.S. power and resolve. Abu Bakr al-Baghdadi believed that the chaos in the Middle East in the aftermath of the Arab uprisings created an opening for a caliphate and that quick success would breed more success until the establishment of the Islamic State could not be reversed. While he was right that the instability in the region, and the weakening of all Arab states in particular, would offer his group a chance to make quick and expansive gains, he underestimated the resolve and capability of the U.S. and its Kurdish and Iraqi allies to roll it all back.

Several implications stem from the operational barrier: first, while jihadi groups may find themselves enjoying a favorable balance of power in some locales, cross-border expansion produces countermobilization by the international community exposing jihadis' inherent power disadvantage. Although preventing a transnational jihadi group from making local gains is desirable, the international community could contain the threat and even role back jihadi gains even if it was slow to respond.

Second, transnational jihadi actors are opportunistic. Since their objectives imply interest in multiple locations, they can be flexible in their arena selection, choosing a target for expansion based on whether particular local conditions are favorable for jihadi advances. Ideally, the international community would search regularly for warning sign that a certain state or region is threatened by jihadi penetration. The African Sahel region in particular is vulnerable because the region's states have only limited control over their porous borders. It is no surprise that of all the al-Qaeda affiliates, its branch in North Africa is the only one that managed to truly operate regionally, as opposed to being restricted to one main area of operation.

In other locations, the agility of transnational jihadi groups could lead them to take surprising moves such as when the Islamic State in the Philippines took over parts of the city of Marawi.[10] But the effects of its surprising moves, especially now that ISIS is a known quality—meaning that it is a threat that all are familiar with and can no longer be dismissed as the "JV team" (to take Barack Obama famous and unfortunate label)[11]—are limited. Determined action could quell local success before the jihadis could capitalize on it to expand.

Third, as long as conditions in weak and unstable states offer jihadi actors opportunities, the international community should be ready to halt any jihadi attempt to expand across borders. Given the little appetite leading members of the international community have for nation building, the vast number of fragile states, and the poor record of external interventions, it would be unrealistic to expect the international community to deny jihadis all opportunities to establish a safe haven. However, once a threat emerges in a particular location, the international community must be ready to contain it and prevent its spread to neighboring countries. The establishment of a multilateral rapid response force could help compensate for a slow recognition of the threat potential for cross-border expansion.

The U.S. could do so, but it does not always have to take the lead. It is undeniable that the U.S. is more capable of fulfilling the task than any other state and that its support is valuable even when other actors take the lead (for example, U.S. assistance to French- and British-led missions in North Africa). But the U.S. is not eager to assume sole responsibility for thwarting jihadi threats and is increasingly aggravated when other nations free ride on its efforts. Moreover, there are many states that have an even greater interest in stopping transnational jihadis. Therefore, while the U.S. must be focused on preventing terrorist attacks against American interests, personnel, and property, it need not always directly intervene in foreign lands.

The U.S. should not enter all conflicts involving jihadis, though it should be willing to offer aid to countries fighting jihadi groups. In the few situations in which a transnational jihadi group evolves to become more than a localized threat, the U.S. should be willing to lead an international effort against the jihadis. Even in such situations, the U.S. should limit its involvement to using its airpower, providing training and weapons to local proxies, and deploying a limited number of special forces to coordinate between the American aerial force and its proxies' ground forces or, in extreme cases, to carry out unique special operations.

INTRA-JIHADI CONFLICTS

As if the systemic ideational and material barriers were not debilitating enough, the inability of transnational jihadi groups to forge unity among all jihadi forces further complicates their efforts. In addition to personal rivalries and ego battles, the jihadi movement also is plagued with divisions over strategy and theology. These divisions could prevent deep cooperation and sometimes even lead to fratricidal violence.

Intra-jihadi disagreements expose a conundrum: these are all rigid ideological actors, but they need unity, which requires willingness to compromise. Moreover, because jihadis couch their disagreements in religious terms, intra-jihadi disagreements could get out of proportion and turn into a zero-sum game in which no compromise is possible. The severity of such conflicts rises as these conflicts become a competition over religious credentials: who has a better understanding of Islam? And who is more committed to its promotion?

At times, disagreements turn into fights over whether members of a rival group should even be considered Muslims. When jihadis lob accusations of apostasy, which is punishable by death, cooperation, let alone unification, becomes highly unlikely.

Thus, not only do intra-jihadi conflicts prevent the jihadi movement from bringing its full collective capabilities to bear, they also cause divisions, distract these groups from their main objective, waste human and material resources, and damage the image of the whole movement. The U.S. and the rest of the international community should take advantage of these cleavages and even try to deepen them. Forcing jihadis to discuss openly their diverging attitudes about who counts as a Muslim, who is a legitimate target for jihadi violence, who is a combatant, what are the conditions under which noncombatants could be killed, and how to treat minorities would magnify internal strife and make any future unification of the forces less likely.

In order to take advantage of the opportunities the disunity of the jihadi movement offers, the international community must avoid bracketing all jihadis together and avoid seeing uncompromising confrontation as the only possible way to deal with them. After all, if all jihadis are made of the same cloth, it is impossible and pointless to separate them. It is true that some jihadis are irreconcilable (consider al-Zarqawi, for example); those who could be influenced to change their thinking still may require a long time and unique circumstances to revise their positions. But the fact remains that many jihadis have changed their positions over time and even denounced their own past actions. Former members of the Egyptian Gama'a Islamiya and the Libyan Islamic Fighting Group even joined the political process in their countries after revolutions deposed Husni Mubarak and Mu'amar Qaddafi.[12] When the right opportunity presented itself, even prominent figures in al-Qaeda, such as Abu Hafz al-Mauritani, sought to abandon the fight and retire to their home countries.[13] Amnesty initiatives in Algeria proved particularly instrumental for ending its civil war and bringing many who had fought the regime back from the mountains and into civilian lives.

Active jihadi actors also could engage in more limited changes, shifting some positions and adopting new strategies. Sensitive to costs and worried about losing public support because ordinary Muslims ended up suffering the brunt of jihadi attack,[14] al-Qaeda altered its strategy to be more appealing to the masses. While hardly a sufficient reason for viewing AQC as a candidate for reconciliation, the shift indicates the limits of rigid uncompromising ideologies and the ability of targeted state policies to shape jihadis' considerations. The efforts of al-Qaeda's affiliates in Yemen and Syria to adopt a less coercive approach in their relations with local populations and tribes are further evidence that some moderation is possible.

While the potential for changing the minds of jihadi leaders is valuable on its own accord, engagement with jihadi figures has perhaps a greater value because it simultaneously produces intra-jihadi acrimony. Fearing the Gama'a Islamya ceasefire initiative, al-Zawahiri, then still the leader of the EIJ, broke an unofficial agreement against intervening in other groups' internal affairs and personally tried—and failed—to persuade Gama'a leaders, especially those located outside of Egypt, to continue planning violent operations, raising the ire of the Gama'a Islamiya's central leadership.[15]

Moreover, often it does not even take an ideological shift to create intra-jihadi conflict; even small changes in a jihadi group's mode of operation could do the trick. In an ironic reflection of al-Qaeda's own critique of Hamas for failing to institute the sharia in Gaza,[16] the Islamic State criticized al-Qaeda for not pressing ahead in locations it enjoyed dominance and for its willingness to expand the circle of potential partners beyond jihadi groups.[17] Although little changed in al-Qaeda ideology, ISIS demanded that AQC reverse its more accommodationist stance and even alter the new vocabulary it adopted. For example, al-Adnani declared that AQC should abandon the terms "popular resistance" and "mass uprising" and return to the language of jihad and reject all peaceful means. Similarly, he demanded that al-Zawahiri would refrain from calling the armies of Egypt, Pakistan, Afghanistan, Libya, Tunisia, and Yemen "Americanized" forces and return to the appropriate Islamic terms of "tyrants," "disbelievers," and "apostates."[18] ISIS's message was clear: the shift in al-Qaeda's position, as reflected in its discourse and in the changes in its behavior, amounts to compromising core beliefs and indicates that the group lacks a true understanding of the Islamic faith.

The prospects for disrupting the march of jihadism are greater whenever the international community manages to split local from transnational jihadi groups, or a branch of a transnational group from its parent organization. In contrast to the uprootedness of transnational jihadis, nation-based jihadi groups and local branches of transnational jihadi groups are more sensitive to local conditions and more constrained by local needs and prevailing social structures. The ability of al-Qaeda and the Islamic State to enter particular locations depends on their ability to rely on local actors, or to at least piggyback on their infrastructure. Expansion often is based on the existence of a local group with sympathy toward the transnational organization and a need for the resources it could provide. But tension between transnational and local agendas never goes away, even when local actors assume the name of the transnational group.

The gap between the two agendas creates friction between a parent organization and its local affiliates. The state directly affected could deepen it (with support from the international community) by forcing local affiliates to confront the tension. In Syria, the universal ostracizing of al-Qaeda has led its branch to search for creative ways to make itself a palatable partner to the rest of the Syrian opposition. After hiding its affiliation at first, the conflict with ISIS forced JN to make its relationship with al-Qaeda public,[19] but the revelation made it harder for other groups in the Syrian opposition camp to cooperate with al-Joulani's people. As long as JN proved a formidable military force, it was able to solicit others' cooperation. However, the relationship with an al-Qaeda branch increasingly became too much of a liability for the rest of the Syrian opposition when the conflict began shifting to the negotiation phase. Al-Qaeda's refusal to negotiate and the dependence of other groups on state patrons (for example, Ahrar al-Sham's dependence on Turkey) that supported the negotiations, made it particularly difficult for the Syrian opposition to maintain close ties with an al-Qaeda affiliate once their state sponsors decided that the relationship with JN was an obstacle to ending the war. Eager to remain relevant JN rebranded and later even abandoned all official ties with al-Qaeda. Attempts to co-opt and even force fellow rebels to unite failed, deepening the rift within the jihadi elements of the Syrian opposition.

In locations where the transnational group either faces a fragmented jihadi field or fails to find an affiliate, expansion depends on local actors' good will (or the benefits they would accrue from allowing it). It is hardly obvious that a transnational jihadi organization would be able to establish itself in regions dominated by local actors. When the latter fears that allowing transnational jihadis in would lead to their own destruction, undermining public support for all jihadis and improving through foreign aid the ability of the state to confront all opposition groups, they would deny support from the transnational group and even outright prevent their entry into the arena. For example, despite al-Qaeda's interest in the Palestinian arena and Hamas's commitment to an armed struggle with Israel, Hamas was not going to let al-Qaeda enter into the Gaza Strip.[20]

Although the threat of terrorist attacks has not dissipated, the overall threat posed by transnational jihadi groups has declined due to determined efforts by the U.S.-led international community. Terrorism is not going away: killing innocents has become easier and jihadis' use of mundane and nearly impossible to defend instruments (such as cars) has become more prevalent. Therefore, terrorism is all but certain to remain a problem that will frustrate states for the foreseeable future.

But containment works! After the 9/11 attacks, the U.S. led the international community to establish a global infrastructure—legal, operational, and technical—to fight al-Qaeda and its ilk. Central to this global campaign was the idea of strengthening states' capacity so that each state would be able to fulfil its responsibility to prevent the use of its territory to harm fellow states.[21] Considerable gaps in states' capabilities made this enterprise necessary and difficult, but under the leadership of the U.S., interstate cooperation (including unprecedented intelligence-sharing) has produced remarkable results, making large-scale terrorist attacks much harder to carry out.

Undoubtedly, this infrastructure could be improved, but it has already made it increasingly difficult for transnational jihadi groups to promote their agendas. Indeed, international cooperation diminished the danger of blind spots in which jihadis could operate undetected, as well as the risk that terrorists would take advantage of dissimilar legal systems and discrepancy in state capacities to challenge states and the state-based order. Finessing and adjustments will always be necessary, but it is high time everyone takes the threat posed by transnational jihadi groups in proper perspective.

The threat posed by transnational jihadi groups has been contained because of the inherent limitations of transnational jihadism, the unrealistic goals its proponents seek, and state actions. The fact that the Islamic State faced the most favorable conditions any jihadi group had ever experienced and still failed is strong evidence of the limitations of transnational jihadism.

A lot of work remains for each country to improve its ability to thwart attacks inside its territory and against its citizens, but the subsiding fear of jihadi territorial expansion allows the U.S. to reduce its involvement in countering jihadism around the world and to divert resources to other, more urgent, needs. In fact, less American involvement could even contribute to reducing jihadi motivation.

At present, states are better positioned to handle domestic threats and prevent their expansion with no more than limited assistance from stronger (and usually Western) powers. When needed, regional powers could come together and cooperate to prevent a jihadi threat from rising and expanding in their neighborhood. Washington could offer them logistical help, provide intelligence, and, in extreme situations, offer air support, but it does not need to go any further. Instead, the U.S. should focus on maintaining its capability to prevent jihadis' cross-border expansion and on organizing a multilateral rapid response force capable of addressing a potential renewed jihadi surge, such as the one that followed the breakdown of regional order in the aftermath of the Arab uprisings. Transnational jihadism has been constrained. It is time to act accordingly.

Notes

INTRODUCTION

1. In this book, I refer to groups that seek Islamic rule or propagate a greater Islamic role in the social, economic, and political realms as Islamist groups. Jihadis represent one strand of Islamism. What separates jihadi groups from other Sunni Islamist groups is their emphasis on armed jihad (rather than political action or bottom-up societal transformation) as the central means for change. In fact, many jihadis elevate the status of jihad to a sixth pillar of Islam (the five recognized pillars are the declaration of faith, charity, pilgrimage, prayer, and fasting).

2. The White House, "Remarks by President Obama in Address to the Nation from Afghanistan," May 1, 2012, https://obamawhitehouse.archives.gov/the-press-office/2012/05/01/remarks-president-obama-address-nation-afghanistan; Phil Stewart, "Leon Panetta Says al Qaeda's Defeat 'Within Reach,'" *Reuters,* July 9, 2011; and Lee Ferran, "Al Qaeda 'Shadow of Former Self,' US Counter-Terror Official Says," *ABC News*, April 30, 2012.

3. For example, see, Raja Abdulrahim and Isabel Coles, "Islamic State Returns to Guerilla Roots," *Wall Street Journal*, January 3, 2018.

4. For example, the Global Terrorism Database (GTD) at the University of Maryland's National Consortium for the Study of Terrorism and Responses to Terrorism (START), http://www.start.umd.edu/gtd/.

5. Matt Bradley, "Rift Grows in Islamic State Between Foreign, Local Fighters," *Wall Street Journal*, March 25, 2016.

6. U.S. Department of State, Bureau of Counterterrorism, "Foreign Terrorist Organizations," https://www.state.gov/j/ct/rls/other/des/123085.htm.

7. Security Council Committee Pursuant to Resolutions 1267 (1999), 1989 (2011), and 2253 (2015) Concerning ISIL (Da'esh) Al-Qaida and Associated Individuals, Groups, Undertakings, and Entities. "ISIL (Da'esh) & Al-Qaida Sanctions List," https://scsanc

tions.un.org/fop/fop?xml = htdocs/resources/xml/en/consolidated.xml&xslt = htdocs/re sources/xsl/en/al-qaida.xsl.

8. Bruce Hoffman, *Inside Terrorism* (New York: Columbia University Press, 2006): 1–41.

9. MEMRI, "Osama bin Laden Speech Offers Peace Treaty with Europe, Says Al-Qa'ida 'Will Persist in Fighting' the U.S." Special Dispatch Series 695, April 15, 2004, www.memri.org.

10. Max Abrahms, "Why Terrorism Doesn't Work," *International Security* 31, no. 2 (Fall 2006): 42–78.

11. On al-Qaeda's quest to remake world order, see, Barak Mendelsohn, *Combating Jihadism: American Hegemony and Interstate Cooperation in the War on Terrorism* (Chicago: University of Chicago Press, 2009).

12. Robert Pape, *Dying to Win: The Strategic Logic of Suicide Terrorism* (New York: Random House, 2005).

13. Christopher Ingraham, "Toddlers Have Shot At Least 23 People This Year," *Washington Post*, May 1, 2016.

14. For example, see, John Mueller and Mark Stewart, *Chasing Ghosts: The Policing of Terrorism* (New York: Oxford University Press, 2016); and John Mueller, *Overblown: How Politicians and the Terrorism Industry Inflate National Security Threats, and Why We Believe Them* (New York: Free Press, 2006).

15. "Worries About Terrorism Subside in Mid-America," Pew Research Center, November 8, 2001, http://www.people-press.org/2001/11/08/worries-about-terrorism-sub side-in-mid-america.

16. "15 Years After 9/11, a Sharp Partisan Divide on Ability of Terrorists to Strike U.S.," Pew Research Center, September 7, 2016, http://www.people-press.org/2016/09/07/15-years-after-911-a-sharp-partisan-divide-on-ability-of-terrorists-to-strike-u-s.

17. Ayman al-Zawahiri, "America Is the First Enemy of the Muslims," SITE Intelligence Group, March 20, 2018.

18. Among the many works some stand out in particular: Cathy Scott-Clark and Adrian Levy, *The Exile: The Stunning Inside Story of Osama bin Laden and al Qaeda in Flight* (New York: Bloomsbury USA, 2017); Jessica Stern and J.M. Berger, *ISIS: The State of Terror* (New York: HarperCollins, 2015); Peter Bergen, *The Osama bin Laden I Know* (New York: Free Press, 2006); Cole Bunzel, *From Paper State to Caliphate: The Ideology of the Islamic State* (Washington, D.C.: Brookings Institution, March 2015); Graham Wood, *The Way of the Strangers: Encounters with the Islamic State* (New York: Random House, 2016); Brian Fishman, T*he Master Plan: ISIS, al-Qaeda, and the Jihadi Strategy for Final Victory* (New Haven: Yale University Press, 2016); Fawaz Gerges, *The Rise and Fall of Al-Qaeda* (New York: Oxford University Press, 2011); Brynjar Lia, *Architect of Global Jihad: The Life of al Qaida Strategist Abu Mus'ab al-Suri* (New York: Columbia University Press, 2008); Thomas Hegghammer, *Jihad in Saudi Arabia: Violence and Pan-Islamism since 1979* (Cambridge: Cambridge University Press, 2010); Charles Lister, *The Syrian Jihad: Al-Qaeda, the Islamic State and the Evolution of an Insurgency* (London: Oxford University Press, 2016); Anne Stenersen, *Al-Qaida in Afghanistan* (Cambridge: Cambridge University Press, 2017); Shiraz Maher, *Salafi-Jihadism: The History of an Idea* (London: Oxford University Press, 2016); William McCants, *The ISIS Apocalypse: The History, Strategy, and Doomsday Vision of the*

Islamic State (New York: Picador, 2016); Joas Wagemakers, *A Quietist Jihadi: The Ideology and Influence of Abu Muhammad al-Maqdisi* (Cambridge: Cambridge University Press, 2012); and Daniel Byman, *Al Qaeda, the Islamic State, and the Global Jihadist Movement: What Everyone Needs to Know* (New York: Oxford University Press, 2015).

19. Jason Burke, *The 9/11 Wars* (London: Penguin Books, 2011); and Peter Bergen, *The Longest War* (New York: Free Press, 2011).

20. Assaf Moghadam and Brian Fishman, eds., *Fault Lines in Global Jihad: Organizational, Strategic, and Ideological Fissures* (London: Routledge, 2011).

21. Vahid Brown, *Cracks in the Foundation: Leadership Schisms in al-Qa'ida from 1989–2006* (West Point: Combating Terrorism Center, September 2007).

22. Nelly Lahoud, *The Jihadis Path to Self-Destruction* (London: Hurst, 2010).

23. For one such comparison between al-Qaeda and the Muslim Brotherhood, see, Barak Mendelsohn, "The Future of al-Qaeda: Lessons From the Muslim Brotherhood," *Survival* 60, no. 2 (2018): 151–78.

CHAPTER ONE

1. Thomas Hegghammer, "The Rise of Muslim Foreign Fighters: Islam and the Globalization of Jihad" *International Security* 35, no. 3 (Winter 2010/11): 61.

2. Rohan Gunaratna, *Inside al Qaeda: Global Network of Terror* (New York: Columbia University Press, 2002): 22–24.

3. Bergen, *The Osama bin Laden I Know*, 76–87.

4. Steve Coll, *Ghost Wars: The Secret History of the CIA, Afghanistan, and bin Laden, from the Soviet Invasion to September 10, 2001* (New York: The Penguin Press, 2004), 222–23.

5. From an interview with bin Laden held on March 18, 1997, Quoted in Simon Reeve, *The New Jackals: Ramzi Yousef, Osama bin Laden and the Future of Terrorism* (Boston: Northeastern University Press, 1999): 262.

6. Mustafa Hamid and Leah Farrall, *The Arabs at War in Afghanistan* (London: Hurst, 2015).

7. World Islamic Front for Jihad Against Jews and Crusaders, "Jihad Against Jews and Crusaders," February 23, 1998.

8. Hamid and Farrall, *The Arabs at War in Afghanistan*, 240–45.

9. Scott-Clark and Levy, *The Exile*, 51–67.

10. Ali Soufan, *Anatomy of Terror: From the Death of Bin Laden to the Rise of the Islamic State* (New York: W. W. Norton & Company, 2017): 93.

11. George W. Bush, "Address to a Joint Session of Congress," *C-Span*, September 20, 2001, https://www.c-span.org/video/?c4498346/george-w-bush-address-congress-september-20-2001.

12. Barton Gellman and Dafna Linzer, "Afghanistan, Iraq: Two Wars Collide," *Washington Post*, October 22, 2004.

13. Barak Mendelsohn, *The al-Qaeda Franchise: The Expansion of al-Qaeda and Its Consequences* (New York: Oxford University Press, 2016).

14. Thomas Hegghammer, *The Failure of Jihadi in Saudi Arabia* (West Point: Combating Terrorism Center, 2010).

15. Ayman al-Zawahiri, "Letter from al-Zawahiri to al-Zarqawi, 9 July, 2005," DNI.gov, October 11, 2005.

16. Mujahideen Shura Council, "Statement of Mujahidin Shura Council on Establishment of 'Islamic State of Iraq,'" Open Source Center, October 15, 2006.

17. Brian Fishman, *Dysfunction and Decline: Lessons Learned From Inside al Qa'ida in Iraq* (West Point: Combating Terrorism Center, 2009): 2–3.

18. Marc Lynch, "Explaining the Awakening: Engagement, Publicity, and the Transformation of Iraqi Sunni Political Attitudes," *Security Studies* 20, no. 1 (2011): 36–72.

19. Gregory Johnsen, "AQAP in Yemen and the Christmas Day Terrorist Attack," *CTC Sentinel*, Special Issue (January 2010): 1–4.

20. Duncan Gardham, "Cargo Plane Bomb Plot: Computer Printer Shows al-Qaeda's Sophistication," *The Telegraph*, November 1, 2010.

21. Al-Qaeda in the Arabian Peninsula, *Inspire* 3 (November 2010).

22. Thomas Joscelyn and Bill, Roggio, "AQAP's Emir Also Serves as al-Qaeda's General Manager," *The Long War Journal*, August 6, 2013.

23. Al-Sahab, "A Glad Tiding from Sheikhs Abu al-Zubeir and Ayman al-Zawahiri, May Allah Protect Them," SITE Intelligence Group, February 9, 2012.

24. Christopher Anzalone, "The Formalizing of an Affiliation: Somalia's Harakat al-Shabab al-Mujahideed & Al-Qa'ida Central," *al-Wasat*, February 10, 2012.

25. Jabhat al-Nusra, "New Jihadist Group Declares Presence in Levant, Calls for Action," SITE Intelligence Group, January 23, 2012.

26. Abu Bakr Al-Baghdadi, "And Give Glad Tidings to the Believers," SITE Intelligence Group, April 8, 2013.

27. Abu Muhammad Al-Joulani, "About the Levantine Front," SITE Intelligence Group, April 10, 2013.

28. Qaedat al-Jihad Organization General Command, "Statement Regarding the Relationship of the Group of Qadat al-Jihad with the Group of the Islamic State in Iraq and the Levant," SITE Intelligence Group, February 3, 2014.

29. Abu Muhammad Al-Adnani, "This is the Promise of Allah," SITE Intelligence Group, June 29, 2014.

30. Bradley, "Rift Grows in Islamic State Between Foreign, Local Fighters."

31. Abu Bakr al-Baghdadi, "Even If the Disbelievers Despise Such," SITE Intelligence Group, November 13, 2014; and Abu Muhammad al-Adnani, "So They Kill and Are Killed," SITE Intelligence Group, March 12, 2015.

32. Hani Amara, "Libyan Forces Clear Last Islamic State Holdout in Sirte," *Reuters*, December 6, 2016.

33. Barack Obama, "Transcript: President Obama's Speech Outlining Strategy to Defeat Islamic State," *Washington Post*, September 10, 2014.

34. Hassan Hassan, "ISIL Sleeper Cells in Iraq Are a Warning Sign the Extremist Group Is Already Reforming," *The National*, March 28, 2018.

35. Amos Harel, "A Daring Assassination Attempt Shows ISIS in Sinai Has the Ultimate Weapon: Intel," *Haaretz*, December 29, 2017; and Bennett Seftel, "Persistent, Expanding and Worrisome: ISIS Rebounds in Afghanistan," *The Cipher Brief*, January 4, 2018.

36. Carlie Winter and Haroro Ingram, "Terror, Online and Off: Recent Trends in Islamic State Propaganda Operations," *War on the Rocks*, March 2, 2018.

37. Al-Sahab, "The Special Production on the Occasion of Unity Among the Ranks of the Mujahideen and Creating 'Qaedat al-Jihad in the Indian Subcontinent,'" SITE Intelligence Group, September 3, 2014.

CHAPTER TWO

1. Ayman al-Zawahiri, "Loyalty and Separation" in *Al Qaeda in Its Own Words*, eds. Gilles Kepel and Jean-Pierre Milelli (Cambridge: Harvard University Press, 2008): 206–9.

2. Mendelsohn, *Combating Jihadism*, 69–77.

3. Among the few exceptions, Virginie Collombier and Olivier Roy, eds., *Tribes and Global Jihadism* (London: Hurst, 2017); and Lahoud, *The Jihadis Path to Self-Destruction*.

4. PEW Research Center, *The World's Muslims: Religion, Politics and Society* (2013), 15–23, http://www.pewforum.org/2013/04/30/the-worlds-muslims-religion-politics-society-overview.

5. Mark Tessler, *Mapping and Explaining Attitudes Toward Political Islam among Ordinary Citizens in the Middle East and North Africa*, Economic Research Forum, Working Paper 902 (January 2015): 3–7.

6. Mark Tessler, "Change and Continuity in Arab Attitudes toward Political Islam: The Impact of Political Transitions in Tunisia and Egypt from 2011 to 2013," in *Values, Political Action, and Change in the Middle East and the Arab Spring*, eds. Mansoor Moaddel and Michele Gelfand (New York: Oxford University Press, 2017): 249–69.

7. "Public Opinion in the Arab World," The Arab Barometer, 2015, http://www.arabbarometer.org/content/public-opinion-arab-world. See, also, 2016 "Arab Opinion Index."

8. PEW Research Center, "Osama bin Laden Largely Discredited Among Muslim Publics in Recent Years," May 2, 2011, http://www.pewglobal.org/2011/05/02/osama-bin-laden-largely-discredited-among-muslim-publics-in-recent-years; PEW Research Center, "On Anniversary of bin Laden's Death, Little Backing of al Qaeda," April 30, 2012, http://www.pewglobal.org/2012/04/30/on-anniversary-of-bin-ladens-death-little-backing-of-al-qaeda.

9. "2016 Arab Opinion Index," The Arab Center for Research and Policy Studies, April 12, 2017, http://arabcenterdc.org/survey/arab-opinion-index-2016.

10. PEW Research Center, "The World's Muslims: Religion, Politics and Society," 29.

11. Mark Tessler, Michael Robbins, and Amaney Jamal, "What Do Ordinary Citizens in the Arab World Really Think About the Islamic State," *Washington Post*, July 27, 2016.

12. In Egypt, those positively replying that they identify themselves primarily by their nationality increased from 10% (2001) to 61% (2014), in Iraq from 24% (2004) to 46% (2013), in Saudi Arabia from 17% (2003) to 48% (2013). See, Mansoor Moaddel and Julie De Jong, "Youth Perceptions and Values During the Arab Spring," in *Values, Political Action, and Change in the Middle East and the Arab Spring*, eds. Moaddel and Gelfand, 25–56.

13. The exceptions are Muslims in central Asia and in eastern and southern Europe

who largely reject the mixing of religion in politics. PEW Research Center, "The World's Muslims: Religion, Politics and Society."

14. Shadi Hamid, "The Roots of the Islamic State's Appeal," *The Atlantic*, October 31, 2014.

15. Note that there have been some weak efforts to promote the Brotherhood as a transnational movement—though even within that transnational structure, the various branches remain largely autonomous and each focused on its own country. See, Alison Pargeter, *The Muslim Brotherhood: From Opposition to Power* (London: Saqi, 2013); and Nathan Brown, "The Irrelevance of the International Muslim Brotherhood," *Foreign Policy*, September 21, 2010.

16. Steven Brooke, "The Muslim Brotherhood in Europe and the Middle East: The Evolution of a Relationship," in *The Muslim Brotherhood in Europe*, eds. Roel Meijer and Edwin Bakker, (New York: Columbia University Press, 2012).

17. When jihadis see the founding of an Islamic emirate as possible, they may follow through, as the Taliban did in Afghanistan. However, for an emirate to survive, it must reduce friction with the international community (something that the Taliban was too slow to do, a factor in its regime's downfall). Increasing the compatibility between an emirate and a state would normally require adapting the emirate to the framework of the state-based order, which means acceptance of limited (state) sovereignty, participation in international organizations and treaties, external recognition, and limitations on one's interference in the affairs of other states.

18. Chris Zambelis, "Ahrar al-Sham: A Profile of Northern Syria's al-Qaeda Surrogate," *Terrorism Monitor* 11, no. 7 (April 2013).

19. Labib al-Nahhas, "The Deadly Consequences of Mislabeling Syria's Revolutionaries," *Washington Post*, July 10, 2015.

20. Sidney Tarrow, *The New Transnational Activism* (Ithaca: Cornell University Press, 2005), 120–40.

21. Alan Cullison, "Inside al-Qaeda's Hard Drive," *The Atlantic Monthly* 294, no. 2 (September 2004); and Montasser al-Zayyat, *The Road to al-Qaeda: The Story of bin Laden's Right-Hand Man* (London: Pluto Press, 2004): 60–72 and 109–10.

22. Stephen Harmon, "From GSPC to AQIM: The Evolution of an Algerian Islamist Terrorist Group Into an Al-Qa'ida Affiliate and Its Implications for the Sahara-Sahel Region," *Concerned Africa Scholars*, Bulletin no. 85 (Spring 2010): 12–29; Stephen Ulph, "Disarray in the Algerian GSPC," *Terrorism Focus* 1, no. 7 (October 2004); and Stephen Ulph, "Declining in Algeria, GSPC Enters International Theater," *Terrorism Focus* 3, no. 1 (January 2006).

23. Hegghammer, "The Rise of Muslim Foreign Fighters," 59–61.

24. Mohammed M. Hafez, "Jihad after Iraq: Lessons from the Arab Afghans Phenomenon," *CTC Sentinel* 1, no. 4 (March 2008): 1–4; and Hegghammer, "The Rise of Muslim Foreign Fighters," 61.

25. Bradley, "Rift Grows in Islamic State Between Foreign."

26. Ayman al-Zawahiri, *Knights Under the Banner of the Prophet,* published by *al-Sharq al-Awsat*, December 2001; and Peter Arnett, "CNN Interview with Osama bin Laden," *CNN*, March 20, 1997.

27. Al-Zawahiri, *Knights Under the Banner of the Prophet.*

28. Mendelsohn, *Combating Jihadism,* 45–54.

29. Abdallah Azzam, *Defense of Muslim Lands* (Birmingham: Maktabah Publications, 2002).

30. Hugh Naylor, "Islamic State Is No Longer So Formidable on the Battlefield," *Washington Post,* February 6, 2016; and Mawassi Lachen, "ISIS Kills Fleeing Fighters," *Magharebia*, January 16, 2015.

31. Al-Shabab, "The Path 2 Paradise: From the Twin Cities to the Land of Two Migrations: Episode 2," SITE Intelligence Service, January 1, 2016.

32. "Letter to All Muslim Brothers in the World," Bin Laden's Bookshelf, January 19, 2017.

33. Osama bin Laden, *Declaration of War*, October 12, 1996, https://ctc.usma.edu/app/uploads/2013/10/Declaration-of-Jihad-against-the-Americans-Occupying-the-Land-of-the-Two-Holiest-Sites-Translation.pdf.

34. Ayman al-Zawahiri, "The Freeing of Humanity and Homelands Under the Banner of the Qur'an," February 11, 2005.

35. Ayman al-Zawahiri, "Let Us Light Them with a Solid Structure," SITE Intelligence Group, November 28, 2017.

36. For example, see, Ayman al-Zawahiri, "Realities of the Conflict between Islam and Unbelief," Open Source Center, December 29, 2006.

37. Abu-Yahya al-Libi, "Democracy, the Modern Idol," Open Source Center, August 5, 2009.

38. Nasir bin Hamd al-Fahd, *A Treatise on the Legal status of Using Weapons of Mass Destructions against the Infidels*, May 2003, https://nsarchive2.gwu.edu/nukevault/ebb270/07.pdf.

39. In the case of WMDs, it means that international law and treaties such as the NPT that prohibit the proliferation of nuclear weapons beyond the five permanent members of the UN Security Council cannot be taken as legal considerations for Muslims who contemplate the acquisition of such weapons. Similarly, the decision to use WMD must take into account Islamic jurisprudence regarding who constitutes non-combatants and the conditions under which they could be targeted, not any definitions offered by international law.

40. Abu Bakr al-Baghdadi, "A Message to the Mujahidin and the Muslim Ummah," al-Hayat Media Center, July 1, 2014.

41. Osama bin Laden, "This War Is Fundamentally Religious," *al-Jazeera*, November 3, 2001; and Bin Laden, *Declaration of War.*

42. Ayman al-Zawahiri, "Unity in the Issue of Tawhid," SITE Intelligence Group, April 6, 2013.

43. "Letter to the Muslim Nation," Bin Laden's Bookshelf, January 19, 2017.

44. Bin Laden, "This War Is Fundamentally Religious."

45. Abu Yahya al-Libi, "Moderation of Islam . . . Moderation of Defeat," Open Source Center, May 22, 2008.

46. Osama bin Laden, "Islamic Website Posts Full Text of Bin Laden 4 January Audio Message," Open Source Center, March 4, 2004; and Abu Yahya al-Libi, "Moderation of Islam."

47. Mohamed Bin Ali, *The Roots of Religious Extremism: Understanding the Salafi Doctrine of al-Wala' wal-Bara'* (Singapore: World Scientific Publishing Company, 2015): 226–31.

48. Rudolph Peters, *Jihad in Classical and Modern Islam* (Princeton: Markus Wiener Publishers, 1996): 120–21.

49. Mendelsohn, *Combating Jihadism,* 64–69.

50. Al-Zawahiri, "Let Us Light Them with a Solid Structure."

51. Azadeh Moaveni, "ISIS Women and Enforcers in Syria Recount Collaboration, Anguish and Escape," *New York Times*, November 21, 2015; Bradley, "Rift Grows in Islamic State Between Foreign, Local Fighters;" and "Europe's Jihadists: What the Paris Attacks Tell Us About IS Strategy," *Der Spiegel*, November 27, 2015.

52. Tamer El-Ghobashy and Ali Nbhan, "Foreign ISIS Fighters Increasingly Isolated in Mosul Battle," *Wall Street Journal*, March 16, 2017.

53. On conflicts between locals and "Arab Afghans" during the 1980s, see, Hamid and Farrall, *The Arabs at War in Afghanistan*; and Vahid Brown, "Foreign Fighters in Historical Perspective: The Case of Afghanistan," in *Bombers, Bank Accounts, & Bleedout*, ed. Brian Fishman (West Point: Combating Terrorism Center, 2008): 27–30. A similar picture emerges from the experience of the Taliban in the following decade. See, Brown, *Cracks in the Foundation*.

54. "Letter from Abu Yahya," Bin Laden's Bookshelf, January 19, 2017.

55. Ibid.

56. Der Spiegel, "Europe's Jihadists."

57. Michael Weiss, "How ISIS Picks Its Suicide Bombers," *The Daily Beast*, November 15, 2015.

58. Olivier Roy defines a tribe as "a segmented solidarity-based group, based on lineage (generally patrilineal and patrilocal), with an internal system of regulation (customary law, mediation to resolve conflicts) which excludes outsiders, an 'ideology' or at least a culture (hospitality, loyalty, honor) and an uneasy connection with state authorities, usually mediated by local notables." See, Olivier Roy, "Introduction," in *Tribes and Global Jihadism*, eds. Collombier and Roy, 5.

59. Roy, "Introduction." Salafism denotes the radicals' commitment to the *salafi* ideology that is based on the emulation of Islam's first three generations when Islam was believed to be implemented in its purest form.

60. This era was characterized by ignorance and barbarism, and the Prophet was sent with God's word to liberate the inhabitants of the Arabian Peninsula from it.

61. Abu Yahya al-Libi, "We Sent Thee Not, But As a Mercy For All Creatures," *Vanguard of Khurasan* 16, Open Source Center, March 12, 2010.

62. Abu Umar al-Baghdadi, "For the Scum Disappears Like Froth Cast Out," Open Source Center, December 5, 2007.

63. Anwar al-Awlaki, "AQAP Releases Interview with Anwar al-Awlaki," Open Source Center, May 23, 2010.

64. Al-Qaeda in Indian Subcontinent, "Land of the Other," *Resurgence Magazine*, October 19, 2014.

65. Virginie Collombier, "Conclusions," in *Tribes and Global Jihadism*, eds. Collombier and Roy, 181–84.

66. Osama bin Laden, "About the Ongoing War Between the Army and the Mujahidin in Swat and the Tribal Areas," Open Source Center, June 4, 2009.

67. Scott-Clark and Levy, *The Exile*, 233–34.

68. Nasir al-Wuhayshi, "They Plot and Plan, and God Plans Too," Open Source Center, February 20, 2009.

69. Ayman al-Zawahiri, "Al-Zawahiri Interviewed on Fighting in Afghanistan, Bin Ladin, Others," Open Source Center, December 16, 2001.
70. Abu Obeida Abdullah Khalid al-'Adam, "The Apostate Awakenings and the Way to Prevent Them," SITE Intelligence Unit, July 25, 2012.
71. Osama bin Laden, "The Way to Foil Plots," Open Source Center, December 30, 2007.
72. "Jihad in Pakistan," Bin Laden's Bookshelf, March 1, 2016.
73. Abu Umar al-Baghdadi, "For the Scum Disappears Like Froth Cast Out," Open Source Center, December 5, 2006.
74. Marc Lynch, "Explaining the Awakening: Engagement, Publicity, and the Transformation of Iraqi Sunni Political Attitudes," *Security Studies* 20, no. 1 (2011): 36–72.
75. "Letter to Abu Bashir," Bin Laden's Bookshelf, January 19, 2017.
76. Nadwa al-Dawsari, *Foe Not Friend: Yemeni Tribes and al-Qaeda in the Arabian Peninsula*, (Washington, D.C.: The Project on Middle East Democracy, 2018): 21–22.
77. Ibid., 22–23.
78. Ibid., 23–27.
79. The Islamic State, "The Punishing of Shu'aytāt for Treachery," *Dabiq* 3, 2014, 12–14; and McCants, *The ISIS Apocalypse*, 136.

CHAPTER THREE

1. "Kind Brother," Bin Laden's Bookshelf, March 1, 2016.
2. For example, Abu Yahya al-Libi, "Moderation of Islam."
3. Al-Zawahiri, "Loyalty and Separation," 206–9.
4. Abu Muhammad Al-Adnani, "O Our People Respond to the Caller of Allah," *Pieter Van Ostaeyen's blog*, June 23, 2015, https://pietervanostaeyen.com/2015/06/23/o-our-people-respond-to-the-caller-of-allah-audio-statement-by-shaykh-abu-muhammad-al-adnani-as-shami.
5. Barak Mendelsohn, "Terrorism and Protean Power: How Terrorists Navigate Uncertainty," in *Protean Power: Exploring the Uncertain and Unexpected in World Politics*, eds. Peter Katzenstein and Lucia Seybert (Cambridge: Cambridge University Press, 2018), 188–208.
6. For example, Abu Musab Al-Zarqawi, "February 2004 Coalition Provisional Authority English Translation of Terrorist Musab al Zarqawi Letter Obtained by United States Government in Iraq, 2001–2009."
7. Kristin Bakke, "Help Wanted? The Mixed Record of Foreign Fighters in Domestic Insurgencies," *International Security* 38, no. 4 (Spring 2014): 150–87; and Jeni Mitchell, "The Contradictory Effects of Ideology on Jihadist War-Fighting: The Bosnia Precedent," *Studies in Conflict and Terrorism* 31, no. 9 (2008): 808–28.
8. "Letter to Abu Basir," Bin Laden's Bookshelf, March 1, 2016.
9. Al-Zawahiri, "Letter from al-Zawahiri to al-Zarqawi."
10. Mark Zacher, "The Territorial Integrity Norm: International Boundaries and the Use of Force," *International Organization* 55, no. 2 (2001): 215–50.
11. Ian Lustick, "The Absence of Middle Eastern Great Powers: Political 'Backward-

ness' in Historical Perspective," *International Organization* 51, no. 4 (Autumn 1997): 653–83.

12. For example, see, United Nations Security Council Resolution 1373, S/RES/1373 (2001), November 28, 2001.

13. Mendelsohn, *Combating Jihadism*.

14. For example, Bill Roggio and Alexandra Gutowski, "Coalition Kills 2 Islamic State External Operations Commanders in Iraq and Syria," *Long War Journal*, November 15, 2017; and Rukmini Callimachi, "3 ISIS Terrorism Planners Killed in Syria Airstrike, Pentagon Says," *New York Times*, December 13, 2016.

15. For example, Abu 'Abd Allah as-Shami, "How Jabhat an-Nusra broke its ties with al-Qaeda," Pieter Van Ostaeyen's blog, October 13, 2017, https://pietervanostaeyen.com/2017/12/01/how-jabhat-an-nusra-broke-its-ties-with-al-qaeda-a-witness-report-by-shaykh-abu-abd-allah-as-shami.

16. Michael W.S. Ryan, *Decoding Al-Qaeda's Strategy: The Deep Battle Against America* (New York: Columbia University Press, 2013); and Lia, *Architect of Global Jihad*.

17. "Letter to All Muslim Brothers in the World," Bin Laden's Bookshelf, January 19, 2017.

18. Ibid.

19. "Letter to Abu Bashir," Bin Laden's Bookshelf, January 19, 2017.

20. The Abbottabad Documents, Combating Terrorism Center, SOCOM-2012-0000017, May 3, 2012.

21. For example, see, "Letter to Abu Bashir."

22. John Esposito and Mogahed Dalia, *Who Speaks for Islam?: What a Billion Muslims Really Think* (New York: Gallup Press, 2007).

23. "Letter About Matter of the Islamic Maghreb," Bin Laden's Bookshelf, March 1, 2016.

24. The Abbottabad Documents, Combating Terrorism Center, SOCOM-2012-0000016, May 3, 2012.

25. Sudarsan Raghavan, "In Yemen, Tribal Militias in a Fierce Battle with al-Qaeda Wing," *Washington Post*, September 10, 2012.

26. "Al-Qaida Papers: The Yemen Letters," *Associated Press*, August 9, 2013, hosted .ap.org/specials/interactives/_international/_pdfs/al-q aida-papers-how-to-run-a-state.pdf.

27. International Crisis Group, *Yemen's al-Qaeda: Expanding the Base*, Middle East Report No. 174 (February 2017): 11–12.

28. Saif Al-'Adl, "Al-'Adl Letter," CTC Harmony Project, https://ctc.usma.edu/app/uploads/2013/10/Al-Adl-Letter-Translation1.pdf.

29. Mendelsohn, *The al-Qaeda Franchise*.

30. "Letter from 'Atiyah to Abu Basir," Bin Laden's Bookshelf, January 19, 2017.

31. Atiyatallah Al-Libi, "Letter to Zarqawi from Senior al Qaeda Leader, 'Atiya,'" Combating Terrorism Center at West Point, https://www.ctc.usma.edu/v2/wp-content/uploads/2013/10/Atiyahs-Letter-to-Zarqawi-Translation.pdf.

32. Ayman al-Zawahiri, "General Guidelines for Jihad," September 13, 2013, https://azelin.files.wordpress.com/2013/09/dr-ayman-al-e1ba93awc481hirc4ab-22general-guidelines-for-the-work-of-a-jihc481dc4ab22-en.pdf.

33. Ayman al-Zawahiri, "We Shall Fight You Until There Is No More Persecution," SITE Intelligence Unit, October 4, 2017.

34. Fishman, *The Master Plan*, 38.

35. "Jihadist Website Posts 'Communique' on Egyptian Islamic Group Joining al-Qa'ida," Open Source Center, August 8, 2006; "Egyptian Al-Jama'ah al-Islamiyah Denies Joining Al-Qa'ida," Open Source Center, August 7, 2006; "Interview with Dr. Najih Ibrahim, Theoretician of the Egyptian Al-Jama'ah Al-Islamiyah," *al-Sharq al-Awast*, August 13, 2006; and Abduh Zaynah, "Egyptian Islamic Group: Al-Zawahiri Wanted to Implicate Us before London Plot Was Uncovered. Said Iran Has Its Own Agenda But Cards in Lebanon Should Not Be Mixed Up," *al-Sharq al-Awsat*, August 14, 2006.

36. Abu Bakr Naji, *The Management of Savagery: The Most Critical Stage Through Which the Umma Will Pass*, trans. William McCants (Boston: The John M. Olin Institute for Strategic Studies at Harvard University, May 2006): 12.

37. Ibid., 15–17.
38. Ibid., 14.
39. Ibid., 13.
40. Ryan, *Decoding al-Qaeda's Strategy*, 162–63.
41. Naji, *The Management of Savagery*, 18–19.
42. Ibid., 76.
43. Ibid., 61.
44. Ibid.
45. Ibid., 32–33.
46. Ibid., 38.
47. Ibid., 81–82.
48. Ibid., 34.
49. Ibid., 35.
50. Lia, *Architect of Global Jihad*, 5–28.
51. Lia, *Architect of Global Jihad*; and Ryan, *Decoding al-Qaeda's Strategy*, 193–254.
52. Lia, *Architect of Global Jihad*, 426.
53. Ibid., 423.
54. Ibid., 426.
55. Ibid., 421–23.
56. Ryan, *Decoding al-Qaeda's Strategy*, 221–24.
57. Lia, *Architect of Global Jihad*, 350–51.
58. Ryan, *Decoding al-Qaeda's Strategy*, 231–32.
59. Ibid., 224–27.
60. Ibid., 227–28.
61. Ibid., 242–48.
62. Ibid., 249.
63. Lia, *Architect of Global Jihad*, 351.
64. Ibid., 402–3.
65. Ibid., 368–70 and 396.

66. Al-Qaeda in the Arabian Peninsula, "How to Make a Bomb in the Kitchen of Your Mother," *Inspire* 1 (2010): 33–40.

67. Daveed Gartenstein-Ross and Nathaniel Barr, "The Myth of Lone-Wolf Terrorism: The Attacks in Europe and Digital Extremism," *Foreign Affairs*, July 26, 2016.

68. Fishman, *The Master Plan*.

69. Scott-Clark and Levy, *The Exile.*
70. Fishman, *The Master Plan*, 33–34.
71. Atiyatallah al-Libi, "Letter to Zarqawi from Senior al Qaeda Leader, 'Atiya'."
72. Al-Zawahiri, "Letter from al-Zawahiri to al-Zarqawi."
73. Fu'ad Husayn, "Al Zarqawi, The Second Generation of al Qa'ida," Serialized in *al Quds al Arabi* (June-July 2005).
74. Ibid.
75. Al-Zarqawi, "February 2004 Coalition Provisional Authority English Translation of Terrorist Musab al Zarqawi Letter."
76. Aymen al Zawahiri, "Open Interview – Part One," Open Source Center, April 3, 2008.
77. Fishman, *The Master Plan*, 250–52.
78. Ibid., 35.
79. Isabel Coles, "Despair, Hardship as Iraq Cuts off Wages in Islamic State Cities," *Reuters*, October 2, 2015.
80. Ibn Rajab al-Hanbalī, "My Provision Was Placed for Me in the Shade of My Spear," *Dabiq* 4, 2014, 10–13; and The Islamic State, "Modern Day Slavery," *Dabiq* 3, 2014, 29–30.
81. Michael Weiss, "How I Escaped From ISIS," *The Daily Beast,* November 18, 2015; and Syrian Observatory for Human Rights, "More Than 1600 Killed Since ISIS Started Its Attack on Ein al-Arab 'Kobane,'" January 16, 2015, http://www.syriahr.com/en/?p=9797.
82. Hani Amara, "Libyan Forces Reduce Islamic State's Grip in Sirte to Final Few Blocks," *Reuters*, October 4, 2016.
83. The Islamic State, *Dabiq* 1, 2014.
84. Al-Adnani, "O Our People Respond to the Caller of Allah."
85. Abu Muhammad al-Adnani, "This Is the Promise of Allah," SITE Intelligence Unit, June 29, 2014.
86. Naji, *The Management of Savagery*, 90–94.

CHAPTER FOUR

1. Lawrence Wright, *The Looming Tower* (New York: Alfred A. Knopf, 2006): 129–31.
2. Mustafa Hamid, "Mustafa Hamid's Analysis of Mujahidin Activities," The Harmony Project, Combating Terrorism Center at West Point; and Mustafa Hamid, "A Mother's Deep Sorrow"/"The Airport Project," The Harmony Project, Combating Terrorism Center at West Point.
3. Alan Cullison and Andrew Higgins, "A Once-Stormy Terror Alliance Was Solidified by Cruise Missiles," *Wall Street Journal*, August 2, 2002; and Brown, *Cracks in the Foundation*, 16–18.
4. Gilles Kepel, *Jihad: The Trail of Political Islam* (Cambridge: Belknap Press of Harvard University Press, 2002): 270–71.
5. Fishman, *Dysfunction and Decline.*
6. Jacob Shapiro, *The Terrorist Dilemma: Managing Violent Covert Organizations*

(Princeton: Princeton University Press, 2013); and Daniel Byman, "Buddies or Burdens? Understanding the Al Qaeda Relationship With Its Affiliate Organizations," *Security Studies* 23, no. 3 (2014): 431–70.

7. Atiyatallah al-Libi, "Letter to Zarqawi from Senior al Qaeda Leader, 'Atiya."

8. Abu Muhammad Al-Adnani, "''Pardon, Emir of al-Qaeda," SITE Intelligence Group, May 12, 2014.

9. Al-Adnani, "This Is the Promise of Allah."

10. Daniel Byman, "Explaining Al Qaeda's Decline," *Journal of Politics* 79, no. 3 (2017): 1107.

11. For example, see, Lahoud, *The Jihadis Path to Self-Destruction*; and Moghadam and Fishman, eds., *Fault Lines in Global Jihad*.

12. For example, see, Al-Zawahiri, "Loyalty and Separation," 206–9.

13. Mark Juergensmeyer, *Global Rebellion: Religious Challenges to the Secular State, from Christian Militias to al Qaeda* (Berkeley: University of California Press, 2008).

14. Coll, *Ghost Wars*, 222–23.

15. For example, al-Zayyat, *The Road to Al Qaeda*, 97.

16. Al-Gama'a al-Islamiya, "The Strategy and Bombings of Al-Qa'ida: Errors and Perils," serialized in *al-Shark al-Awsat*, January 2004.

17. Yotam Feldner, Yigal Carmon, and Daniel Lev, "The Al-Gama'a Al-Islamiyya Cessation of Violence: An Ideological Reversal," *MEMRI, Inquiry and Analysis Series— No. 309*, December 21, 2006; and Paul Cruickshank, "LIFG revisions Posing Critical Challenge to al-Qa'ida," *CTC Sentinel* 2, no. 10 (December 2009).

18. Al-Makalaat, "Thoughts on the Ideology of the Global Jihad Movement Embodied By al-Qaeda, part 2," *Pieter Van Ostaeyen Blog*, June 26, 2016, https://pietervanostaeyen.com/2016/06/26/thoughts-on-the-ideology-of-the-global-jihad-movement-embodied-by-al-qaeda-2.

19. Ibid.

20. Al-Makalaat, "Thoughts on the Ideology of the Global Jihad Movement Embodied By al-Qaeda, part 4," *Pieter Van Ostaeyen Blog*, August 6, 2016, https://pietervanostaeyen.com/2016/08/06/thoughts-on-the-ideology-of-the-global-jihad-movement-embodied-by-al-qaeda-4.

21. Al-Makalaat, "Thoughts on the Ideology of the Global Jihad Movement Embodied By al-Qaeda, part 2."

22. Ibid.

23. Al-Zawahiri, "Letter from al-Zawahiri to al-Zarqawi."

24. Ibid.

25. Brown, *Cracks in the Foundation*, 8.

26. Hamid, "A Mother's Deep Sorrow"/"The Airport Project," 61–62.

27. "The Ogaden File: Operation Holding," AFGP-2002–600104, The Harmony Project, Combating Terrorism Center at West Point, 19–21. Cited at Anne Stenersen, "Arabs and Non-Arab Jihadis," in *Fault Lines in Global Jihad*, eds. Moghadam and Fishman, 120.

28. Brown, *Cracks in the Foundation*, 13–16; and Stenersen, "Arabs and Non-Arab Jihadis," 128.

29. Lia, *Architect of Global Jihad*, 240.

30. Stenersen, "Arabs and Non-Arab Jihadis," 132–33.
31. Hamid, "A Mother's Deep Sorrow"/"The Airport Project," 61.
32. Al-Zawahiri, "Knights Under the Banner of the Prophet."
33. "Meeting Notes," The Harmony Project, Combating Terrorism Center at West Point, 6 and 29.
34. Al-Zarqawi, "February 2004 Coalition Provisional Authority English Translation of Terrorist Musab al-Zarqawi Letter."
35. Fishman, *Dysfunction and Decline*, 16–8; and "Analysis of State of ISI," Harmony Project at West Point, https://ctc.usma.edu/app/uploads/2013/09/Analysis-of-the-State-of-ISI-Translation.pdf.
36. For example, see, "What the Paris Attacks Tell Us about IS Strategy," *Der Spiegel*, November 27, 2015.
37. Hanin Ghaddar, "ISIS Strategy of Terror," *NOW*, July 14, 2015.
38. Bradley, "Rift Grows in Islamic State Between Foreign, Local Fighters"; Maria Abi-Habib, "Splits in Islamic State Emerge as Its Ranks Expand," *Wall Street Journal*, March 9, 2015; Azadeh Moaveni, "ISIS Women and Enforcers in Syria Recount Collaboration, Anguish and Escape," *New York Times*, November 21, 2015; and "What the Paris Attacks Tell Us About IS Strategy," *Der Spiegel*.
39. Abi-Habib, "Splits in Islamic State Emerge as Its Ranks Expand."
40. Bradley, "Rift Grows in Islamic State Between Foreign, Local Fighters."
41. Lahoud, *The Jihadis Path to Self-Destruction*, 246–47.
42. Al-Zawahiri, "Knights Under the Banner of the Prophet."
43. I distinguish between pledges to jihadi groups, which are based on adopting a group's ideology, from a *bay'a* to the Taliban leader as representing the ruling regime in a country hosting jihadis. Thus, Hamid's allegiance to the Taliban does not reduce his independence outside Afghanistan.
44. For example, see, Mustafa Hamid, "Chatting on Top of the World," Harmony Project, Combating Terrorism Center at West Point.
45. Vahid Brown, "The Façade of Allegiance: Bin Laden's Dubious Pledge to Mullah Omar," *CTC Sentinel* 3, no. 1 (2010): 1–6.
46. Cullison, "Inside al Qaeda's Hard Drive;" and "Letters to Abu Khabab," Harmony Project, Combating Terrorism Center at WestPoint.
47. Lia, *Architect of Global Jihad*.
48. Steven Brooke, "The Preacher and the Jihadi," in *Current Trends in Islamist Ideology* 3, eds. Hillel Fradkin, Husain Haqqani, and Eric Brown (Washington, D.C.: Hudson Institute, 2006): 52–66; Nibras Kazimi, "A Virulent Ideology in Mutation: Zarqawi Upstages Maqdisi," in *Current Trends in Islamist Ideology* 2, eds. Hillel Fradkin, Husain Haqqani, and Eric Brown (Washington, D.C.: Hudson Institute, 2005): 59–73.
49. Al-Adnani, "Pardon, Emir of al-Qaeda."
50. Abu Muhammed al-Adnani, "This Was Not Our Method, and It Will Not Be," SITE Intelligence Group, April 18, 2014.
51. For example, Bruce Hoffman, "The Coming ISIS-al Qaeda Merger," *Foreign Affairs*, March 29, 2016.
52. For example, Graham Wood, "What ISIS Really Want and How to Stop It," *The Atlantic Monthly*, March 2015.
53. Quintan Wiktorowicz, "Anatomy of the Salafi Movement," *Studies in Conflict and Terrorism* 29 (2006): 207–39.

54. I would like to thank Sam Helfont for this observation.
55. For example, see, Brynjar Lia, "Jihadis Divided Between Strategists and Doctrinarians," in *Fault Lines in Global Jihad*, eds. Moghadam and Fishman, 74–79.
56. Tore Hamming, "The Increasing Extremism Within the Islamic State: Interview with Ahmed al-Hamdan, Part 5," *Jihadica*, November 19, 2016, http://www.jihadica.com/the-increasing-extremism-within-the-islamic-state.
57. Al-Makalaat, "Thoughts on the Ideology of the Global Jihad Movement Embodied By al-Qaeda, part 4."
58. Mohammed Hafez, "Armed Islamist Movements and Political Violence in Algeria," *Middle East Journal* 54, no. 4 (2000): 582.
59. Camille Tawil, *Brothers in Arms: The Story of Al-Qa'ida and the Arab Jihadists* (London, UK: SAQI, 2010): 84–87 and 120–24.
60. Kepel, *Jihad*, 270–71.
61. Hamming, "The Increasing Extremism Within the Islamic State."
62. Christopher Anzalone, "Revisiting Shaykh Atiyyatullah's Works on Takfir and Mass Violence," *CTC Sentinel* 5, no. 4 (April 2012).
63. Gama'a Islamiya, "Authority: Shari'ah View and Realistic Vision," Serialized in *al-Sharq al-Awsat*, July-August 2005.
64. Al-Zawahiri, "Letter from al-Zawahiri to al-Zarqawi."
65. Hamming, "The Increasing Extremism Within the Islamic State."
66. Cited in Bunzel, *From Paper State to Caliphate*, 38–41.
67. Notably, the recanting Gama'a Islamiya warned of the implications of falling into a chain of takfir. See, Gama'a Islamiya, *Authority*.
68. Cole Bunzel, "Caliphate in Disarray: Theological Turmoil in the Islamic State," *Jihadica*, October 3, 2017, http://www.jihadica.com/caliphate-in-disarray.
69. Hamming, "The Increasing Extremism Within the Islamic State."
70. For example, see, Ayman al-Zawahiri, "America Is the First Enemy of the Muslims," SITE Intelligence Group, March 20, 2018.
71. Joas Wagemakers, "The Concept of Bay'a in the Islamic State's Ideology," *Perspectives on Terrorism* 9, no. 4 (2015): 99–100.
72. Allegiance to a caliph is considered a "greater *bay'a*," while for other authority figures, a "smaller *bay'a*." Anne Stenersen and Philipp Holtmann, "The Three Functions of UBL's "Greater Pledge" to Mullah Omar (2001–2006–2014), *Jihadology*, January 8, 2015, http://jihadology.net/2015/01/08/guest-post-the-three-functions-of-ubls-greater-pledge-to-mullah-omar-2001-2006-2014.
73. Although Muslim rulers also perform ceremonial *bay'a*-taking to legitimize their rule. See, Elie Podeh, "The Bay'a: Modern Political Uses of Islamic Ritual in the Arab World," *Die Welt des Islams* 50, no. 1 (2010): 117–52.
74. As will be discussed below, the case of ISI is somewhat different. If we take ISIS's claim that it has been independent of al-Qaeda since the announcement of ISI in 2006, then al-Qaeda experienced a defection without being aware of it.
75. Ayman al-Zawahiri, "Testimony to Stop the Bloodshed of the Mujahideen in al-Sham," SITE Intelligence Group, May 2, 2014.
76. Al-Shabab, "Shabaab Appoints New Leader After Death of Godane, Renews Pledge to Zawahiri," SITE Intelligence Group, September 6, 2014; and Qassim al-Rimi, "But They Never Lost Heart for that which Did Befall Them," SITE Intelligence Unit, July 9, 2015.

77. Jason Warner and Caleb Weiss, "A Legitimate Challenger? Assessing the Rivalry between al-Shabaab and the Islamic State in Somalia," *CTC Sentinel* 10, no. 10 (November 2017): 27–32; and Greg Miller, "Fighters Abandoning Al-Qaeda Affiliates to Join Islamic State, U.S. officials say," *Washington Post*, August 9, 2014.

78. Ayman al-Zawahiri, "We Shall Fight You Until There Is No More Persecution," SITE Intelligence Group, December 4, 2017.

79. Al-Adnani, "This Was Not Our Method, and It Will Not Be."

80. Aaron Zelin, "The War Between ISIS and al-Qaeda for Supremacy of the Global Jihadist Movement," Washington Institute for Near East Policy, Research Notes no. 20 (June 2014): 3.

81. Bunzel, *From Paper State to Caliphate*, 21.

82. Al-Baghdadi, "And Give Glad Tidings to the Believers."

83. Al-Adnani, "Pardon, Emir of al-Qaeda."

84. Brian Fishman, "Fourth Generation Governance: Sheikh Tamimi Defends the Islamic State of Iraq," Combating Terrorism Center, March 23, 2007, https://ctc.usma.edu/app/uploads/2010/06/ISI-Fourth_Gen4.pdf.

85. Bunzel, *From Paper State to Caliphate*, 19–20.

86. Fishman, *Dysfunction and Decline*, 6.

87. Abu Muhammad al-Joulani, "Allah, Allah, in the Field of al-Sham," SITE Intelligence Group, January 7, 2014; Abu Khalid al-Suri, "Message Attributed to Zawahiri's Arbiter in Syria Gives Advice to ISIL," SITE Intelligence Group, January 17, 2014; and Thomas Joscelyn, "Saudi Cleric's Reconciliation Initiative for Jihadists Draws Wide Support, Then a Rejection," *The Long War Journal*, January 27, 2014.

88. Cited in Bunzel, *From Paper State to Caliphate*, 29.

89. Al-Zawahiri, "Testimony to Stop the Bloodshed of the Mujahideen in al-Sham."

90. Al-Sahab, "Zawahiri Denies Changing His Ideology, Speaks in Interview on Syrian Conflict, Egypt, War with the U.S.," SITE Intelligence Group, April 18, 2014.

91. For ISIS's claim, see al-Adnani, "Pardon, Emir of al-Qaeda."

92. Al-Zawahiri, "Testimony to Stop the Bloodshed of the Mujahideen in al-Sham."

93. Barak Mendelsohn, "ISIL's Bold Caliphate Roll-Out: Objectives and Risks." *War on the Rocks*, July 8, 2014.

94. Thomas Hegghammer, "Calculated Caliphate," *Lawfare*, July 6, 2014.

95. Al-Adnani, "This Is the Promise of Allah."

96. Ibid.

97. Ibid.

98. Abu Muhammed Al-Adnani, "So Leave Them Alone with their Fabrications," SITE Intelligence Group, June 20, 2013.

99. Ibid.

100. Al-Sahab, "Zawahiri Denies Changing His Ideology."

101. Al-Adnani, "Pardon, Emir of al-Qaeda."

102. Al-Adnani, "So Leave Them Alone with their Fabrications."

103. Abu Muhammad al-Joulani, "About the Levantine Front," SITE Intelligence Group, April 10, 2013.

104. Brown, "The Façade of Allegiance."

105. Stenersen and Holtmann, "The Three Functions of UBL's 'Greater Pledge' to Mullah Omar."

106. Bunzel, *From Paper State to Caliphate*, 32–34.

107. Stenersen and Holtmann, "The Three Functions of UBL's 'Greater Pledge' to Mullah Omar."

108. Cited in Cole Bunzel, "Al-Qaeda's Quasi-Caliph: The Recasting of Mullah Omar," *Jihadica*, July 23, 2014.

109. Barak Mendelsohn, "Al-Qaeda After Omar: Why His Death Could Hurt the Terrorist Group and Empower ISIS," *Foreign Affairs*, August 9, 2015.

110. "Taliban Admits Covering Up Death of Mullah Umar," *BBC*, August 31, 2015, http://www.bbc.com/news/world-asia-34105565.

111. Ayman al-Zawahiri, "A Biography of Faithfulness," SITE Intelligence Group, August 13, 2015.

112. Tore Hamming and Olivier Roy, "Al-Zawahiri's Bay'a to Mullah Mansoor: A Bitter Pill but a Bountiful Harvest," *CTC Sentinel* 9, no. 5 (May 2016): 19.

113. Ibid., 18.

114. Mendelsohn, "Al-Qaeda After Omar."

115. "Audio Message by Shaykh Ahmad Hassan Abu al-Khayr," *Pieter Van Ostaeyen Blog*, July 26, 2016, https://pietervanostaeyen.com/2016/07/28/janhat-an-nusra-audio-message-by-shaykh-ahmad-hassan-abu-al-khayr.

116. "Last Video Message of Abū Muhammad al-Jūlānī as leader of Jabhat an-Nusra," *Pieter Van Ostaeyen Blog*, July 28, 2016, https://pietervanostaeyen.com/2016/07/28/jabhat-an-nusra-last-video-message-of-abu-muhammad-al-julani-as-leader-of-an-al-qaeda-affiliate; and Jabhat Fath as-Sham, "Founding Declaration," *Pieter Van Ostaeyen Blog*, July 29, 2016, https://pietervanostaeyen.com/2016/07/29/jabhat-fath-as-sham-founding-declaration.

117. Cole Bunzel, "Abandoning al-Qaida: Tahrir al-Sham and the Concerns of Sami al-'Uraydi," *Jihadica*, May 12, 2017, http://www.jihadica.com/abandoning-al-qaida.

118. Hay'at Tahrir al-Sham, "An Announcement Of the Formation of Hayat Tahrir al-Sham," SITE Intelligence Group, January 28, 2017.

119. "The First Speech of the General Leader of Hayy'at Tahrir as-Sham Shaykh Hashem Al-Shaykh Abu Jaber," *Pieter Van Ostaeyen Blog*, February 11, 2017, https://pietervanostaeyen.com/2017/02/11/first-statement-by-the-general-leader-of-hayyat-tahrir-as-sham.

120. Charles Lister, "How al-Qa'ida Lost Control of Its Syrian Affiliate: The Inside Story," *CTC Sentinel* 11, no. 2 (February 2018): 6–7.

121. Hay'at Tahrir al-Sham, "Administrative Decision," SITE Intelligence Group, October 1, 2017; and Aymenn Jawad al-Tamimi, "Harakat Nour al-Din al-Zinki Splits from Hay'at Tahrir al-Sham," July 20, 2017, http://www.aymennjawad.org/2017/07/harakat-nour-al-din-al-zinki-splits-from-hayat.

122. Ayman al-Zawahiri, "Let Us Fight Them with a Solid Structure," SITE Intelligence Group, November 28, 2017; and Aymenn Jawad Al-Tamimi, "The Hay'at Tahrir al-Sham-al-Qaeda Dispute: Primary Texts (I)," December 6, 2017, http://www.aymennjawad.org/2017/12/the-hayat-tahrir-al-sham-al-qaeda-dispute-primary.

123. Aymenn Jawad Al-Tamimi, "The Hay'at Tahrir al-Sham-al-Qaeda Dispute: Primary Texts (II)," December 10, 2017, http://www.aymennjawad.org/2017/12/the-hayat-tahrir-al-sham-al-qaeda-dispute-primary-1.

124. Bunzel, "Abandoning al-Qaida."

125. For example, see, al-Zawahiri, "Let Us Fight Them with a Solid Structure."
126. Tore Hamming and Pieter Van Ostaeyen, "The True Story of al-Qaeda's Demise and Resurgence in Syria," *Lawfare*, April 8, 2018, https://bit.ly/2qdGKDi; and Lister, "How al-Qa'ida Lost Control of Its Syrian Affiliate," 7–8.
127. Charles Lister, "Al-Qaeda's Turning Against Its Syrian Affiliate," The Middle East Institute, May 18, 2017, http://www.mei.edu/content/article/al-qaeda-s-turning-against-its-syrian-affiliate; and Hamming and Van Ostaeyen, "The True Story of al-Qaeda's Demise and Resurgence in Syria."

CHAPTER FIVE

1. Steven Metz, "Rethinking Insurgency," in *The Routledge Handbook of Insurgency and Counterinsurgency*, eds. Paul Rick and Isabelle Duyvesteyn (London: Routledge, 2012): 38.
2. Assaf Moghadam, Ronit Berger, and Polina Beliakova, "Say Terrorist, Think Insurgent: Labeling and Analyzing Contemporary Terrorist Actors," *Perspectives on Terrorism* 8, no. 5 (October 2014): 2–17.
3. Audrey Cronin, "ISIS Is Not a Terrorist Group: Why Counterterrorism Won't Stop the Latest Jihadi Threat," *Foreign Affairs* 94, no. 2 (March/April 2015).
4. For example, Ishaan Tharoor, "Turkey's Erdogan Would Label Even More People as Terrorists," *Washington Post*, March 17, 2016.
5. Note Max Abrahms' controversial argument that terrorists are actually much more focused on the social function of membership in a terrorist organization than on attaining political goals. However, his argument is more relevant for foot soldiers than to the goals of a group and its leadership. For his argument, see, Max Abrahms, "What Terrorists Really Want: Terrorist Motives and Counterterrorism Strategies," *International Security* 32, no. 4 (Spring 2008): 78–105.
6. Anne Speckhard, "Inside the ISIS Machine Turning Children to 'Monsters,'" *The Daily Beast*, August 25, 2017.
7. The Islamic State, "The Extinction of the Grayzone," *Dabiq* 7, 2015, 54–66.
8. Al-Zawahiri, "Knights Under the Banner of the Prophet."
9. Lister, "How al-Qa'ida Lost Control of Its Syrian Affiliate."
10. Tom Allard, "Looted Cash, Gold Help Islamic State Recruit in Philippines," *Reuters*, January 22, 2018.
11. David Remnick, "Going the Distance: On and off the road with Barack Obama," *The New Yorker*, January 27, 2014.
12. Bradley Hope, "Egypt's Islamists: A Troubled Path From Violence to Peaceful Politics," *The National*, March 23, 2012; and Sudarsan Raghavan "These Libyans Were Once Linked to al-Qaeda. Now They Are Politicians and Businessmen," *Washington Post*, September 28, 2017.
13. Scott-Clark and Levy, *The Exile*.
14. Scott Helfstein, Nassir Abdullah, and Muhammad al-Obaidi, *Deadly Vanguards: A Study of al-Qa'ida's Violence Against Muslims* (West Point: Combating Terrorism Center, 2009).
15. Muhammad al-Shafi'I, "Al-Zawahiri's Secret Papers, part 3," *Al-Sharq al-Awsat*,

December 15, 2002; and Muhammad al-Shafi'I, "Al-Zawahiri's Secret Papers, part 5," *Al-Sharq al-Awsat*, December 17, 2002.

16. Al-Zawahiri, "Open Interview – Part One."
17. Al-Adnani, "This Was Not Our Method, and It Will Not Be."
18. Al-Adnani, "Pardon, Emir of al-Qaeda."
19. Al-Joulani, "About the Levantine Front."
20. Barak Mendelsohn, "Al Qaeda's Palestinian Problem," *Survival* 51, no. 4 (2009): 71–86.
21. Barak Mendelsohn, "Bolstering the State: A Different Perspective on the War on the Jihadi Movement," *International Studies Review* 11, no. 4 (2009): 663–86.

Bibliography

Abdulrahim, Raja, and Isabel Coles. "Islamic State Returns to Guerrilla Warfare in Iraq and Syria." *Wall Street Journal*, January 2, 2018.

Abi-Habib, Maria. "Splits in Islamic State Emerge as Its Ranks Expand." *Wall Street Journal*, March 9, 2015.

Abrahms, Max. "What Terrorists Really Want: Terrorist Motives and Counterterrorism Strategy." *International Security* 32, no. 4 (2008): 78–105.

———. "Why Terrorism Does Not Work." *International Security* 31, no. 2 (2006): 42–78.

Abu-Bader, Soleman, Imad K. Harb, and Tamara Kharroub. "2016 Arab Opinion Index." The Arab Center for Research and Policy Studies, Executive Summary, April 11, 2017.

"The Abbottabad Documents: Harmony Document, SOCOM-2012–0000017." Combating Terrorism Center at West Point, May 3, 2012.

Al-'Adam, Abu Obeida Abdullah Khalid. "The Apostate Awakenings and the Way to Prevent Them." SITE Intelligence Group, July 25, 2012.

Al-'Adl, Saif. "Al-'Adl Letter." The Harmony Project, Combating Terrorism Center at West Point.

Al-Adnani, Abu Muhammad. "O Our People Respond to the Caller of Allah." *Blog of Pieter Van Ostaeyen*, July 23, 2015.

———. "Pardon, Emir of Al-Qaeda." SITE Intelligence Group, May 12, 2014.

———. "So Leave Them Alone with Their Fabrications." SITE Intelligence Group, June 20, 2013.

———. "So They Kill and Are Killed." SITE Intelligence Group, March 12, 2015.

———. "This Is the Promise of Allah." SITE Intelligence Group, June 29, 2014.

———. "This Was Not Our Method, and It Will Not Be." SITE Intelligence Group, April 18, 2014.

Al-Awlaki, Anwar. "AQAP Releases Interview with Anwar Al-Awlaki." Open Source Center, May 23, 2010.

Al-Baghdadi, Abu Bakr. "A Message to the Mujahidin and the Muslim Ummah." Al-Hayat Media Center, July 1, 2014.

———. "And Give Glad Tidings to the Believers." SITE Intelligence Group, April 8, 2013.

———. "Even If the Disbelievers Despise Such." SITE Intelligence Group, November 13, 2014.

Al-Baghdadi, Abu Umar. "For the Scum Disappears Like Froth Cast Out." *Al-Furqan Media Production*, December 5, 2007.

Al-Dawsari, Nadwa. *Foe Not Friend: Yemeni Tribes and Al-Qaeda in the Arabian Peninsula*. Washington DC: Project on Middle East Democracy, Feburary 1, 2018.

Al-Fahd, Nasir bin Hamd. "A Treatise on the Legal Status of Using Weapons of Mass Destructions against the Infidels." The National Security Archive at The George Washington University, May 2003.

Al-Gama'a al- Islamiya. "Authority: Shari'ah View and Realistic Vision." Serialized in *al-Sharq al-Awsat*, July-August 2005.

———. "Egyptian Al-Jama'ah Al-Islamiyah Denies Joining Al-Qa'ida." Open Source Center, August 7, 2006.

———. "The Strategy and Bombings of Al-Qa'ida: Errors and Perils." Serialized in *al-Shark al-Awsat*, January 2004.

Al-Hanbali, Ibn Rajab. "My Provision Was Placed for Me in the Shade of My Spear." *Dabiq*, October 11, 2014, 10.

Al-Joulani, Abu Muhammad. "About the Levantine Front." SITE Intelligence Group, April 10, 2013.

———. "Allah, Allah, in the Field of Al-Sham." SITE Intelligence Group, January 7, 2014.

———. "Last Video Message of Abū Muhammad Al-Jūlānī as Leader of Jabhat an-Nusra." *Blog of Pieter Van Ostaeyen*, July 28, 2016.

Allard, Tom. "Looted Cash, Gold Help Islamic State Recruit in Philippines." *Reuters*, January 22, 2018.

Al-Libi, Abu-Yahya. "Democracy, the Modern Idol." Open Source Center, August 5, 2009.

———. "Letter from Abu Yahya." Bin Laden's Bookshelf, Office of the Director of National Intelligence, January 19, 2017.

———. "Moderation of Islam . . . Moderation of Defeat." Open Source Center, May 22, 2008.

———. "We Sent Thee Not, But As a Mercy For All Creatures." *Vanguard of Khurasan*, Open Source Center, March 12, 2010.

Al-Libi, Atiyatallah. "Kind Brother." Bin Laden's Bookshelf, Office of the Director of National Intelligence, March 1, 2016.

———. "Letter to Zarqawi from Senior Al Qaeda Leader, 'Atiya." Combating Terrorism Center at West Point, December 12, 2005.

———. "Letter from 'Atiyah to Abu Basir." Bin Laden's Bookshelf, Office of the Director of National Intelligence, January 19, 2017.

Al-Makalaat. "Thoughts on the Ideology of the Global Jihad Movement Embodied By Al-Qaeda, Part 2." *Blog of Pieter Van Ostaeyen*, June 26, 2016.

———. "Thoughts on the Ideology of the Global Jihad Movement Embodied By Al-Qaeda, Part 4." *Blog of Pieter Van Ostaeyen*, August 6, 2016.

Al-Nahhas, Labib. "The Deadly Consequences of Mislabeling Syria's Revolutionaries." *The Washington Post*, July 10, 2015.

Al-Qaeda in the Arabian Peninsula. "How to Make a Bomb in the Kitchen of Your Mother." *Inspire*, June 2010.

———. *Inspire,* November 2010.

Al-Qaeda in the Indian Subcontinent. "Land of the Other." *Resurgence Magazine*, October 19, 2014.

"Al-Qaida Papers: The Yemen Letters." *The Associated Press*, August 9, 2013.

Al-Rimi, Qassim. "But They Never Lost Heart for That Which Did Befall Them." SITE Intelligence Group, July 9, 2015.

Al-Shabab. "Shabaab Appoints New Leader After Death of Godane, Renews Pledge to Zawahiri." SITE Intelligence Group, September 6, 2014.

———. "The Path 2 Paradise: From the Twin Cities to the Land of Two Migrations: Episode 2." SITE Intelligence Group, January 1, 2016.

Al-Sahab. "A Glad Tiding from Sheikhs Abu Al-Zubeir and Ayman Al-Zawahiri, May Allah Protect Them." SITE Intelligence Group, February 9, 2012.

———. "The Special Production on the Occasion of Unity Among the Ranks of the Mujahideen and Creating 'Qaedat Al-Jihad in the Indian Subcontinent.'" SITE Intelligence Group, September 3, 2014.

———. "Zawahiri Denies Changing His Ideology, Speaks in Interview on Syrian Conflict, Egypt, War with the U.S." SITE Intelligence Group, April 18, 2014.

Al-Shafi'I, Muhammad. "Al-Zawahiri's Secret Papers, Part 3." *Al-Sharq Al-Awsat*, December 15, 2002.

———. "Al-Zawahiri's Secret Papers, Part 5." *Al-Sharq Al-Awsat*, December 17, 2002.

Al-Shami, Abu 'Abd Allah. "How Jabhat An-Nusra Broke Its Ties with Al-Qaeda." *Blog of Pieter Van Ostaeyen*, October 13, 2017.

Al-Suri, Abu Khalid. "Message Attributed to Zawahiri's Arbiter in Syria Gives Advice to ISIL." SITE Intelligence Group, January 16, 2014.

Al-Tamimi, Aymenn Jawad. "Harakat Nour Al-Din Al-Zinki Splits from Hay'at Tahrir Al-Sham." *Blog of Aymenn Jawad Al-Tamimi*, July 20, 2017.

———. "The Hay'at Tahrir Al-Sham-Al-Qaeda Dispute: Primary Texts (I)." *Blog of Aymenn Jawad Al-Tamimi,* December 6, 2017.

———. "The Hay'at Tahrir Al-Sham-Al-Qaeda Dispute: Primary Texts (II)." *Blog of Aymenn Jawad Al-Tamimi*, December 10, 2017.

Al-Wuhayshi, Nasir. "They Plot and Plan, and God Plans Too." Open Source Center, February 20, 2009.

Al-Zarqawi, Abu Musab. "February 2004 Coalition Provisional Authority English Translation of Terrorist Musab Al Zarqawi Letter Obtained by United States Government in Iraq, 2001–2009." United States Department of State, 2004.

Al-Zawahiri, Ayman. "A Biography of Faithfulness." SITE Intelligence Group, August 13, 2015.

———. "Al-Zawahiri Interviewed on Fighting in Afghanistan, Bin Ladin, Others." Open Source Center, December 16, 2001.

———. "America Is the First Enemy of the Muslims." SITE Intelligence Group, March 20, 2018.

———. "Dr. Ayman Al-Zawahiri: The Freeing of Humanity and Homelands Under the Banner of the Qur'an." Jihad Unspun, February 11, 2005.

———. "General Guidelines for Jihad,"As-Sahab media, September 14, 2013.

———. "Knights Under the Banner of the Prophet." Serialized in *al-Sharq al-Awsat*, December 2001.

———. "Let Us Light Them with a Solid Structure." SITE Intelligence Group, November 28, 2017.

———. "Letter from Al-Zawahiri to Al-Zarqawi." Office of the Director of National Intelligence, July 9, 2005.

———. Kepel, Giles, and Jean-Pierre Milelli, eds. *Al Qaeda in Its Own Words*. Cambridge, MA: Harvard University Press, 2009.

———. "Open Interview – Part One." Open Source Center, April 3, 2008.

———. "Realities of the Conflict between Islam and Unbelief." Open Source Center, December 29, 2006.

———. "Testimony to Stop the Bloodshed of the Mujahideen in Al-Sham." SITE Intelligence Group, May 2, 2013.

———. "Unity in the Issue of Tawhid." SITE Intelligence Group, April 6, 2013.

———. "We Shall Fight You Until There Is No More Persecution." SITE Intelligence Group, October 4, 2017.

Amara, Hani. "Libyan Forces Clear Last Islamic State Holdout in Sirte." *Reuters*, December 6, 2016.

———. "Libyan Forces Reduce Islamic State's Grip in Sirte to Final Few Blocks." *Reuters*, October 4, 2016.

"Analysis of State of ISI." NMEC-2008–612449. The Harmony Project, Combatting Terrorism Center at West Point.

Anzalone, Christopher. "Revisiting Shaykh Atiyyatullah's Works on Takfir and Mass Violence." *CTC Sentinel* 5, no. 4 (April 2012): 10–12.

———. "The Formalizing of an Affiliation: Somalia's Harakat Al-Shabab Al-Mujahideed & Al-Qa'ida Central." *Al-Wasat*, February 10, 2012.

Azzam, Abdallah. *Defense of Muslim Lands*. Birmingham: Maktabah Publications, 2002.

Bakke, Kristin M. "Help Wanted?: The Mixed Record of Foreign Fighters in Domestic Insurgencies." *International Security* 38, no. 4 (2014): 150–87.

Bergen, Peter L. *The Longest War: The Enduring Conflict between America and Al-Qaeda*. New York: Free Press, 2011.

———. *The Osama Bin Laden I Know: An Oral History of Al Qaeda's Leader*. New York: Free Press, 2006.

Bin Ali, Mohamed. *The Roots of Religious Extremism: Understanding the Salafi Doctrine of Al-Wala' Wal Bara'*. Singapore: World Scientific Publishing Company, 2015

Bin Laden, Osama. "About the Ongoing War Between the Army and the Mujahidin in Swat and the Tribal Areas." Open Source Center, June 4, 2009.

———. "Bin Ladin Warns Iraqis Against Joining Anti-Al-Qa'ida Tribal Councils, Unity Govt." Open Source Center, December 30, 2007.

———. "CNN Interview with Osama Bin Laden." By Peter Arnett, CNN, March 20, 1997.

———. "Declaration of War," October 12, 1996.

———. "Islamic Website Posts Full Text of Bin Laden 4 January Audio Message." March 2004.

———. "Letter to Abu Basir." Bin Laden's Bookshelf, Office of the Director of National Intelligence, January 19, 2017.

———. "Letter to Abu Basir." Bin Laden's Bookshelf, Office of the Director of National Intelligence, March 1, 2016.

———. "Letter to All Muslim Brothers in the World." Bin Laden's Bookshelf, Office of the Director of National Intelligence, January 19, 2017.

———. "Letter to the Muslim Nation." Bin Laden's Bookshelf, Office of the Director of National Intelligence, January 19, 2017.

———. "Osama Bin Laden Speech Offers Peace Treaty with Europe, Says Al-Qa'ida 'Will Persist in Fighting' the U.S." MEMRI. April 15, 2004.

———. "This War Is Fundamentally Religious." *al-Jazeera*, November 3, 2001.

Bradley, Matt. "Rift Grows in Islamic State Between Foreign, Local Fighters." *Wall Street Journal*, March 25, 2016.

Brooke, Steven. "The Muslim Brotherhood in Europe and the Middle East: The Evolution of a Relationship." In *The Muslim Brotherhood in Europe*. Edited by Roel Meijer and Edwin Bakker, 27–50. New York: Columbia University Press, 2012.

———. "The Preacher and the Jihadi." In *Current Trends in Islamist Ideology* 3. edited by Hillel Fradkin, Husain Haqqani, and Eric Brown, 52–66. Washington DC: Hudson Institute, 2006.

Brown, Nathan. "The Irrelevance of the International Muslim Brotherhood." *Foreign Policy*, September 21, 2010.

Brown, Vahid. *Cracks in the Foundation: Leadership Schisms in Al-Qa'ida from 1989–2006*. The Harmony Project, Combatting Terrorism Center at West Point, September 2007.

———. "Foreign Fighters in Historical Perspective: The Case of Afghanistan." In *Bombers, Bank Accounts, & Bleedout*, edited by Brian Fishman, West Point: Combating Terrorism Center, 2008, 27–30.

———. "The Façade of Allegiance: Bin Laden's Dubious Pledge to Mullah Omar." *CTC Sentinel* 3, no. 1 (2010): 1–6.

Bunzel, Cole. "Abandoning Al-Qaida: Tahrir Al-Sham and the Concerns of Sami Al-'Uraydi." *Jihadica*, May 12, 2017.

———. "Al-Qaeda's Quasi-Caliph: The Recasting of Mullah Omar." *Jihadica*, July 23, 2014.

———. "Caliphate in Disarray: Theological Turmoil in the Islamic State." *Jihadica*, October 3, 2017.

———. *From Paper State to Caliphate: The Ideology of the Islamic State*. Washington DC: The Brookings Institution, 2015.

Burke, Jason. *The 9/11 Wars*. London: Penguin Books, 2012.

Bush, George W. "Address to a Joint Session of Congress." *C-Span*, September 20, 2001.

Byman, Daniel. *Al Qaeda, the Islamic State, and the Global Jihadist Movement: What Everyone Needs to Know*. New York: Oxford University Press, 2015.

———. "Buddies or Burdens? Understanding the Al Qaeda Relationship With Its Affiliate Organizations." *Security Studies* 23, no. 3 (2014): 431–470.

———. "Explaining Al Qaeda's Decline." *Journal of Politics* 79, no. 3 (2017): 1106–1117.

Callimachi, Rukmini. "3 ISIS Terrorism Planners Killed in Syria Airstrike, Pentagon Says." *The New York Times*, December 13, 2016.

Coles, Isabel. "Despair, Hardship as Iraq Cuts off Wages in Islamic State Cities." *Reuters*, October 2, 2015.

Coll, Steve. *Ghost Wars: The Secret History of the CIA, Afghanistan, and Bin Laden, from the Soviet Invasion to September 10, 2001*. London: Penguin Books, 2005.
Collombier, Virginie. "Conclusion." In *Tribes and Global Jihadism*, edited by Olivier Roy and Virginie Collombier. London: Hurst, 2017.
Collombier, Virginie, and Olivier Roy, eds. *Tribes and Global Jihadism*. London: Hurst, 2017.
Cronin, Audrey Kurth. "ISIS Is Not a Terrorist Group: Why Counterterrorism Won't Stop the Latest Jihadist Threat." *Foreign Affairs* 94, no. 2 (2015): 87–98.
Cruickshank, Paul. "LIFG Revisions Posing Critical Challenge to Al-Qa'ida." *CTC Sentinel* 2, no. 10 (December 2009): 5–8.
Cullison, Alan. "Inside Al-Qaeda's Hard Drive." *The Atlantic Monthly* 294, no. 2 (September 2004): 55–70.
Cullison, Alan, and Andrew Higgins. "A Once-Stormy Terror Alliance Was Solidified by Cruise Missiles." *Wall Street Journal*, August 2, 2002.
El-Ghobashy, Tamer, and Ali Nbhan. "Foreign ISIS Fighters Increasingly Isolated in Mosul Battle." *Wall Street Journal*, March 16, 2017.
Esposito, John L., and Dalia Mogahed. *Who Speaks for Islam? What a Billion Muslims Really Think*. New York, NY: Gallup Press, 2007.
"Europe's Jihadists: What the Paris Attacks Tell Us About IS Strategy." *Der Spiegel*, November 27, 2015.
Feldner, Yotam, Yigal Carmon, and Daniel Lev. "The Al-Gama'a Al-Islamiyya Cessation of Violence: An Ideological Reversal." *MEMRI*, Inquiry and Analysis Series, no. 309, December 21, 2006.
Ferran, Lee. "Al Qaeda 'Shadow of Former Self', US Counter-Terror Official Says." *ABC News Investigative*, April 30, 2012.
Fishman, Brian. *Dysfunction and Decline: Lessons Learned From Inside Al Qa'ida in Iraq*. West Point: Combating Terrorism Center, 2009.
———. *The Master Plan: ISIS, Al Qaeda, and the Jihadi Strategy for Final Victory*. New Haven: Yale University Press, 2016.
———. "Fourth Generation Governance: Sheikh Tamimi Defends the Islamic State of Iraq." Combating Terrorism Center at West Point, March 23, 2007.
"Foreign Terrorist Organizations." U.S. Department of State, Bureau of Counterterrorism and Countering Violent Extremism.
Gardham, Duncan. "Cargo Plane Bomb Plot: Computer Printer Shows Al-Qaeda's Sophistication." *The Telegraph*, November 1, 2010.
Gartenstein-Ross, Daveed, and Nathaniel Barr. "The Myth of Lone-Wolf Terrorism: The Attacks in Europe and Digital Extremism." *Foreign Affairs*, July 26, 2016.
Gellman, Barton, and Dafna Linzer. "Afghanistan, Iraq: Two Wars Collide." *The Washington Post*, October 22, 2004.
Gerges, Fawaz A. *The Rise and Fall of Al-Qaeda*. New York: Oxford University Press, 2011.
Ghaddar, Hanin. "ISIS Strategy of Terror." *NOW* (blog). July 14, 2015.
Gunaratna, Rohan. *Inside Al Qaeda: Global Network of Terror*. New York: Columbia University Press, 2002.
Hafez, Mohammad. "Armed Islamist Movements and Political Violence in Algeria." *Middle East Journal* 54, no. 4 (2000): 582–598.

———. "Jihad after Iraq: Lessons from the Arab Afghans Phenomenon." *CTC Sentinel* 1, no. 4 (March 2009): 1–4.
Hamid, Mustafa. "A Mother's Deep Sorrow/ The Airport Project." The Harmony Project, Combatting Terrorism Center at West Point.
———. "Chatting on Top of the World." The Harmony Project, Combatting Terrorism Center at West Point.
———. "Mustafa Hamid's Analysis of Mujahidin Activities." The Harmony Project, Combatting Terrorism Center at West Point.
Hamid, Mustafa, and Leah Farrall. *The Arabs at War in Afghanistan*. London: Hurst & Company, 2015.
Hamid, Shadi. "The Roots of the Islamic State's Appeal." *The Atlantic*, October 31, 2014.
Hamming, Tore. "The Increasing Extremism Within the Islamic State: Interview with Ahmed Al-Hamdan, Part 5." *Jihadica*, November 19, 2016.
Hamming, Tore, and Olivier Roy. "Al-Zawahiri's Bay'a to Mullah Mansoor: A Bitter Pill but a Bountiful Harvest." *CTC Sentinel* 9, no. 5 (May 2016): 16–20.
Hamming, Tore, and Pieter Van Ostaeyen. "The True Story of Al-Qaeda's Demise and Resurgence in Syria." *Lawfare*, April 8, 2018.
Harel, Amos. "A Daring Assassination Attempt Shows ISIS in Sinai Has the Ultimate Weapon: Intel." *Haaretz*, December 29, 2017.
Harmon, Stephen. "From GSPC to AQIM: The Evolution of an Algerian Islamist Terrorist Group Into an Al-Qa'ida Affiliate and Its Implications for the Sahara-Sahel Region." *Concerned Africa Scholars* Bulletin no. 85 (Spring 2010): 12–29.
Hassan, Hassan. "ISIL Sleeper Cells in Iraq Are a Warning Sign the Extremist Group Is Already Reforming." *The National*, March 28, 2018.
Hay'at Tahrir al-Sham. "Administrative Decision." SITE Intelligence Group, October 1, 2017.
———. "An Announcement Of the Formation of Hayat Tahrir Al-Sham." SITE Intelligence Group, January 28, 2017.
Hegghammer, Thomas. "Calculated Caliphate." *Lawfare*, July 6, 2014.
———. *Jihad in Saudi Arabia: Violence and Pan-Islamism since 1979*. Cambridge, UK: Cambridge University Press, 2010.
———. *The Failure of Jihad in Saudi Arabia*. West Point: Combating Terrorism Center, February 25, 2010.
———. "The Rise of Muslim Foreign Fighters: Islam and the Globalization of Jihad." *International Security* 35, no. 3 (Winter 2010/2011): 53–94.
Helfstein, Scott, Nassir Abdullah, and Muhammad al-Obaidi. *Deadly Vanguards: A Study of Al-Qa'ida's Violence Against Muslims*. West Point: Combating Terrorism Center, December 1, 2009.
Hoffman, Bruce. *Inside Terrorism*. New York: Columbia University Press, 2006.
———. "The Coming ISIS-Al Qaeda Merger." *Foreign Affairs*, March 29, 2016.
Hope, Bradley. "Egypt's Islamists: A Troubled Path From Violence to Peaceful Politics." *The National*, March 23, 2012.
Husayn, Fu'ad. "Al Zarqawi, The Second Generation of al Qa'ida," Serialized in *al-Quds al-Arabi*, 2005.
Ingraham, Christopher. "Toddlers Have Shot at Least 23 People This Year." *The Washington Post*, May 1, 2016.

International Crisis Group. *Yemen's Al-Qaeda: Expanding the Base*. Middle East and North Africa, Report No. 174. February 2017.

"Interview with Dr. Najih Ibrahim, Theoretician of the Egyptian Al-Jama'ah Al-Islamiyah." *al-Sharq al-Awsat*, August 13, 2006.

ISIL (Da'esh) & Al-Qaida Sanctions Committee. "ISIL (Da'esh) & Al-Qaida Sanctions List." United Nations Security Council Subsidiary Organs: Security Council Committee pursuant to resolutions 1267 (1999) 1989 (2011) and 2253 (2015) concerning ISIL (Da'esh) Al-Qaida and associated individuals groups undertakings and entities. Accessed May 22, 2018.

The Islamic State. *Dabiq*, vol. 1. 2014.

———. "The Extinction of the Grayzone." *Dabiq*, 2015.

———. "Modern Day Slavery." *Dabiq*, 2014.

———. "The Punishing of Shu'aytāt for Treachery." *Dabiq*, 2014.

Jabhat al-Nusra. "New Jihadist Group Declares Presence in Levant, Calls for Action." SITE Intelligence Group, January 23, 2012.

Jabhat Fath as-Sham. "Founding Declaration." *Blog of Pieter Van Ostaeyen*, July 29, 2016.

"Jihad in Pakistan." Bin Laden's Bookshelf, Office of the Director of National Intelligence, March 1, 2016.

"Jihadist Website Posts 'Communique' on Egyptian Islamic Group Joining Al-Qa'ida." Open Source Center, August 8, 2006.

Johnsen, Gregory D. "AQAP in Yemen and the Christmas Day Terrorist Attack." *CTC Sentinel*, special issue January 2010.

Joscelyn, Thomas. "Saudi Cleric's Reconciliation Initiative for Jihadists Draws Wide Support, Then a Rejection." *The Long War Journal*, January 27, 2014.

Joscelyn, Thomas, and Bill Roggio. "AQAP's Emir Also Serves as Al-Qaeda's General Manager." *The Long War Journal*, August 6, 2013.

Juergensmeyer, Mark. *Global Rebellion: Religious Challenges to the Secular State from Christian Militias to Al Qaeda*. Berkeley: University of California Press, 2008.

Kazimi, Nibras. "A Virulent Ideology in Mutation: Zarqawi Upstages Maqdisi." In *Current Trends in Islamist Ideology* 2, edited by Hillel Fradkin, Husain Haqqani and Eric Brown. Washington DC: Hudson Institute, 2005.

Kepel, Gilles. *Jihad: The Trail of Political Islam*. Cambridge, Mass: Harvard University Press, 2003.

Kepel, Gilles, and Jean-Pierre Milelli. *Al Qaeda in Its Own Words*. Cambridge, Mass.: Cambridge University Press, 2008.

Lachen, Mawassi. "ISIS Kills Fleeing Fighters." *Magharebia*, January 16, 2015.

Lahoud, Nelly. *The Jihadis' Path to Self-Destruction*. London: Hurst, 2010.

"Letter About Matter of the Islamic Maghreb." Bin Laden's Bookshelf, Office of the Director of National Intelligence, March 1, 2016.

"Letters to Abu Khabab." The Harmony Project, Combatting Terrorism Center at West Point.

Levy, Adrian, and Catherine Scott-Clark. *The Exile: The Stunning Inside Story of Osama Bin Laden and Al Qaeda in Flight*. New York: Bloomsbury, 2017.

Lia, Brynjar. *Architect of Global Jihad: The Life of Al-Qaida Strategist Abu Mus'ab Al-Suri*. New York: Columbia University Press, 2008.

———. "Jihadis Divided Between Strategists and Doctrinarians." In *Fault Lines in*

Global Jihad: Organizational, Strategic and Ideological Fissures, edited by Assaf Moghadam and Brian Fishman. New York: Routledge, 2011.

Lister, Charles. "Al-Qaeda's Turning Against Its Syrian Affiliate." *Middle East Institute*, May 18, 2017.

———. "How Al-Qa'ida Lost Control of Its Syrian Affiliate: The Inside Story." *CTC Sentinel* 11, no. 2 (February 2018): 1–9.

———. *The Syrian Jihad: Al-Qaeda, the Islamic State and the Evolution of an Insurgency*. London: Oxford University Press, 2016.

Lustick, Ian. "The Absence of Middle Eastern Great Powers: Political 'Backwardness' in Historical Perspective." *International Organization* 51, no. 4 (1997): 658–683.

Lynch, Marc. "Explaining the Awakening: Engagement, Publicity, and the Transformation of Iraqi Sunni Political Attitudes." *Security Studies* 20, no. 1 (2011): 36–72.

Maher, Shiraz. *Salafi-Jihadism: The History of an Idea*. London: Oxford University Press, 2016.

McCants, William F. *The ISIS Apocalypse: The History, Strategy, and Doomsday Vision of the Islamic State*. New York: Picador, 2016.

"Meeting Notes." AFGP-2002-600086. The Harmony Project, Combatting Terrorism Center at West Point.

Mendelsohn, Barak. "Al-Qaeda After Omar: Why His Death Could Hurt the Terrorist Group and Empower ISIS." *Foreign Affairs*, August 9, 2015.

———. *The Al-Qaeda Franchise: The Expansion of Al-Qaeda and Its Consequences*. New York: Oxford University Press, 2016.

———. "Al-Qaeda's Palestinian Problem." *Survival* 51, no. 4 (September 1, 2009): 71–86.

———. "Bolstering the State: A Different Perspective on the War on the Jihadi Movement." *International Studies Review* 11, no. 4 (2009): 663–686.

———. *Combating Jihadism: American Hegemony and Interstate Cooperation in the War on Terrorism*. Chicago: University of Chicago Press, 2009.

———. "The Future of Al-Qaeda: Lessons from the Muslim Brotherhood." *Survival* 60, no. 2 (March 4, 2018): 151–178.

———. "ISIL's Bold Caliphate Roll-Out: Objectives and Risks." *War on the Rocks*, July 8, 2014.

———. "Terrorism and Protean Power: How Terrorists Navigate Uncertainty." In *Protean Power: Exploring the Uncertain and Unexpected in World Politics*, edited by Peter Katzenstein and Lucia Seybert. Cambridge: Cambridge University Press, 2018.

Metz, Steven. "Rethinking Insurgency." In *The Routledge Handbook of Insurgency and Counterinsurgency*, edited by Paul Rick and Isabelle Duyvesteyn. London: Routledge, 2012.

Miller, Greg. "Fighters Abandoning Al-Qaeda Affiliates to Join Islamic State, U.S. Officials Say." *The Washington Post*, August 9, 2014.

Mitchell, Jeni. "The Contradictory Effects of Ideology on Jihadist War-Fighting: The Bosnia Precedent." *Studies in Conflict & Terrorism* 31, no. 9 (September 10, 2008): 808–828.

Moaddel, Mansoor, and Julie De Jong. "Youth Perceptions and Values During the Arab Spring." In *Values, Political Action, and Change in the Middle East and the Arab Spring*, edited by Mansoor Moaddel and Michele Gelfand. New York: Oxford University Press, 2017.

Moaveni, Azadeh. "ISIS Women and Enforcers in Syria Recount Collaboration, Anguish and Escape." *The New York Times*, November 21, 2015.

Moghadam, Assaf, Ronit Berger, and Polina Beliakova. "Say Terrorist, Think Insurgent: Labeling and Analyzing Contemporary Terrorist Actors." *Perspectives on Terrorism* 8, no. 5 (2014): 2–17.

Moghadam, Assaf, and Brian Fishman, eds. *Fault Lines in Global Jihad: Organizational, Strategic and Ideological Fissures*. London: Routledge, 2011.

"More Than 1600 Killed Since ISIS Started Its Attack on Ein Al-Arab 'Kobane." The Syrian Observatory for Human Rights, January 16, 2015.

Mueller, John. *Overblown: How Politicians and the Terrorism Industry Inflate National Security Threats, and Why We Believe Them*. New York: Free Press, 2006.

Mueller, John E., and Mark G. Stewart. *Chasing Ghosts: The Policing of Terrorism*. New York: Oxford University Press, 2016.

Mujahideen Shura Council. "Statement of Mujahidin Shura Council on Establishment of 'Islamic State of Iraq." Open Source Center, October 15, 2006.

Naji, Abu Bakr. *The Management of Savagery: The Most Critical Stage Through Which the Umma Will Pass*. Translated by McCants William. The John M. Olin Institute for Strategic Studies at Harvard University, May 2006.

Naylor, Hugh. "Islamic State Is No Longer So Formidable on the Battlefield." *The Washington Post*, February 6, 2016.

Obama, Barack. "Transcript: President Obama's Speech Outlining Strategy to Defeat Islamic State." *The Washington Post*, September 10, 2014.

"The Ogaden File: Operation Holding." The Harmony Project, Combatting Terrorism Center at West Point.

Pape, Robert. *Dying to Win: The Strategic Logic of Suicide Terrorism*. New York: Random House, 2005.

Pargeter, Alison. *The Muslim Brotherhood: From Opposition to Power*. London: Saqi, 2013.

Peters, Rudolph. *Jihad in Classical and Modern Islam: A Reader*. Princeton: Markus Wiener, 1996.

Pew Research Center. "15 Years After 9/11, a Sharp Partisan Divide on Ability of Terrorists to Strike U.S." *U.S. Politics and Policy* (blog), September 7, 2016.

———. "On Anniversary of Bin Laden's Death, Little Backing of Al Qaeda," April 30, 2012.

———. "Osama Bin Laden Largely Discredited Among Muslim Publics in Recent Years," May 2, 2011.

———. "The World's Muslims: Religion, Politics and Society." *Religion and Public Life* (blog), April 30, 2013.

———. "Worries About Terrorism Subside in Mid-America: Ratings of Government Efforts Slips." *U.S. Politics and Policy* (blog), November 8, 2001.

Podeh, Ellie. "The Bay'a: Modern Political Uses of Islamic Ritual in the Arab World." *Die Welt Des Islams* 50, no. 1 (2010): 117–152.

"Public Opinion in the Arab World." The Arab Barometer, 2015.

Qaedat al-Jihad Organization General Command. "Statement Regarding the Relationship of the Group of Qadat Al-Jihad with the Group of the Islamic State in Iraq and the Levant." SITE Intelligence Group, February 3, 2014.

Raghavan, Sudarsan. "In Yemen, Tribal Militias in a Fierce Battle with Al-Qaeda Wing." *The Washington Post*, September 10, 2012.

———. "These Libyans Were Once Linked to Al-Qaeda. Now They Are Politicians and Businessmen." *The Washington Post*, September 28, 2017.

Reeve, Simon. *The New Jackals: Ramzi Yousef, Osama bin Laden and the Future of Terrorism*. Boston: Northeastern University Press, 1999.

"Remarks by President Obama in Address to the Nation from Afghanistan." The White House, May 1, 2012.

Remnick, David. "Going the Distance: On and Off the Road with Barack Obama." *The New Yorker*, January 27, 2014.

Roggio, Bill, and Alexandra Gutowski. "Coalition Kills 2 Islamic State External Operations Commanders in Iraq and Syria." *Long War Journal*, November 15, 2017.

Roy, Olivier. "Introduction." In *Tribes and Global Jihadism*, edited by Olivier Roy and Virginie Collombier. London: Hurst, 2017.

Ryan, Michael W. S. *Decoding Al-Qaeda's Strategy: The Deep Battle against America*. New York: Columbia University Press, 2013.

Seftel, Bennett. "Persistent, Expanding and Worrisome': ISIS Rebounds in Afghanistan." *The Cipher Brief*, January 4, 2018.

Shapiro, Jacob N. *The Terrorist's Dilemma: Managing Violent Covert Organizations*. Princeton: Oxford: Princeton University Press, 2015.

Shaykh Ahmad Hassan Abu al-Khayr. "Audio Message by Shaykh Ahmad Hassan Abu Al-Khayr." *Blog of Pieter Van Ostaeyen*, July 26, 2016.

Shaykh Hashem Al-Shaykh Abu Jaber. "The First Speech of the General Leader of Hayy'at Tahrir as-Sham Shaykh Hashem Al-Shaykh Abu Jaber." *Blog of Pieter Van Ostaeyen*, February 11, 2017.

Soufan, Ali H. *Anatomy of Terror: From the Death of Bin Laden to the Rise of the Islamic State*. New York: W. W. Norton & Company, 2017.

Speckhard, Anne. "Inside the ISIS Machine Turning Children to 'Monsters'." *The Daily Beast*, August 25, 2017.

Stenersen, Anne. *Al-Qaida in Afghanistan*. Cambridge: Cambridge University Press, 2017.

———. "Arabs and Non-Arab Jihadis." In *Fault Lines in Global Jihad*, edited by Assaf Moghadam and Brian Fishman. New York: Routledge, 2011. 117–137

Stenersen, Anne, and Philipp Holtmann. "The Three Functions of UBL's 'Greater Pledge' to Mullah Omar (2001–2006–2014)." *Jihadology*, January 8, 2015.

Stern, Jessica, and J.M. Berger. *ISIS: The State of Terror*. New York: Ecco Press, 2015.

Stewart, Phil. "Leon Panetta Says Al Qaeda's Defeat 'Within Reach.'" *Reuters*, July 9, 2011.

"Taliban Admits Covering Up Death of Mullah Umar." *BBC News*, August 31, 2015.

Tarrow, Sidney. *The New Transnational Activism*. Cambridge: Cambridge University Press, 2005.

Ṭawīl, Kamīl. *Brothers in Arms: The Story of Al-Qa'ida and the Arab Jihadists*. London: Saqi, 2010.

Tessler, Mark. "Change and Continuity in Arab Attitudes toward Political Islam: The Impact of Political Transitions in Tunisia and Egypt from 2011 to 2013." In *Values, Political Action, and Change in the Middle East and the Arab Spring*, edited by Mansoor Moaddel and Michele Gelfand. New York: Oxford University Press, 2017.

———. "Mapping and Explaining Attitudes Toward Political Islam among Ordinary Citizens in the Middle East and North Africa." Working Paper No. 902, Economic Research Forum, Cairo, Egypt, 2015.
Tessler, Mark, Michael Robbins, and Amaney Jamal. "What Do Ordinary Citizens in the Arab World Really Think About the Islamic State." *Washington Post*, July 27, 2016.
Tharoor, Ishaan. "Turkey's Erdogan Would Label Even More People as Terrorists." *Washington Post*, March 17, 2016.
Ulph, Stephen. "Declining in Algeria, GSPC Enters International Theater." *Terrorism Focus* 3, no. 1 (January 2006).
———. "Disarray in the Algerian GSPC." *Terrorism Focus* 1, no. 7 (October 2004).
"United Nations Security Council Resolution 1373." United Nations Security Council, November 28, 2001.
Wagemakers, Joas. *A Quietist Jihadi: The Ideology and Influence of Abu Muhammad Al-Maqdisi*. Cambridge: Cambridge University Press, 2012.
———. "The Concept of Bay'a in the Islamic State's Ideology." *Perspectives on Terrorism* 9, no. 4 (2015): 98–106.
Warner, Jason, and Caleb Weiss. "A Legitimate Challenger? Assessing the Rivalry between Al-Shabaab and the Islamic State in Somalia." *CTC Sentinel* 10, no. 10 (November 2017): 27–32.
Weiss, Michael. "How I Escaped From ISIS." *The Daily Beast*, November 18, 2015.
———. "How ISIS Picks Its Suicide Bombers." *The Daily Beast*, November 15, 2015.
Wiktorowicz, Quintan. "Anatomy of the Salafi Movement." *Studies in Conflict & Terrorism* 29 (2006): 207–239.
Winter, Charlie, and Haroro Ingram. "Terror, Online and Off: Recent Trends in Islamic State Propaganda Operations." *War on the Rocks*, March 2, 2018.
Wood, Graeme. *The Way of the Strangers: Encounters with the Islamic State*. New York: Random House, 2017.
———. "What ISIS Really Want and How to Stop It." *The Atlantic Monthly*, March 2015.
World Islamic Front for Jihad Against Jews and Crusaders. February 23, 1998.
Wright, Lawrence. *The Looming Tower: Al-Qaeda and the Road to 9/11*. New York: Alfred A Knopf, 2006.
Zacher, Mark. "The Territorial Integrity Norm: International Boundaries and the Use of Force." *International Organization* 55, no. 2 (2001): 215–250.
Zambelis, Chris. "Ahrar Al-Sham: A Profile of Northern Syria's Al-Qaeda Surrogate," *Terrorism Monitor* 11:7 (April 2013).
Zaynah, Abduh. "Egyptian Islamic Group: Al-Zawahiri Wanted to Implicate Us before London Plot Was Uncovered. Said Iran Has Its Own Agenda But Cards in Lebanon Should Not Be Mixed Up." *al-Sharq al-Awsat*, August 14, 2006.
Zayyāt, Montasser. *The Road to Al-Qaeda: The Story of Bin Lāden's Right-Hand Man*. London: Pluto Press, 2004.
Zelin, Aaron Y. "The War Between ISIS and Al-Qaeda for Supremacy of the Global Jihadist Movement: Research Notes No. 20." Washington Institute for Near East Policy, June 2014.

Index

Abd al-Wahhab, Muhammad Ibn, 90
Abu Bakr, 38
al-Adl, Sayf, 48, 66
al-Adnani, Abu Muhammad, 49–50, 73, 88, 100–101, 121, 128, 133
Afghanistan, 3, 60, 84; centrality of, 83; role in jihad, 9–10, 36, 56, 68, 80; U.S. invasion of, 12, 80; al-Zawahiri arrival in, 87
Afghan-Soviet War of 1980's, 9–10, 36–37, 55, 77
aggregation problem, 48, 50–54, 60–61, 71–74
Ahrar al-Sham, 24, 104–5
allegiance (*bay'a*), 7, 34, 39, 49–50, 89; to al-Baghdadi, Abu Bakr, 17, 97; conflict surrounding, 84–86; elements of agreement surrounding, 96; as instrument for maintaining order, 94; Islamic pledge of, 79, 95; primary, of Muslims, 83; reaffirming of, 96; shifts in, 105
Ansar al-Sharia Libya (ASL), 16
Ansar al-Sharia Tunisia (AST), 16
apostasy: permissible declaration of, 90; as punishable by death, 89
AQAP. *See* al-Qaeda in the Arabian Peninsula
AQC. *See* al-Qaeda Central

Arabic language, knowledge of, 36–37
Armed Islamic Group (GIA), 25, 91–92
ASL. *See* Ansar al-Sharia Libya
al-Assad, Bashar, 24, 69
AST. *See* Ansar al-Sharia Tunisia
authority: internal conflicts over, 79; ISIS claiming, over Muslims, 17; refusal of acceptance of, 88; relationships of, within al-Qaeda, 97–98. *See also* divine authority; religious authority; sovereign authority
Awakening Councils, 41–42, 110
Azzam, Abdallah, 27, 77, 80, 86

al-Baghdadi, Abu Bakr, 7, 14–16, 118; acceptance of, 78; allegiance to, 17, 97; sermon delivered by, 31; strategies of, 74; al-Zawahiri rivalry with, 88–89
al-Baghdadi, Abu Omar, 39, 42
bay'a. *See* allegiance
Bin Laden, Osama, 1, 9, 26, 36, 41–42, 57; ceasefire offer by, 3; death of, 16, 88, 96; hostility toward U.S., 10; master plan and, 66–67, 71; media interviews by, 87–88; resistance from, 15; as revered, 101; strategic vision of, 48; U.S.-first strategy of, 54, 117–18; view of, 11

157

Bonaparte, Napoleon, 49
Brown, Vahid, 5, 84
Bush, George W., 1, 12

caliphate, 83; developing of, 71–75; founding of, 32; as global, 108; reception of, by jihadi groups, 13, 19, 24, 50; reception of, by Muslims, 3, 20–23; restoration by ISIS, 81–82, 99–100; role in ISIS strategy, 17, 43–45, 48, 99–100; supremacy of, 36
The Call to Global Islamic Resistance Call (al-Suri), 54, 62–66
chauvinism, Arab, 84, 106
China, 69
civil war among Muslims (*fitna*), 84, 94
Cosmic battle, 49
counterterrorism, 5, 48, 111
Cracks in the Foundation (Brown), 5
Cronin, Audrey, 110
cross-border activities, 6, 28, 52–53, 72; expansion of, 119, 123; strategic effects through, 47, 81, 83–86

al-Dawsari, Nadwa, 42–43
decentralization of jihad, 57–58
defensive jihad, 34–35
divine authority, 19
drones, 52–53

Egypt, 25
Egyptian Islamic Jihad (EIJ), 25, 77, 85, 115
electronic surveillance, 53
ethnic identity, 19–20, 44–45
ethnicity, 20, 108
excommunication (*takfir*), 7, 79, 89–93

al-Fahd, Nasir bin Hamd, 30
falsehood, forces of, 49, 79, 113
Fault Lines of Global Jihadi (Moghadam and Fishman), 5
al-Filistini, Abu Qatada, 86
Fishman, Brian, 5, 66–67, 70–71, 98
fitna (civil war among Muslims), 84, 94

France: headscarf ban, 35; terrorist attacks on, 25
franchising, of al-Qaeda, 13–14, 18
freedom: of action, 29; to design foreign policy, 30

Gama'a Islamiya, 25, 59, 77, 120–21
GIA. *See* Algerian Armed Islamic Group
GSPC. *See* Salafist Group for Preaching and Combat

al-Hamdan, Ahmed, 91
Hamid, Mustafa, 77, 84, 86
Hay'at Tahrir al-Sham (HTS), 105
Hazimis, 93
headscarf ban, 35
Hegghammer, Thomas, 26
Hitler, Adolf, 49
Hoffmann, Bruce, 3
HTS. *See* Hay'at Tahrir al-Sham
Husayn, Fu'ad, 66–67

ideational barrier, 5, 33, 45, 74, 95, 112–17
immigration, 39
international relations theory, 5
Internet, 64–65
Iran, 66–68; and al-Qaeda, 69; relations with al-Zawahiri/ISIS, 104–5; role in master plan, 66–68
Iraq, 2, 16, 68–69, 96–97; Awakening Councils, 41–42, 110; corrupt government in, 71–72; sectarian violence in, 14–16, 24, 50; U.S. invasion of, 12–13, 48, 80; violence in, 88
ISIS. *See* Islamic State
Islam: aggression against, 35; boundaries of Muslims and, 91; compatibility between, and nationalism, 21; emergence of, 38; five pillars of, 21; legitimacy of, derived from religion, 32; morality and, 30; nullifiers of, 90; role of, in political life, 22; superiority of, 28–30; tolerant versions of, 114
Islamic emirates, 56–58, 61, 73, 97, 100, 103, 130n17

Islamic identity, 23; elevating of, 36; production of, 45; role of, 20
Islamic resistance, 62–63
Islamic revival, promotion of, 23
Islamic schools of thought, 21, 91
Islamic State (ISIS), 1–2, 5, 14, 16; affiliates of, 116; aggregation problem and, 71–73; AQC, JN and, 97–101; AQC and Taliban against, 102–4; authority over Muslims claimed by, 17; caliphate restoration by, 81, 99–100; collective punishment from, 43; in conflict with tribes, 44; as corrupt, 27–28; danger posed by, 108; economic plan of, 72–73; excommunication inclination of, 93; expansion of, 24–25; global aspirations of, 48–50; imperialist agenda of, 20; language used by, 37–38; limited appeal of, 70–71; lone wolf terrorism and, 62–66; mobilization called for by, 35–36; Obama vow to destroy, 17; overreach of, 117; al-Qaeda comparison with, 7, 36; al-Qaeda conflict with, 78; al-Qaeda rejecting expansion of, 99; rejection of, by Muslims, 22; religious-based world order intention of, 108, 112–13; structural obstacles faced by, 9; violence focus of, 82
Islamist groups, 1, 6; beliefs of, 21–22; foreign fighters within, 26; interpersonal conflicts within, 86–89, 92, 119–22
Islamophobia, 115
Israel, 30, 55, 68–70
Israeli-Palestinian conflict, 29–30

Jabhat al-Nusra (JN), 7, 16–17, 53; AQC, ISIS and, 97–101; AQC against, 104–6; attack on, 101; rebranding of, 104, 122
jahiliya, 39, 90
JN. *See* Jabhat al-Nusra
al-Joulani, Abu Muhammad, 88, 101, 104–5

khawarij, 7, 101
kidnapping-for-ransom, 15, 17

Lahoud, Nelly, 5, 87
al-Libi, Abu Yahya, 33, 36–37, 39
al-Libi, Atiyatallah, 49, 58, 92
Libyan Islamic Fighting Group (LIFG), 20, 77, 120
LIFG. *See* Libyan Islamic Fighting Group
localism, 5, 59
localization trap, 2, 48, 109, 116
London, terrorist attacks on, 13
lone-wolf terrorism, 62–66
Loyalty and Enmity: An Inherited Doctrine and a Lost Reality (al-Zawahiri), 33–34

Madrid, terrorist attacks on, 3, 13
The Management of Savagery (Abu Bakr Naji), 54, 59–62
al-Maqdisi, Abu Muhammad, 86, 87–88
master plan, 48, 66–75
material power, 50, 75
media coverage: of Bin Laden interviews, 87–88; of terrorist attacks, 4
Moghadam, Assaf, 5
morality, Islam and, 30
Mubarak, Hosni, 25
Mueller, John, 4
al-Muhajir, Abu Hamza, 13–15, 98
Mullah Omar, 77, 84, 87, 97–98, 102–4
multiculturalism, 114
multinationalism, 58, 86
Muslim Brotherhood, 23, 28, 90, 130n15
Muslims, entire community of (*umma*), 69; acceptance of al-Qaeda by, 55–56; boundaries of Islam and, 91; defense for, 80; elite groups within, 91; as enraged, 60; inclusion of, 114–15; ISIS claiming authority over, 17; ISIS rejected by, 22; mobilization of, 35–36, 41–42, 50, 54, 73, 100; national identity of, 21; 9/11 terrorist attacks reaction of, 56–57; obligations governing behavior of, 31; primary allegiance of, 83; as prohibited from befriending non-Muslims, 34; religious ideologies of, 108; rights of, 99; solidarity among, 22–23, 35, 62

Naji, Abu Bakr, 48, 54, 59–62, 74
national identity, 19; giving up of, 61; of Muslims, 21; religious identity as superior to, 30, 56; shedding of, 36; strengthening of, 113–14
nationalism, 65, 108; accommodating of, 20; arrival of, in Middle East, 23; compatibility between, and Islam, 21; exclusionary nature of, 28; as foreign scheme, 37–38; power of, 33–37; al-Qaeda argument on, 29; tribalism, ethnic identity and, 44–45; weak sense of, 59. *See also* multinationalism; transnationalism
nation-state, 5, 19; attitudes towards, 20, 24; rejection of, 33; transnational movements and, 21
9/11 terrorist attacks, 1–3, 6, 60, 122–23; international response to, 63; Muslims reaction to, 56–57; perceived as inspiring, 55–56; as provoking U.S. involvement, 11–12; U.S. failure to understand threat of, 52–53
Nour al-Din Zinki, 105

Obama, Barack, 1, 17, 118
offensive jihad, call for, 35–36
open fronts, 63–64
operational barrier, 117–19

Pakistan, 40, 85
Palestinian Authority, 29–30
pashtunwali (tribal code of behavior), 40
Peters, Rudolph, 34
pluralism, 91
power: of nationalism, 33–37; overextension of, 60; of U.S., as myth, 11. *See also* material power
propaganda: as seductive, 28; from terrorist attacks, 11
provinces (*wilayas*), 17, 73

al-Qaeda, 1, 4–5, 116–17; abandoning of, 97; authority relationships within, 97–98; branches of, 6–7, 58; communication as problem for, 53; danger posed by, 108; defensive focus of, 82; denouncing of, 84; efforts against, by U.S., 2; establishment of, 10; failures of, 14; first operation of, 47; founding of, 37; franchising of, 13–14, 18; global aspirations of, 48–50; ideology of, 85; importance of public support to, 51; Internet use by, 65; ISIS comparison with, 7, 36; ISIS conflict with, 78; ISIS expansion rejected by, 99; master plan and, 66–71; mobilization efforts by, 41–42; Muslims acceptance of, 55–56; nationalism argument of, 29; organizational expansion of, 57; popularity of, 11; religious-based world order intention of, 108, 112–13; rise of, 26; strategies of, 54–59, 120; strategy disagreements with, 80–81; structural obstacles faced by, 9; support offered by, 11; U.S.-first strategy of, 54, 58–59
al-Qaeda Central (AQC), 14, 42, 58, 66–67; ISIS, JN and, 97–101; JN *versus*, 104–6; Taliban and, *versus* ISIS, 102–4
al-Qaeda in the Arabian Peninsula (AQAP), 14, 43, 57–58
al-Qaeda in the Islamic Maghreb (AQIM), 15, 57
Quran, 36
Qutb, Sayyid, 90
Qutbism, 90

race, 20
religious authority: absence of, 90; as not shared, 32
religious identity: attachment to, 74; guarding of, 34; as superior to national identity, 30, 56
religious ideology: betrayal of, 40–41; conflict magnified by, 106, 119–22; legitimacy of Islam derived from, 32; of Muslims, 108; prioritization of, 19–20; as source of division, 79, 86–93
Ridda Wars (wars of apostasy), 38
Roy, Olivier, 38, 132n58

Salafist Group for Preaching and Combat (GSPC). *See* al-Qaeda in the Islamic Maghreb
Salafization, of tribes, 38
Saudi Arabia, 14–15, 27, 80
Second World War, 1
segmentation: of jihadi action, 53; manifestation of, in tribal divisions, 38–39; rejection of, by state borders, 28
self-defense, actions triggering, 59
self-destruction, 5
sharia law, 21–22, 28; implementation of, 30–32, 50, 81, 89; opposition to, 61
social media, 64
solidarity, 58–59; expression of, as prohibited, 31; among Muslims, 22–23, 35, 62
sovereign authority, 19
Soviet Union, collapse of, 55
Stewart, Mark, 4
suicide bombing, 58
al-Suri, Abu Musab, 48, 54, 62–66, 74, 86
Syria, 4, 16, 36, 71–72, 96–98, 122; borders of, 13; change in, 24; civil war in, 117; liberation of, 82; violence in, 88

takfir. See excommunication
Taliban, 2, 77; AQC and, against ISIS, 102–4; collapse of, 13; negative views of, 84; opposition to, 92; al-Qaeda alliance with, 11–12; reputation of, damaged, 103–4
al-Tawhid wal-Jihad (TWJ), 13–15
technology, 52, 55. *See also* drones; Internet
television: attack value enhanced through, 64
terrorism, 4, 75; containment of, 122–23; by disconnected perpetrators, 63–64; fear of, 5, 107; financing for, 53; reflection of threat level of, 107–8; success rates of, 111–12; use of terminology for, 109–11. *See also* lone-wolf terrorism
terrorist attacks, 2, 122; call for, 73; failure of campaign for, 107; on France, 25; frequency of, 18; on London, 13; on Madrid, 3, 13; as means to goal, 111; media coverage of, 4; propaganda from, 11; public exposure to, 64
Tessler, Mark, 22
transnational ideologies, 25, 45
transnationalism, 28, 117
transnational movements, 5, 21
tribal code of behavior (*pashtunwali*), 40
tribal identities, 6, 19
tribalism, 65, 108; as foolish, 39; nationalism, ethnic identity and, 44–45; as pillar of social order, 37–38; rejecting of, 21; transforming of, 20
tribal traditions, 38
tribes: aggressive leaders of, 42; centrality of, 51; excessive violence rejected by, 43; global agenda disinterest of, 51–52; as hostile, 40; ISIS in conflict with, 44; methods for preventing conflict with, 41; support from, as necessary, 41–42. *See also* Awakening Councils
truth, forces of, 49, 79
TWJ. *See* al-Tawhid wal-Jihad

umma. See Muslims
United States (U.S.), 123; Afghanistan invasion by, 12, 80; Bin Laden hostility towards, 10; efforts against al-Qaeda by, 2; as enemy, 44, 65; failure of, to understand threat of 9/11 terrorist attacks, 52–53; international order investment of, 54; Iraq invasion by, 12–13, 48, 80; Israel alliance with, 70; 9/11 terrorist attacks provoking involvement from, 11–12; power of, as myth, 11; resilience of, 61; resource investment of, 78–79; strategy to exhaust resources of, 55, 68; targeting of, 27; as weakened, 56–57, 69
U.S.-first strategy, 54, 58–59, 117–18

Vietnam War, 1
violence, 2–4; in Iraq, 88; ISIS focus on, 82; as only available course of action, 110; restrictions on, 65; spread of, 107; in Syria, 88; tribes rejecting excessive,

43; as unbounded, 27–28; as used to bring change, 24

Wahhabism, 90
al-wala'wal-bara', 33–34, 92–93
War on Terrorism, 5, 65, 80, 107
wars of apostasy. *See* Ridda Wars
weapons of mass destruction (WMD), 30–31, 53, 131n39
wilayas (provinces), 17, 73
WMD. *See* weapons of mass destruction
World Islamic Front for Jihad Against Jews and Crusaders, 11
al-Wuhayshi, Nasir, 15, 57, 96

al-Zarqawi, Abu Musab, 13–14, 42, 48; criticism of, 42, 58; criticisms from, 85; death of, 98; frustration with, 78; al-Maqdisi relationship with, 87–88; master plan and, 66–67, 69–71; suicide bombing ordered by, 58
al-Zawahiri, Ayman, 16, 25–26, 29–30, 32; ability of, to provide instructions, 53; accusations towards, 100–101; Afghanistan arrival of, 87; al-Baghdadi, Abu Bakr, rivalry with, 88–89; *Loyalty and Enmity: An Inherited Doctrine and a Lost Reality* by, 33–34; marriage of, 40; master plan and, 66–67; on public support importance, 51; rise of, 92
Zelin, Aaron, 98
Zionist Crusader alliance, 33, 113
Zoubari, Antar, 91

About the Author

Barak Mendelsohn is associate professor of political science at Haverford College and a Senior Fellow at the Philadelphia-based Foreign Policy Research Institute (FPRI). He holds a doctoral degree in government from Cornell University, MA in security studies from Tel Aviv University, and BA in Middle East studies from the Hebrew University, Jerusalem. He specializes in radical Islamist organizations, with an emphasis on al-Qaeda and the Islamic State. His research interests also cover Middle East security, terrorism and counterterrorism, U.S. foreign policy, and questions of international order. Mendelsohn is the author of *The al-Qaeda Franchise: The Expansion of al-Qaeda and Its Consequences* (2016) and of *Combating Jihadism: American Hegemony and Interstate Cooperation in the War on Terrorism* (2009). In addition, Mendelsohn has published numerous articles in a variety of academic and policy journals, as well as in prominent media outlets.

www.ingramcontent.com/pod-product-compliance
Lightning Source LLC
Chambersburg PA
CBHW031553300426
44111CB00006BA/291